MAY 0 8 2009

The Only Superpower

The Only Superpower

Reflections on Strength, Weakness, and Anti-Americanism

Paul Hollander

LEXINGTON BOOKS

A division of
ROWMAN & LITTLEFIELD PUBLISHERS, INC.
Lanham • Boulder • New York • Toronto • Plymouth, UK

LEXINGTON BOOKS

A division of Rowman & Littlefield Publishers, Inc.
A wholly owned subsidiary of The Rowman & Littlefield Publishing Group, Inc.
4501 Forbes Boulevard, Suite 200
Lanham, MD 20706

Estover Road
Plymouth PL6 7PY
United Kingdom

Copyright © 2009 by Lexington Books

The acknowledgments section of this book constitutes an official extension of the copyright page.

All rights reserved. No part of this publication may be reproduced, stored in a retrieval system, or transmitted in any form or by any means, electronic, mechanical, photocopying, recording, or otherwise, without the prior permission of the publisher.

British Library Cataloguing in Publication Information Available

Library of Congress Cataloging-in-Publication Data

Hollander, Paul, 1932–
 The only super power : reflections on strength, weakness, and anti-Americanism / Paul Hollander.
   p. cm.
 Includes index.
 ISBN-13: 978-0-7391-2543-4 (cloth : alk. paper)
 ISBN-10: 0-7391-2543-5 (cloth : alk. paper)
 ISBN-13: 978-0-7391-3133-6 (electronic)
 ISBN-10: 0-7391-3133-8 (electronic)
 1. United States—Civilization—21st century. 2. United States—Social conditions—21st century. 3. United States—Relations—Foreign countries. 4. Political culture—United States. 5. Anti-Americanism. I. Title.
 E169.12.H637 2009
 973.931—dc22   2008029077

Printed in the United States of America

∞™ The paper used in this publication meets the minimum requirements of American National Standard for Information Sciences—Permanence of Paper for Printed Library Materials, ANSI/NISO Z39.48-1992.

Contents

Acknowledgments		vii
Introduction: The Pleasures of Hate and the New Anti-Americanism		1

PART I: THE NEW ANTI-AMERICANISM

1	Anti-Americanism and a World-Class Hate Crime	33
2	Anti-Americanism: Murderous and Rhetorical	36
3	The Politics of Envy	41
4	Anti-Americanism and Moral Equivalence	49

PART II: AMERICANA

5	Our Society and Its Celebrities	59
6	Watching Celebrities	62
7	Michael Moore: The New Political Celebrity	65
8	SUVs and Americans	71
9	The Chronic Ailments of Television News	73
10	Stereotyping and the Decline of Common Sense	77
11	Tawana Brawley and the "Exotic Dancer" at Duke	81
12	An Islamic Requirement on Campus	85
13	Rehabilitating the Great Books: Literature and Life	88

| 14 | The Counterculture of the Heart | 102 |
| 15 | Old and Busier Than Ever | 118 |

PART III: FOREIGN MATTERS

16	American Travelers to the Soviet Union	123
17	Alexander Yakovlev	141
18	Violence of Higher Purpose	150
19	The North Korean Gulag	164
20	Admiring North Korea	167
21	The Fiftieth Anniversary of the Hungarian Revolution	170
22	Crossing the Moral Threshold: The Rejection of Communist Systems in Eastern Europe	174
23	Ambivalent in Amsterdam	184
24	Travel in the Peloponnesos	189

PART IV: THE SURVIVAL AND REPLENISHMENT OF THE ADVERSARY CULTURE

25	The Resilience of the Adversary Culture	203
26	The Chomsky Phenomenon	216
27	The Banality of Evil and the Political Culture of Hatred	225
28	The Left and the Palestinians	229
29	The Personal and the Political in Lessing's Fiction	233
30	Haven in Cuba	237
31	Demystifying Marxism	242
32	Public Intellectuals and the God That Failed	246

PART V: IN CONCLUSION

| 33 | From a "Builder of Socialism" to "Free-Floating Intellectual": My Politically Incorrect Career in Sociology | 257 |

| Index | 281 |
| About the Author | 291 |

Acknowledgments

I gratefully acknowledge the assistance of the Bradley Foundation, longtime supporter of my work, in contributing to the expenses associated with the creation of this volume. Erika Pfaff, (formerly of Smith College) was an exemplary research assistant and performed with exceptional competence a variety of tasks required for collecting and producing these essays. Raquel Manzanares (also of Smith College) was similarly helpful in the preparation of the index.

In some instances the titles were modified either to restore the original title (changed by the publications concerned) or in order to better reflect the contents of the piece.

A number of the chapters in this book were originally published elsewhere. I gratefully acknowledge those publications and the permission to reprint my material.

"It's a Crime That Some Don't See This as Hate." *Washington Post*, October 28, 2001.

"Anti-Americanism: Murderous and Rhetorical." *Partisan Review* 1 (2002).

"The Politics of Envy." *The New Criterion* (November 2002).

"On Moral Equivalence." Special pamphlet, *The New Criterion* (2005).

"Our Society and Its Celebrities." *National Review Online* (October 11, 2002). Copyright © 2002 by National Review, Inc. Used by permission of the publisher.

"Watching Celebrities." *New York Sun*, January 2007.

"Just Who Really Needs an SUV?" *Daily Hampshire Gazette*, January 18–19, 2003.

"Chronic Ailments of Television News." *FrontPage*, November 18, 2002.

"Stereotyping and the Decline of Common Sense." *FrontPage*, July 19, 2002.

"Tawana Brawley and the 'Exotic Dancer' at Duke." *FrontPage*, December 29, 2006.

"Requiring Islam." *FrontPage*, April 27, 2002.

"The Counterculture of the Heart." *Society* 41, no. 2 (January/February 2004). Copyright © 2004 by Springer. Used with kind permission of Springer Science and Business Media.

"Old and Busier Than Ever." *New York Sun*, December 27, 2006.

"American Travelers to the Soviet Union in the Cold War Era." *Society* 44, no. 3 (March/April 2007). Copyright © 2007 by Springer. Used with kind permission of Springer Science and Business Media.

Preface to *A Century of Violence in Soviet Russia*. By Alexander Yakovlev. New Haven, Conn.: Yale University Press, 2002. Copyright © 2002 by Yale University Press. Used by permission of the publisher.

Introduction to *From the Gulag to the Killing Fields: Personal Accounts of Political Violence and Repression in Communist States*. Edited by Paul Hollander. Wilmington, Del.: Intercollegiate Studies Institute, 2007.

"Inside the Aquarium." *New York Sun*, February 11, 2004.

"Pariah Lies." *National Review* (February 9, 2004). Copyright © 2004 by National Review, Inc. Used by permission of the publisher.

"Hungary for Personal Freedom." *New York Sun*, October 26, 2006.

"Crossing the Moral Threshold and the Rejection of Communist Systems in Eastern Europe." In *Resistance, Rebellion, and Revolution in Hungary and Central Europe: Commemorating 1956*, edited by Laszlo Peter and Martyn Rady. London: UCL SSEES, 2008.

"Ambivalent in Amsterdam." *The National Interest* (November–December 2006). Copyright © 2006 by The National Interest. Used by permission of the publisher.

"Travel in the Peloponnesos." *Modern Age* (Winter 2007). Copyright © 2007 by Intercollegiate Studies Institute. Used by permission of the publisher.

"The Resilience of Adversary Culture. "*The National Interest* (Summer 2002). Copyright © 2002 by The National Interest. Used by permission of the publisher.

"The Chomsky Phenomenon." *Society* 42, no. 3 (March/April 2005). Copyright © 2005 by Springer. Used with kind permission of Springer Science and Business Media.

"The Banality of Evil and the Political Culture of Hatred." *FrontPage*, June 27, 2002.

"The Left's Love Affair with the Palestinians." *FrontPage*, November 6, 2003.

"Aspiration and Reality." *The New Criterion* (March 2003).

"A Tombstone for Utopias." *New York Sun*, October 31, 2005.

"Clinging to Faith: Public Intellectuals and the God That Failed." *The National Interest* (Spring 2006). Copyright © 2006 by The National Interest. Used by permission of the publisher.

"From a 'Builder of Socialism' to 'Free-Floating Intellectual': My Politically Incorrect Career in Sociology." *The American Sociologist* 32, no. 3 (Fall 2001). Copyright © 2001 by Springer. Used with kind permission of Springer Science and Business Media.

Introduction: The Pleasures of Hate and the New Anti-Americanism

I

The writings that follow reflect both recent and longstanding interests.[1] They include worldwide anti-Americanism, American culture, and mass culture; the persisting political influence of the 1960s; and the controversial relationship between the personal and political realms. Also prominent among these interests are the emotional components of political conflicts (hatred foremost among them), the peculiarities of Islamic fanaticism, and finally, the remnants and reverberations of former communist systems and their supporting ideologies.

American society and its perceptions cannot be understood without reminding ourselves that from its earliest days it has been marked by high and questionably realistic hopes and expectations; it is these expectations that lend a distinctive quality to American society and culture. These qualities have been reflected in both the attitudes and activities of an unusually large number of idealistic and decent Americans as well as in those of a violent, unscrupulous and amoral disposition. Quantitative support for these assertions can be found in the vast number of voluntary organizations and the activities of their members, in the largesse of charitable foundations, in the readiness of all such organizations (as well as of U.S. government agencies) to make their presence felt around the globe whenever disaster strikes, in the admission of refugees of various kinds from all corners of the world, and in the countless social, political, and legislative efforts undertaken over time to improve American society. American idealism also found expression in the proliferation of churches and do-it-yourself religious sects and in the expansion and accessibility of educational institutions. Last but not least, the idealism here noted is also manifest in the behavior of the proverbial "ordinary" Americans, in their trusting and helpful attitude toward strangers (unless short-circuited by racial or ethnic bias).

Notwithstanding the more recent denunciations it has stimulated around the world, this country remains the focus of attraction and hopeful curiosity of countless millions seeking to gain entry to it. These multitudes persist in seeing the United States as the land of promise and opportunity. If all of these immigrants and would-be immigrants have been suffering false consciousness, it is a historically unique and unprecedented case of mass delusion. (At the time of this writing, Congress and public opinion are preoccupied with finding ways to control the relentless influx of millions of illegal immigrants.)

As to the darker sides of America and its residents, the most obvious evidence comes from crime statistics, ranging from the large number of brutal and matter-of-fact killings to rape and robbery and zestful and often imaginative schemes for defrauding consumers, especially the poor and the old,[2] prompted by dreams of wealth. Equally prominent has been white-collar crime, especially in recent times, committed by CEOs of huge corporations with huge incomes, further illuminating the elasticity of human wants and the part played by amassing wealth in the pursuit of a positive and expansive self-conception. There is also the long list of social pathologies that are not by themselves criminal: alcoholism, drug addiction, homelessness, illegitimacy, dropping out of school, and a wide variety of mental illnesses.

American individualism—"radical individualism," if you will—can be held responsible for both a good deal of unscrupulous behavior and for some of the high-minded varieties. The frenzied efforts of Americans to make and remake themselves cut both ways: they find expression in ruthless competition, unbridled ambition, and grotesque, egomaniacal status-seeking as well as in praiseworthy efforts to earn respect and self-respect by helping others. Celebrities are an interesting example of this polarity, as their behavior oscillates between feverish self-aggrandizement and idealistic, if often uninformed, noblesse oblige.[3] They are morbidly fascinating products of American-style modernity stimulating sociological and social historical thought.[4]

Anti-Americanism has always been associated with the contradictory aspects of American society. In the new century it combines murderous violence with lofty and heartfelt religious and political sentiments and justifications. The most striking attribute of the new anti-Americanism is its origin in, and fusion with, an exceptionally pure and intense hatred and the apparent pleasure that hatred provides to those consumed by and acting on it. Rarely before (in more recent times, at any rate) have the pleasures of hatred been so openly displayed, indeed flaunted, and the rhetoric of violence so elaborate and explicit.[5] Islamic terrorists and their supporters proudly and cheerfully proclaim their murderous beliefs, intentions, and actions; Arab crowds joyously display these sentiments in their body language and facial expressions contorted by hatred. Arab political culture reliably supports these attitudes. As a British journalist remarked, "There would be few if any suicide bombers in the Middle East if 'martyrdom' were not glorified by Imams and politicians, if pictures of local 'martyrs' were not proudly displayed in West Bank grocery stores, if Muslim banks did not offer special 'martyrdom' accounts to the relics thereof, if schools did not run essay competitions on 'Why I want to grow up to be a martyr.'"[6] These attitudes have been exemplified by, among others, "Mariam Farhat the mother of three Hamas supporters killed by Israelis. She bade one son goodbye in a home-made videotape, before he stormed an Israeli settlement killing five people, then being shot dead. She said later . . . that she wished she had 100 sons to sacrifice that way. Known as the 'mother of martyrs' she was seen in a campaign video toting a gun."[7] Farhat was elected to the new parliament in Gaza. Closer to home, an Iranian-born graduate of the University of North Carolina at Chapel Hill rented a Jeep for the explicit purpose of "taking some kind of retaliatory action" against the United States by running down as many people as he could on the same campus: "he said he was disappointed that more people were not in the commons crowd around noon when it is typically crowded and he told a detective . . . that he rented the four wheel drive vehicle so he could inflict as much damage as possible." He injured nine people and was arrested. He told the judge that he was "thankful for the opportunity to spread the will of Allah. . . ."[8]

Once a group is branded "infidels," questions of guilt and innocence linked to actual behavior cease to arise. In this, as in some other respects, present-day Islamic political culture has much in common with both Nazi and communist totalitarian ideologies and the practices they had inspired and sanctioned. Each of these belief systems has sweepingly categorized and classified human beings, persecuting or killing them not for what they did but for what they stood for, what they symbolized: various imputed incarnations of evil. As a commentator put it

> the lesson of today's terrorism is that if God exists, then everything, including blowing up thousands of innocent bystanders, is permitted—at least to those who claim to act directly on behalf of God, since, clearly a direct link to God justifies the violation of any merely human constraints and considerations. In short fundamentalists have become no different from the "godless" Stalinist Communists, to whom everything was permitted since they perceived themselves as direct instruments of their divinity, the Historical Necessity of Progress Toward Communism.[9]

As David Brooks also noted, "today's jihadists have a lot in common with the left-wing extremists of the 1930s and 1960s. Ideologically Islamic neo-fundamentalism occupies the same militant space that was once occupied by

Marxism."[10] In both cases there is room for disputing the precise nature of the relationship between theory and practice. Just as it has often been said by advocates of Marxism that the Soviet Union and other "actually existing" socialist states had little or nothing to do with Marxism (or "true Marxism"), it has been argued that the Islamic terrorists claiming to implement Muslim religious commandments through violence had misappropriated and distorted their religious heritage. Both denials are questionable: there was a connection between Marxism and the policies of communist states, and there is one between Islamic beliefs and the activities of Islamic terrorists. What can be disputed is the extent of these connections or the specific ways in which these ideas influenced behavior or policy.

Further parallels may be found between the Western disputes about the threat the Soviet Union and its allies used to represent and present-day positions taken toward the threats of Islamic terrorism and expansionism. The Soviet Union was, of course, a superpower outfitted with nuclear weapons and ballistic missiles and commanded armed forces numbering in the millions; Osama bin Laden has fewer divisions and no nuclear weapons so far but—as has often been pointed out—his followers and supporters may be a greater threat than the Soviet Union used to be, given bin Laden's supporters' deeper and more irrational commitment to the destruction of the West. These groups also enjoy support in the growing Islamic communities in Western Europe and large portions of them are disinclined to adopt Western cultural and political values and practices.

It is of particular significance that Islamic fanatics are fortified by the serene conviction that their murderousness (often combined with unhesitating self-destruction) is divinely sanctioned and rewarded—as was the gunman in Jordan shooting at Western tourists while shouting "Allah-u akbar" or God is Great."[11] These terrorists rejoice in their destructiveness because it rests on the determination to wipe out the evildoers identified as responsible for all the ills and corruptions of the world. Contrary to the "root cause" argument[12] these attitudes are held by many who are far from destitute but are well-educated and of middle- or upper-middle-class background. Education does not provide immunity to the rise and indulgence of the murderous fanaticism here discussed. The violence-prone include those "looking to strike a vague blow against the system and so give their lives (and death) shape and meaning."[13] Hostility to Western values and societies is not necessarily a result of unfamiliarity with them; many prominent Islamic terrorists have been radicalized by living in the West, by their encounter with modernity and secularity and by the difficulty of finding an identity defined by neither tradition nor modernity.[14] Pankaj Mishra, the American Indian author observed, "Uprooted from societies that were once small and close-knit, trying to organize themselves into large collectivities; a people falsifying their past and turning a privately and diversely followed faith into political ideology; focusing their rage against such imagined entities as 'America' and the 'West' and working to rouse people the world over for the sake of revolution—it was hard not to see these men as trying to find their being within history and only floundering in vast empty spaces."[15]

This "rage against imagined entities" finds expression in the demonstrations, protests, and rampages of Arab or Muslim crowds protesting alleged offenses to their religious sensibilities, as for example the notorious Danish cartoons. These protests, as recorded by television, suggest that their major, indeed singular, purpose is the venting of a deep, underlying hatred and resentment shaped by a political culture and only marginally related to some specific grievance or precipitating event. A major theme of these outbursts is the demand for "respect" and outrage over being "disrespected." These outbursts are reminiscent of the violent behavior of American juvenile gangs displaying an extreme sensitivity to alleged slights and expressions of disrespect to which they respond with instant, retributive violence intended to salvage honor. Neither these Arab mobs nor American gang members can claim an abundance of compelling reason for the respect they demand or could boast of demonstrable accomplishments to bolster the claim. In both cases the demand for respect is compensatory, its intensity and emotional quality proportional to the lack of realistic grounds upon which respect or deference could be granted.

The pleasure human beings take in the location, specification, and denunciation of evil cannot be overestimated. A major source of this pleasure is the gratification of the scapegoating impulse that appears to be universal and timeless and signals a determination to hold others—individuals, groups, social, or political forces—responsible for personal difficulties, whatever they are. Human beings appear to have a marked preference for not taking responsibility for those of their actions or attitudes which have unpleasant consequences. Nor is it sufficient to blame bad luck, impersonal social forces, or genetic factors for personal failures or misfortunes; it is far more agreeable to locate a specific human being or group or personalized abstraction that can be blamed with gusto, directly and fully. Identifying evil and evil-doers offers the additional, quasi-spiritual gratification of feeling that there is an ordered and meaningful moral universe where good can be readily distinguished from evil, and in which evil—when located and unmasked—can be crushed without hesitation or regret. Most human beings are deeply averse to moral relativism including the sophisticates who claim to subscribe to it, mostly intellectuals (in our times the so-called postmodernists) whose views and beliefs, on closer examination, also turn out to have a pronounced moral-judgmental component.

In contemporary Western societies the scapegoating impulse is connected to the belief in the social-environmental influences shaping personal lives and to the often-exaggerated connections discerned between the personal and the public or political realm. If society, culture, social forces, the ruling class, the power elite, the military-industrial complex, and so on (take your pick) are responsible for the bad things that befall us, then our personal responsibility for unhappiness is gratifyingly diminished. Blaming social forces or entities is insufficiently gratifying unless human faces or forms can be affixed to them; evil must be personified in order to be hated and destroyed. The nature of political propaganda and its visual images of "the enemy" bear out this proposition.[16]

Somewhat counterintuitively, hatred and compassion are often complementary. Radicals and extremists of all stripes legitimate their hatred by their professed or genuine compassion for the downtrodden and victimized; the victimizers, real or imaginary, inspire fierce hatred on behalf of their victims. Jews have been hated and held guilty of exploiting and corrupting the world of upright gentiles; capitalists for victimizing the poor; whites for the subjugation of "people of color"; men for the inferior social status of women; and so on. At the present time it is the fate of Palestinians that opens the floodgates of anti-Israeli sentiment, and, some would argue, of anti-Semitism.

The complex relationship between compassion and hatred and the part played by intensely personalized hatreds in social-political conflicts have not received the social scientific or historical attention they deserve. Why is the capacity to dehumanize human beings so readily forthcoming? Why is the public infliction of pain and even death entertaining, as indicated by the historical popularity of public executions, tortures, and humiliations? Why do brutal athletic events invariably draw large audiences? Why is so much of popular culture devoted to displays of violence? Those entertaining a benign view of human nature cannot easily dismiss such phenomena or blame them on the "environment" since, after all, the latter is composed and shaped by human beings. While at the present time Islamic political movements and cultures excel in the public endorsement and celebration of righteous hatred and violence—both in their embrace of terrorism and in the continued performance of public executions and mutilations—many other political systems and movements around the world, from Srebrenica to Rwanda, have made use of the same human potential for hate and dehumanization. From the smiling SS executioners on the edge of mass graves (their photos displayed in the Holocaust Museum in Washington, D.C.), to the youthful mobs of the Chinese "Cultural Revolution" thrilled by the violence and humiliation they inflicted, to the cheerful American lynch mobs further in the past, there is ample evidence that political objectives sanctioning violence are nurtured by the subjective enjoyment of inflicting it or observing its infliction. In recent times even children have been enlisted in armed conflicts (mostly in Africa and Palestine), and many seem to enjoy such participation. Juvenile gangs in the United States and other modern societies further illustrate the appeal and enjoyment of violence deployed matter-of-factly in criminal enterprises and in the building of reputation and positive self-conception.

Che Guevara, a cult figure of our times, prompts further reflections on the blend of attitudes that nurture and sanction political violence. In 1964 when he witnessed the overthrow of the Arbenz government in Guatemala he wrote, "It was all a lot of fun, what with the bombs, speeches, and other distractions to break the monotony I was living in." In 1987 he extolled "hatred as an element of struggle: unbending hatred for the enemy, which pushes a human being beyond his natural limitations, making him into an effective, violent, selective, and cold-blooded killing machine." When he gained power he ordered the execution of many alleged or real enemies of the revolution. Following a tour of communist states in 1960, "Kim Il Sung's North Korea was the country that impressed him the most."[17] Neither his pronouncements on hatred and violence nor the actions and policies testifying to their authenticity have discouraged the rise of the Guevara cult (and its commercialization) in the West. He remains to this day a curious amalgam of secular saint and "a quintessential capitalist brand. His likeness adorns mugs . . . key chains, wallets, baseball caps, denim jeans, and . . . [the] omnipresent T-shirts. . . ."[18] He may be seen as both a champion of ideologically sanctioned political violence and an emblem of Western projections of secular sainthood resting on seemingly inexhaustible reservoirs of ignorance, gullibility, and wishful thinking. Reverence to Che Guevara has not been limited to Western intellectuals. The president of Bolivia, Evo Morales, following his swearing-in ceremony "asked for a moment of silence for Inca martyrs, for . . . Che Guevara." He averred that there was a continuity between "the fight of Tupuc Katari" and "the fight of Che Guevara."[19]

While the massive, institutionalized violence and repression communist states carried out is now mainly of historical interest (not that Western historians have shown much interest), the regimes in North Korea and Cuba demonstrate the survival of the genre and its distinctive characteristics discussed in some of the writings in part III of this volume. Particularly noteworthy is the largely intact preservation of totalitarian repression in North Korea and the modest moral indignation and condemnation it has inspired in the West among liberal intellectuals, churches, investigative journalists, and all those concerned with human rights violations around the globe.

II

A paradox underlies a great deal of anti-Americanism: it is the contradictory perception of the United States as both powerful and weak. Its power prompts fear, the weakness moral indignation.

The power of the United States is self-evident deriving from its size, population, unsurpassed economic and military strength, and a global political, military, and cultural presence. So much power, and especially its singular superpower status (attained since the fall of the Soviet Union), is conducive to apprehension. The fearsome superpower image is bolstered by another longstanding perception of the United States as a country that is morally, ethically, or civilizationally underdeveloped, populated by barbarians of sorts or by immature, childish human beings who blundered into an excess of power, wealth, and technology but lack the proper cultural restraints or guidelines for using these assets wisely. An observation made decades ago about American military pilots captures this point of view:

> To the observer outside the fences, a major U.S. airbase is a strange, different, alien and menacing world.... In the officer's mess at Mildenhall [in Britain], a champagne brunch is laid on ... a young pilot clad in a very zippy flying suit festooned with bright badges, flashes, emblems, decals, numbers and bars, sits at a table covered with fine linen eating a giant cream puff with a silver fork. He has champagne there and three other types of cream cake, and, as he quaffs at both, he is deeply absorbed in the pages of a child's comic.[20]

The quote aptly encapsulates the image of the awesome power incongruously possessed by childlike, simple-minded pilots who read comics and devour pastries. Even George Kennan, not given to thoughtless stereotyping, entertained similar notions of the American character: "Here it is easy to see that when man is given ... freedom from both political restraint and want, the effect is to render him childlike ... fun-loving, quick to laughter and enthusiasm, unanalytical, unintellectual ... given to seizures of aggressiveness, driven constantly to protect his status ... by an eager conformism.... Southern California together with all that tendency of American life which it typifies, is childhood without the promise of maturity."[21]

The weakness of America is usually located in the moral-ethical, characterological realm; American society in this perspective is seen as decadent, hedonistic, morally depraved, undisciplined, and riddled with social pathologies such as crime, drug addiction, family disintegration, declining standards of education, and moral relativism; it is a society symbolized by gangsters, cowboys, ruthless capitalists, and corrupt preachers and politicians. Once more George F. Kennan memorably expressed such sentiments during the Cold War:

> Show me first an America which has successfully coped with the problems of crime, drugs, deteriorating educational standards, urban decay, pornography and decadence of one sort or another—show me an America that pulled itself together and is what it might be, then I will tell you how we are going to defend ourselves from the Russians. But as things are I can see very little merit in organizing ourselves to defend from the Russians the porno-shops in central Washington. In fact the Russians are much better in holding pornography at bay than we are.[22]

The concept of the "great Satan" current in the Islamic world and among the most avid haters of the United States also captures the threatening combination of power and evil, that is, power and moral depravity.

The resurgent anti-Americanism in Europe (and its domestic version in the United States) can be readily distinguished from the Islamic variety by its secular and far less violent quality. It has largely been a response to the emergence of the United States as the only superpower following the collapse of the Soviet Union.[23] The United States as the singular superpower and ubiquitous cultural presence[24] has become an inviting target of both diffuse scapegoating impulses and specific grievances around the globe. The European anti-Americanism, "once no more than an expression of the Old World's condescension toward the New . . . has soured into a deep-seated resentment . . . ultimately fueled by the long-term decline in European power."[25] This new anti-Americanism has also been bolstered by the intense anti-Americanism radiating from the Islamic countries and the Muslim populations in Western Europe, while in the United States it feeds on feelings of guilt, on the plausible notion that "if we are so much hated there must be good reasons for it."

The collapse of Soviet communism and the decline of global revolutionary fervor deprived those on the radical left of the apparent promise of alternative social-economic systems but did not dislodge their deep and embittered anti-Americanism. Harold Pinter in England and Noam Chomsky in the United States, as well as their audiences and followers, exemplify these attitudes. On the occasion of receiving the Noble Prize Pinter said, "The crimes of the United States have been systematic, constant, vicious, remorseless but very few people have actually talked about them"—a strange proposition given the huge volume of denunciations of the United States in recent times. Perhaps he meant that these utterances were insufficiently virulent or venomous. He further added, thereby illuminating an important theme of anti-Americanism (and more generally of political hatreds), "It [America] has exercised a quite clinical manipulation of power worldwide while *masquerading* [my emphasis] as a force for universal good . . . brutal, indifferent, scornful and ruthless it may be but it is also very clever."[26] Pinter probably wished to convey that evil is particularly detestable when it is concealed, conspiratorial, and manipulative. The fervent social critic finds particular satisfaction in denouncing evil that is hidden and requires his services to unmask and expose it. The by now venerable notion of "repressive tolerance" (devised by Herbert Marcuse) also appeals to the conspiratorial mindset by suggesting that repression is more sinister and reprehensible when it is masked as tolerance.

As for Chomsky, already in 1966 he believed that unsurpassable misdeeds were integral to American culture and institutions: "[American] schools are the first training ground for troops that will enforce the muted, unending terror of the status quo in the coming years . . . for the technicians who will be developing the means for the American extension of power; for the intellectuals who can be counted on . . . to provide the ideological justification for this particular form of barbarism. . . ."[27]

The old and new anti-Americanism share a major tool of denigration, namely the attribution of moral equivalence between the United States and its enemies, or between the United States and some other, widely acknowledged, self-evident embodiment of evil. In the 1960s and 1970s the Soviet Union was such an entity, and for the most radical anti-Americans, Nazi Germany. Most recently Arab terrorists became morally equivalent. After 9/11 Gore Vidal wrote, "The awesome physical damage Osama and company did to us . . . is as nothing compared to the knockout blow to our vanishing liberties—the Anti-Terrorism Act of 1996. . . ." He also suggested that American pretexts for "the unremitting violence of the United States against the rest of the world . . . might have even given Hitler pause. . . ."[28] Chomsky, in turn, proposed that "in comparison to the conditions imposed by U.S. tyranny and violence, East Europe under Russian rule was practically a paradise."[29] More recently Lewis Lapham, editor of *Harper's Magazine*, explained with heavy-handed irony, why the United States is a fascist state:

> It does no good to ask . . . "Is America a fascist state?" We must ask instead . . . "Can we make America the best damned fascist state the world has ever seen," an authoritarian paradise deserving the admiration of the international capital markets. . . . We're Americans; we have the money and the know-how to succeed where Hitler failed. . . . We can count it as a blessing that we don't bear the burden of an educated citizenry. The systematic destruction of the public-school and library systems over the last thirty years, a program wisely carried out under administrations both Republican and Democratic, protects the market for the sale and distribution of the government's propaganda posters. . . . Thanks to the diligence of our news media and the structure of our tax laws, our affluent and

suburban classes have taken to heart the lesson taught to the aspiring serial killers rising through the ranks at West Point and the Harvard Business School — think what you're told to think.... we are blessed with a bourgeoisie that will welcome fascism as gladly as it welcomes rain in April and sun in June.... We don't have to gag the press or seize the radio stations. People trained to the corporate style of thought ... have no further use for free speech.... Who better than the Americans to lead the fascist renaissance...."[30]

The sentiments shared by Lapham, Chomsky, and Pinter belong to what an author called "fundamentalist anti-Americanism"[31] that finds expression in the sweeping and impassioned denunciation of what is seen as a comprehensively and fundamentally evil and corrupt entity rather than one characterized by specific and potentially corrigible failings. Paul Trout linked this kind of anti-American rhetoric to the prophetic tradition of "righteous fury" and the conviction that "wealth corrupts" and "acquisitiveness is the root of much evil." He further observed, "These vituperative accusations ... are nothing like the routine, predictable complaints and gripes that arise from partisan politics and from the chronic conflicts of a heterogeneous and dynamic society. These accusations vilify the nation as a whole: its institutions, its history, its basic values, its very existence."[32]

A noteworthy feature of the new anti-Americanism is its growing confluence with anti-Israeli attitudes and sentiments not only in Arab countries but also among Western intellectuals. Andre Markovits wrote, "Anti-Zionism, together with anti-Americanism is a new litmus test of progressive politics.... If one is not at least a serious doubter of the legitimacy of the state of Israel ... one runs the risk of being excluded from the entity called 'the left.'"[33] Boycotts of Israel have been proposed and enacted.[34] Such sentiments can also be found among Israeli academic intellectuals who developed a rejection of their society comparable to sentiments of American intellectuals in the 1960s and 1970s including "passions of anger and indignation, bitterness and repudiation.... Israel in their eyes is guilty of a great betrayal and should be punished."[35] Their disappointment is strikingly similar to the longstanding American belief that the United States failed to live up to its founding promises and hopes. Similarly disposed Israeli intellectuals support, in effect, the dissolution of Israel by proposing to make it a binational state (in which the Arab population would soon submerge the Jewish portion). These attitudes also resemble the leftist support for "multiculturalism" in the United States that is hoped to dilute and eventually submerge white, Western, Eurocentric culture. There has been a commingling in recent years of anti-American and anti-Israeli attitudes among both American and Israeli intellectuals. Some of the most prominent Western anti-Israeli voices have been Jewish, such as Chomsky and Eric Hobsbawm. They and other Western intellectuals abhor

Israel because it is an ally and protégé of the United States and because it is a Western outpost in the third world and a major military power in the region. It is difficult to determine to what degree undercurrents of anti-Semitism merge with and nurture these anti-Israeli attitudes in the West.

It is a notable paradox that this new and strident anti-Americanism in the West has unfolded against a cultural background saturated with moral relativism. If this relativism had been serious and consistent its upholders, postmodernists and deconstructionists, would have refrained from the frequent, highly judgmental denunciations of American society, U.S. foreign policy, capitalism, and globalization. But the "deconstruction" of reality (or of certain texts) has always been selective and governed by political-ideological preferences: "theory was seen as a political weapon with which to challenge the status quo. . . . The hope was to revolutionize the world" observed Stanley Fish,[36] who in his earlier philosophical incarnation had contributed to the proliferation of these attitudes and theories. What these theories actually promoted was a *selective relativism* allied to identity politics, multiculturalism, and antirationalist positions. Richard Wolin wrote, "An entire generation of post-Communist thinkers on the left have rushed to embrace 'difference' ethics, identity politics and other celebrations of 'heterogeneity' at the expense of . . . universal principles. They have been only too eager . . . to blame reason itself . . . for the multiple catastrophes of the twentieth century."[37] The roots of this "neotribalist ethos" were discernible in the protest movements of the 1960s, in their preoccupation with and overreaction to the evils of homogenization, uniformity, and conformity, as well as in the quest for community that paradoxically combined with assertions of radical individualism. It is a further paradox that many if not most intellectuals consider the foundation of their moral identity their social critical activities that are hardly compatible with moral relativism.

III

The moral relativism here sketched has also been boosted by and is reflected in the relentless entertainment orientation of American culture, mass as well as elite. The *New York Times*, once considered the voice of reason and seriousness has joined the scramble for diverting, attention-getting stories and formats; increasingly it fills its op-ed pages and book review section with "cute" illustrations wasting space and sacrificing content. In 2005 its front page included lengthy articles about stuffed toy animals decorating long distance trucks and a floating island in an unremarkable small pond in Springfield, Massachusetts. The magazine section introduced cartoons and supposedly entertaining (very) short stories in addition to regularly featuring articles about athletes, fashion designers, and popular entertainers. The magazine also took it upon itself to acquaint its readers regularly with the "favorite take-out food," "the morning routine," the "clothing item he cannot live without," and other indispensable information about assorted celebrities such as Drew Nieporent, "the force behind 15 restaurants."[38] In turn the Sunday style section was apparently designed to cater in its entirety to the more mindless forms of consumerism, status seeking, and celebrity cult.

Another remarkable example of these trends was the prominent coverage by the *New York Times* and the major television networks (ABC, CBS, and NBC) on their evening news of the story of a man whose Corvette sports car stolen thirty-seven years ago was "miraculously" recovered.[39] It was meant to be a heart-warming report of lifelong attachment, albeit attachment to a piece of machinery, with a happy ending. Each of these stories took for granted that there was nothing peculiar about harboring feelings toward a car that used to be reserved for human beings or at least pets; lavishing such affection on an inanimate object was considered perfectly normal and preeminently newsworthy. It did not occur to the reporters of this story (or to their editors) that people who allegedly "love" a machine may have difficulties with human attachments and it is the latter difficulty that may deserve discussion.

The entertainment orientation of the mass media also reflects relativism and the diminished capacity of the American public to make important distinctions, moral or aesthetic. Our system of education has made a substantial contribution to this state of affairs through its campaigns against "elitism" and "judgmental" dispositions and by increasingly distancing itself from Western cultural traditions. One result has been the spectacular decline in literary reading especially among the young influenced by the educational reforms inspired by the 1960s. As a critic of these trends wrote "young Americans today are not encouraged to love their . . . tradition, their language, their literature, for fear that they will offend someone who does not 'identify' with them. . . ."[40] The politically colored rejection of the cultural traditions in question provides further explanation of these trends.

The search for maximizing audiences or readership undertaken by television producers and publishers is helped along by the idea that everything is a matter of subjective interpretation and the pursuit of objective truth is pointless as well as unhelpful for attracting larger audiences. The best-selling and much discussed memoirs of a former drug addict and petty criminal (James Frey), which misrepresented and embellished his life to make it more dramatic and saleable, is a case in point. It is easier to erase the distinction between fact and fiction when the belief in objective truth and a hierarchy of moral and aesthetic values is shaky or nonexistent. As the critic Michiko Kakutani wrote,

> By focusing on the "indeterminacy" of texts and the crucial role of the critic in imputing meaning, deconstructionists were purveying a fashionably nihilistic view of the world suggesting that all meaning is relative, all truth elusive. . . . When people assert that there is no ultimate historical reality an environment is created in which the testimony of a witness to the Holocaust . . . can actually be questioned. . . . Postmodernists do not merely acknowledge the obstacles that stand in the way of objectivity but also celebrate those obstacles, elevating relativism into a kind of end in itself.[41]

Of the broader significance of these trends Daniel Mendelsohn remarked, "Perhaps the most dismaying response to the James Frey scandal was the feeling on the part of many readers, that true or false, his book had given them the feel-good 'redemptive' experience. . . ." Mendelsohn also noted that the notion of a subjective reality, or "'my reality' raises even more far-reaching and dire questions about the state of our culture, one in which the very concept of reality seems to be in danger."[42]

A different kind of attack on objective reality and, arguably, on the enterprise of making differentiated moral judgments was mounted by the novelist Nicholson Baker in his purported history of World War II (*Human Smoke*). The volume sought to convey that there was no moral distinction to be made between the Nazis and the Allies or between Hitler and Roosevelt. Anne Applebaum wrote, "He [Baker] has used his license as a 'novelist' to excuse himself from all of the tedious work of genuine knowledge. By way of research he has read back issues of the *New York Times* and *New York Herald Tribune*. . . . From them he has plucked bits of information . . . that he finds compelling. . . ." He accumulated an arbitrary "set of anecdotes" as a basis of his pronouncements and insinuations.[43]

Also characteristic of the trends discussed here is the fact that on occasion intellectuals themselves (especially those considering themselves public intellectuals) take the role of entertainer and become willing participants in, or purveyors of, popular culture. Cornel West records rap CDs and appears at benefits with movie starts and famous athletes; the late Jean Baudrillard (described as "one of France's most celebrated philosophers") "some years ago . . . appeared on the stage of Whiskey Pete's, near Las Vegas, wearing a gold lame suit with mirrored lapels, and read a poem."[44] George Galloway, the British member of parliament and prominent critic of the United States and his own society (a public figure, if not exactly an intellectual) appeared on a British television game show called *Celebrity Big Brother*, "imitating a cat, nuzzling and purring on all fours and licking imaginary cream from the hands of . . . [an] actress. . . ."⁴⁵ Norman Mailer and Gore Vidal appeared in movies in cameo roles; Susan Sontag made movies.

Two explanations may be suggested. One is that such individuals yearn for publicity and celebrity status that can be furthered by exposure in the more accessible mass media. The other explanation may be found in the embrace of the relativism that erases the distinctions between entertainment and intellectual expression, entertainment, and social criticism.

If supposedly serious public intellectuals sometimes act like entertainers, even more frequently entertainers act like serious public intellectuals, portentously offering their opinions on a wide range of political, social, economic, and cultural issues and policies. They have been encouraged to play this role by the respectful public attention they receive and the frequent invitations to appear before various congressional committees.⁴⁶ Politicians seeking to enlarge their own visibility rejoice in the association with popular entertainers. As Leon Wieseltier observed, "Not since the 1960s have so many entertainers believed that they can rescue the world." While their uninformed idealism is not in doubt, their influence is a good measure of the flaws of American political culture. Again, Wieseltier wrote, "they [celebrities] corrupt the consciousness that they raise, because they confirm them in their belief in the moral authority of fame. . . . Nothing more disfigures personal authenticity in America than the veneration of celebrities. . . . It teaches Americans to live vicariously passively, alienated from the possibilities of their lives, in slavish imitation of people luckier than themselves."⁴⁷

Celebrities thus play multiple social roles: they dominate popular entertainments, pronounce on weighty social, political, and economic issues, and are also intimately involved in the world of commerce through their participation in advertising, endorsing a wide range of products and services.

The celebrity phenomenon brings together three major strands in American culture: individualism, egalitarianism, and relativism. Individualism propels people to engage in the single-minded pursuit of success (testified to by both material rewards and recognition), and it underlies the desire to emerge from anonymity; it also encourages the pursuit of one's "true self." The importance placed upon the self, the craving for personal fame and success, has been instrumental in the rise of the public relations "industry," dedicated to the unbridled pursuit of publicity. Egalitarianism and antielitism in turn promote the quest for celebrity status by promising that it can be accomplished by virtually anybody, that no specific talents, qualifications, or prerequisites are needed. Finally, relativism muddles the criteria as to the grounds on which a person may deserve acclaim and admiration; it provides assurance that it matters little for what reason, on what grounds celebrity status is acquired and promoted. Thus the self becomes a product to be sold, promoted, invented, and reinvented. Celebrity status is not merely gratifying for those who attain it, it is also highly marketable in advertising and political campaigns.

While most celebrities are entertainers, broadly defined (including those in competitive sports), no occupation is immune to the phenomenon: academics like Cornel West may qualify, as does the real estate operator Donald Trump; models and "supermodels" too can join their ranks, as do TV anchormen and women of no discernible qualification or talent, as well as wealthy hostesses appearing on the society pages of major newspapers—anybody capable of generating and commanding publicity for virtually any reason. The proliferation of celebrities also reflects the demand for novelty in the entertainment business and popular demand for the "services" they provide as short-term role models and objects of vicarious gratification. Celebrities fulfill fantasies of being beautiful, rich, famous, powerful, and recipients of vast amounts of attention.

Celebrity worship has something in common with the fleeting and artificial sense of community conjured by the shared support of a football or baseball team. It is not a uniquely American phenomenon but one of the by-products of modernity stimulated by the convergence of mass entertainments, diminished social ties, eroding communities, high expectations, and aspirations unsupported by genuine talent or ability.

Popular culture, although primarily dedicated to entertainment, is not wholly apolitical. It has been influenced by political correctness during the last decades of the past century, especially in its presentation of "role models" for minorities, women, and those of alternative sexual orientation.

IV

A collection of my writings published twenty years ago was entitled *The Survival of the Adversary Culture*. There are many indications that this culture has endured in the twenty-first century, replenished by new causes, movements, and grievances while some of the old ones refuse to fade away. Jerold Auerbach wrote, "arguments over American politics and culture still divide along fault lines that opened during the sixties. . . . The sixties are long gone, but the struggle over their meaning endures." The revival of the adversarial attitudes of the 1960s in recent American movies was shown by Ross Douthat. In turn Wendy Kaminer observed that "New Age rhetoric . . . permeates our culture."[48] There are no better indicators of the connection between the present and the not-so-distant past than the persisting reverence for the problematic idealism of the 1960s. For Studs Terkel, unrepentant Weathermen activist Bill Ayers personified this lost idealism. Terkel characterized Ayers's memoirs (*Fugitive Days*) as "a deeply moving elegy to all those young dreamers who tried to live decently in an indecent world."[49]

Faith in the essential innocence of the Rosenbergs (executed for spying for the Soviet Union) is another illustration of the durability of these attitudes—a faith that has withstood the accumulation of all evidence to the contrary. A recent Fordham University Law School Forum was devoted to them and their supposed "artistic influence." Tony Kushner, one of the featured speakers, argued that they were "murdered" while E. L. Doctorow proposed that the Rosenberg case was fabricated to fan the flames of the Cold War and to impose on the American public "a Puritan, punitive civil religion." The moderator warned the audience that they must not ask "disrespectful" questions."[50]

In December 2005 a "landmark" conference on the state of American psychotherapy took place in California attended by nine thousand psychologists, social workers, and students. In the opening convocation "Dr. Hunter 'Patch' Adams—charismatic therapist played on screen by Robin Williams—displayed on a giant projection screen photos from around the world of burned children, starving children, diseased children. . . . He called for a 'a last stand of loving care' to prevail over the misery in the world . . . and 'our fascistic government.' Overcome by his own message, Dr. Adams eventually fell to the floor of the stage in tears."[51]

If the casual attribution of "fascistic" to the U.S. government by the keynote speaker provoked neither protest nor astonishment it might have been because for many of those in the audience the atmosphere brought back happy memories of the 1960s. Said one participant, "this is like a rock concert for most of us"—offering another illustration of the entertainment orientation of our times. A similar emblematic incident occurred at the Modern Language Association meeting in December 2006 when Ariel Dorfman delivered what he called a "whimsical literary invention" intended as a parable of what *might happen* in the United States if it were hit by "an even more devastating and lethal terrorist attack" than that of 9/11. The "whimsical literary invention"—that is, Dorfman's imagined mistreatment by an already well-established American police state—"had tapped into a deep paranoia": his "fictional account of detention . . . had resonated with unbridled fantasies" of his audience. "Not one of my friends and associates at the convention . . . dismissed my tall tale as patently absurd. . . . My fraudulent yarn was apparently all too terrifyingly plausible. . . ."[52] That is to say, the assembled academics were convinced that they already lived in a police state; they were the type of people who (as Christopher Hitchens put it) considered John Ashcroft (or his successor) a greater threat than Osama bin Laden.[53] It may be recalled here that in the 1960s too it was conventional wisdom among many on the left that the United States was a police state.

The victim culture as a whole remains well and alive. Its more unusual manifestations include a long confessional article of Naomi Wolf, the popular feminist author, recalling an incident twenty years ago that traumatized her for life: one of her professors in college put his hand on her thigh. Anne Applebaum commented: "Wolf's article is not merely about that event (a secret that she 'can't bear to carry around anymore'). The article is also about the lasting damage that this single experience has wrought on a woman who has since written a number of bestsellers, given hundreds of lectures, been featured on dozens of talk shows and photographed in various glamorous postures. . . . Not that she mentions her achievements. On the contrary she implies that this terrible experience left on a lasting mark on her . . . career."[54] Such wallowing in the victim role is apparently fueled by self-pity and an evident satisfaction derived from magnifying and nurturing the sufferings experienced. The attachment to victimhood also rests on the moral distinction conferred by the acknowledged victim status and, at another level, the tangible benefits of preferential treatment accorded to those in the certified victim categories. Persisting in the self-conception of victim yields further benefit by reducing responsibility for one's life and especially its difficulties; it also helps to legitimize the rejection of the entire social system and perpetuate the role of the righteous social critic that would be undermined by admitting to personal successes and accomplishments.

Alongside the attachment to victimhood (or at any rate, its politically correct varieties), "the inequality taboo"[55] has also retained its prominence, especially in educational institutions as was manifest in the furor the president of Harvard University created by cautiously entertaining the *possibility* that the unequal scientific achievements of women may *in part* be explained by genetic dispositions.[56] The "inequality taboo" finds further expression in the continued aversion to the rigorous evaluation of student performance in both colleges and schools since such evaluations reveal substantial differences between the performance and aptitudes of students; it is also objected to on the grounds that it enhances competition and penalizes minorities. A manifestation of this aversion has been the abandonment in many high schools of class ranking, in order to "cut down on competition" as some school administrators saw it. A school principal observed that "when they don't rank, then they have to look at the total child."[57] He did not explain how the "total child" was to be evaluated and by what criteria. Such hankering "for the total child" (or the total human being)—entailing the reluctance to recognize differences among human beings and the aversion to making critical evaluations of them—was, of course, also emblematic of the 1960s.

"Multiculturalism," another article of faith of our times, can also be linked to egalitarian values given its alleged belief in the equality of all cultures— "alleged" because it routinely deprecates Western culture, produced by "dead white males." Closer inspection also reveals that the egalitarian-relativist message of multiculturalism is contradicted and outweighed by affirmations of pride in group identity based on some unique cultural heritage. In the final analysis multiculturalism has little to do with culture; it is a political rather than cultural phenomenon: "the multiculturalist's real interest is not pedagogy but power, not teaching but advocacy, not the history of the past but the politics of the present." Moreover, the "multicultural belief in the impossibility of transcending your point of view applies in particular to . . . moral and political preferences."[58]

In the final analysis, the declarations of an impartial relativism supporting a nonjudgmental multiculturalism are negated by strongly held, and highly judgmental, beliefs and convictions.

A recent expression of multiculturalism has been a new solicitousness on campuses toward Islamic religion and culture. Following 9/11 faculties and administrators often appeared to evince greater concern with a possible anti-Islamic (or anti-Arab) backlash than with the dangers and threats of Islamic terrorism. A notable manifestation of such attitudes was the newly required freshmen reading assignment of the Koran at the University of North Carolina (discussed in one of the writings in part II of this volume).

Identity politics is another legacy of the 1960s and a prominent feature of the current political and cultural landscape. It rests on the belief that political attitudes and allegiances are, or ought to be, rooted in a shared group identity—racial, ethnic, or sexual. This belief is linked to a compensatory pursuit of identity ("black is beautiful," "gay pride") on the part of racial, ethnic, and sexual minorities who used to be (and sometimes still are) devalued and who suffered discrimination. The victim status (former, current, or avowed) is an important contributor to this sense of identity. Even physical handicaps can be enlisted in this pursuit. Deaf students at Gallaudet University in Washington, D.C., consider " deafness not a disability but . . . an identity" and many reject implants and hearing aids "arguing that they undermine a strong deaf identity and pride." Such technologies are further rejected since they supposedly imply that "deaf people are not good enough, they need to be fixed." These students insist that sign language is the only authentic communication among the deaf compatible with their culture and identity.[59] There were protests against a new president not considered "deaf enough,"[60] a notion similar to the critiques of some black politicians not considered "black enough." The Gallaudet trustees eventually gave in to the protestors "in the forefront of deaf-rights movement" who viewed the appointment as "an assault on deaf culture and deaf identity."[61]

The transformation of deafness from an affliction or disability into a "culture" and source of prideful identity illustrates not only the rise of identity culture and its affinity with victimhood but also a desperate, and somewhat confused, quest for identity and community in modern American society in which a sense of identity and community has become increasingly difficult to attain or retain.

The attempts to change one's sexual identity (with or without surgery) is another manifestation of the same phenomenon—the problematic pursuit of identity—most recently demonstrated by a proposal in New York City that "would have allowed people to alter sex on their birth certificate without sex change surgery."[62] These beliefs and attitudes are also closely related to cultural relativism and the notion that sexual identity is "socially constructed" and has a negligible or irrelevant biological basis. Thus identity becomes a matter of personal (or group) definition and preference.

At last, the protests against the current war in Iraq also bring back memories of both the anti-Vietnam war protests of the 1960s and 1970s and those against the 1991 Gulf War. All these antiwar protests rapidly mutated into broad and impassioned critiques of American society and its major institutions and often into expressions of warmth toward the adversaries of the United States: the Vietcong and communist North Vietnam during the 1960s and 1970s and, to a lesser extent, Sadam Hussein's Iraq during the two Iraq wars. An observer of a major antiwar demonstration in October 2005 wrote, "the sheer number of grievances on offer overwhelmed the only one that counted, what Washington endured this weekend wasn't exactly an antiwar march. It was anti-everything: Israel, the U.S. military, capitalism, colonialism, Wal-Mart. . . . [A] catalogue of fringe causes and well-advertised sympathy for dictatorships. . . ."[63] Similar attitudes were apparent during the "counterinaugural events" sponsored by the International Socialist Organization that offered its support to the insurgents in Iraq.[64] Characteristic of the anticapitalist animus of the recent protests (recalling similar sentiments from the 1960s and 1970s) has been the slogan and imagery of "blood for oil." The symbolic use of blood in the recent antiwar protests (as in the 1960s) was revived by left-wing Catholic activists who "poured vials of their own blood . . . onto the walls, windows and American flag" [in an Army recruiting center in upstate New York]. They had activist parents of the 60s generation and modeled themselves on the Berrigan brothers." Frida Berrigan, daughter of the late Philip Berrigan (famed 1960s protestor) was among them.[65]

Reminiscent of the radical Vietnam war protestors, Cindy Sheehan, prominent present-day war protestor (and mother of a soldier killed in Iraq), was led to embrace, literally and figuratively, Hugo Chavez of Venezuela, a prominent enemy of her enemy (President Bush) as she appeared with him at a rally in Caracas. Chavez assured her, "Cindy, we are with you in your fight. . . ." As the *New York Times* noted, "Mr. Chavez has become a voice for many opponents of the Bush administration policies who are drawn to his self-styled socialist revolution and his close alliance with . . . Fidel Castro."[66] Presumably Sheehan, radicalized by the loss of her son, gave little thought to the propaganda services she rendered to Chavez or to the kind of political system he has been creating in Venezuela. She is among the growing number of new political pilgrims who discovered Venezuela under Chavez as the current embodiment of their hopes for a new socialist-revolutionary society. Cuba too continues to claim the loyalties of many Western intellectuals and entertainers including Harold Pinter, Nadine Gordimer, Harry Belafonte, and Tariq Ali, who "signed a letter claiming that in Cuba 'there has been not a single case of disappearance, torture or extrajudicial execution since 1959. . . .'" [67] Even North Korea was occasionally given the benefit of doubt. In the spring of 2006 the Harvard Alumni Association organized a tour of North Korea (costing $636 per night), unlikely to be a critical fact-finding mission since all such tours are strictly controlled by the North Korean authorities. The tour memo instructed the tourists that they "will be expected to bow as a gesture of respect at the statue of Kim Il Sung" and explained that such bowing is the normal thing to do because "North Korea like every country, has its unique protocols."[68] It is unlikely that the Harvard Alumni Association would have organized a tour of apartheid-era South Africa and advise the travelers to observe apartheid since it was part of the "unique protocols" in that country.

As to my own views of the war in Iraq, I was pleased by the removal of Sadam Hussein and his regime from power—an exceptionally brutal and repressive dictatorship presided over by an exceptionally repellent human being.[69] I was inclined to believe that almost anything that replaced his system would be an improvement, including an Iraq splintered along ethnic lines. Events following the initial American military success made clear that the United States did not properly plan and conduct this intervention. Not enough troops were used for keeping the peace after the victory, borders went unguarded, there was easy access to leftover military equipment; the insurrection was not anticipated, nor the pouring in of suicidal Islamic terrorists. The proverbial unintended consequences have overwhelmed praiseworthy goals (which might have been unrealizable to begin with) as the human and material costs of this war continued to erode its initial accomplishments.[70] There also remains the difficult and unresolved question of whether it is possible to bring democracy to places like Iraq where intolerant political-religious cultures and traditions and ethnic hostilities are deeply entrenched. At the same time, the elections held since the overthrow of Saddam have been accomplishments and Iraq currently appears to have a democratically elected government of otherwise dubious credentials and modest accomplishments. Unlike in Vietnam, where the forces opposed to the United States had (at least initially) substantial popular support, the Saddam regime was widely detested except on the part of the Sunni minority, beneficiaries of his rule. There remains a remote possibility that the recent troop "surge" could accomplish something. In short I am not yet willing to conclude that the U.S. invasion was a *totally* misguided effort, although at times (depending on the daily news) I feel so.

V

Some of the writings in this volume (mostly in part II) should make clear that notwithstanding my longstanding critiques of the adversary culture I am well aware of numerous flaws of American culture and society and of various policies of George W. Bush's administration. I find its energy and environmental policies particularly irresponsible, although it must be acknowledged that they are congruent with widespread popular attitudes and preferences. These popular attitudes find expression in indifference to conservation, specifically in the popularity of SUVs driven by approximately half of the American public. And while I do not consider capitalism the source of all, or most, evil, capitalism's tendency to glorify consumption and its encouragement of the relentless pursuit of material gain (recently testified to by the notorious corporate scandals) taint many accomplishments of American society. I also find misleading and wrongheaded the notion—zealously promoted by the advertising industry—that a solution for every human need and problem can be found in the purchase of the appropriate goods or services.

While I do not believe that human beings are inherently or potentially equal in their abilities or ethical dispositions, or that a wide range of inequalities among them can be erased by well-intentioned government policies, neither do I believe that the survival of democratic capitalism requires or justifies the exorbitant income differentials that exist in our society. The astronomical incomes of the CEOs of major corporations and popular entertainers (including athletes) seems to have little moral or economic justification. At the same time I do not believe that these excesses and the underlying, apparently insatiable, human desires are peculiar to Americans or the times we live in. It may be, however, that American society provides more favorable conditions and greater incentives for the unfettered expression of these impulses and inclinations by encouraging a notion that there should be no limitation placed upon the material rewards reaped by successful individuals. The pursuit of self-expression by elaborate consumption is as old as the end of subsistence economy or access to a discretionary income. What is new is that in this society (and some others in Western Europe) such impulses can be expressed and gratified by larger numbers of people than in the past and that people are routinely provided with an extraordinary range of choice in the realm of consumption that was not available at other times, nor was such choice available in other realms of life unrelated to consumption.

"Self-realization" pursued by owning and driving a Hummer (the large, gas-guzzling vehicle originally designed for military use) and other similar vehicles is a good example of the misguided expression of these impulses. It represents not just conspicuous consumption and status seeking but also a longing for at least symbolic power. Such yearnings found expression in the apparent craze for the Toyota Land Cruiser, "the vehicle of choice for the Taliban . . . and for Hollywood honchos like Tom Hanks and fashion executives like Millard Drexler of J. Crew. . . ." One of these enthusiasts, "on his third Land Cruiser," was quoted saying, "If there's a car to be crazy about, this is it. . . . It's easy to park because you can just push the other car out of the way." The article I quote from also discussed the great expenses incurred in the acquisition of these vehicles, even when used and dilapidated. The writer confessed with some pride to having bought one and getting it transported from Los Angeles to New York at great expense, followed by spending "the equivalent of a month's rent on a studio apartment to park it in a 24-hour garage." She "felt this kind of desire before—for, say, a pair of Prada sandals."[71] There was no attempt to explain what exactly accounted for the veneration of these vehicles; it was implied that such devotion to a hunk of movable metal was a romantic whimsy, something not fully rational but nonetheless to be readily understood and indulged.

VI

Most of the pieces in this volume were written after I retired from teaching, and the first draft of this introduction was written while I was staying temporarily in a retirement community called "Leisure World" in Laguna Woods, California. These circumstances were conducive to musings about living and growing old in American society and about the advantages and disadvantages of aging in a modern, as opposed to a more traditional, society.

Insofar as most traditional societies were (and are) poor, life expectancies were much shorter and medical care inferior, which made aging more unpleasant from the physical and material point of view. While the ranks of the old in America continue to include many who are poor, most of them are far from destitute; tens of millions of the old can afford to pursue a life of leisure and attempted personal fulfillment that was not available earlier in their own lives or for similar age groups at other times. The "Leisure World" mentioned above is an example of such comforts and conveniences. It is a gated community for slightly over 20,000 people who must be over fifty-five; it was established in the early 1960s, thoroughly and well planned, attractively landscaped, provided with several clubhouses and workshops offering a wide range of recreational opportunities and the pursuit of hobbies. There are numerous large swimming pools, golf courses, and tennis courts and a well-equipped computer center, as well as scores of clubs and associations. Just outside the gates are a large hospital, medical offices, and shopping malls. The children and grandchildren of the residents live elsewhere but come to visit. Few of the residents were born in the area. In this setting the old are as comfortable and carefree as can be; the inhabitants of Leisure World have been freed of the routines and exertions of work; leisure is indeed in unlimited supply. In some ways the place reminds one of the half-baked notions of Marx and his successors of what communist society would be like and (in Soviet terminology) its projected fostering the "all round development" of the lucky people who will live in it.

While medically and economically far more deprived, it appears that the old in traditional societies fared better in regard to more intangible benefits. They occupied a more generously defined social space, had higher status, and were accorded respect on account of their age—quite possibly undeserved on rational, meritocratic grounds but nonetheless agreeable for those upon whom it was bestowed. The second great advantage these elders enjoyed in more traditional societies was the possession of religious beliefs and certitudes that made the approaching end of life easier to accept. By contrast, I strongly suspect that—notwithstanding widespread affirmations of belief in God, heaven, and hell (repeatedly found in survey research)—most Americans, indeed most of those living in modern secular societies, have no similarly comforting beliefs and correspondingly are poorly equipped to deal with their own death and the deaths of those close to them. Quite possibly a large, deeply religious minority of Americans believes, and takes solace in the belief (as most people did and still do in traditional societies), that death is not the irrevocable and meaningless end and that there is some kind of continuity between life, death, and afterlife. Notwithstanding the beliefs of this minority, modern American society is replete with death-denying propensities and a youth cult; it is the setting of the frenzied and often unseemly efforts of the old (under pressure by this culture) to act and appear young. The latest notable addition to the long list of these overreaching exhortations and assurances has been the (2006) book by Gail Sheehy entitled *Sex and the Seasoned Woman*, which attempts to persuade and reassure readers that aging is no obstacle to superb sexual performance and fulfillment and that nothing should prevent Americans from endlessly reinventing themselves. As Daphne Merkin observed, Sheehy is a virtuoso "in keeping with the desires of a culture frantically dedicated to the pursuit of silver linings—ever on the lookout for evidence that life is not hard, death is not final and it is never too late to make another, better choice. . . ."[72] In a similar spirit Eric Cohen and Leon R. Cass pointed out that

> there is something weird about treating old age as a time of life when things should always be "getting better." While aging affords some people new possibilities for learning and "growth" it also means—eventually and inevitably—the loss of one's vital powers. Some people may ride horses or climb mountains in their seventies and eighties, just like in the commercials for anti-arthritis medication but such . . . images offer a partial and misleading picture of the realities

of senescence. . . . Endless chatter about "healthy aging" is at bottom a form of denial. . . . The nursing home refutes the dream of limitless progress toward ageless bodies. . . ."[73]

Death and dying are still largely taboo topics; the old in America are encouraged to frolic and mimic the young; extending one's life remains a major preoccupation. Increasing numbers of people exchange or renovate body parts for aesthetic and psychological, rather than medical, reasons. Selling medications, cosmetics, and recreational services to the old and aging is a big and growing business. The prevalent denial of death is, of course, a contradiction in a supposedly religious society. But Americans manage to combine a robust, acted-out secularity with a less than fully convincing spirituality.

The paradoxes and incongruities of American social and cultural values and practices mirror those of human nature. Like human beings, and especially those shaped by modernity, American society seeks to reconcile a wide range of contradictory values, impulses, and desires. It is the most highly evolved embodiment of these contradictory and mutually exclusive human attributes and efforts, as well as the most determined to bridge the gaps between them; therein lies its historical distinctiveness, strength, and weaknesses.

NOTES

1. See Paul Hollander, *The Many Faces of Socialism* (New Brunswick, N.J.: Transaction, 1984); *The Survival of the Adversary Culture* (New Brunswick, N.J.: Transaction, 1988); *Decline and Discontent* (New Brunswick, N.J.: Transaction, 1992); *Discontents: Postmodern and Postcommunist* (New Brunswick, N.J.: Transaction, 2002).

2. See, for example, Charles Duhigg, "Bilking the Elderly, with a Corporate Assist," *New York Times*, May 20, 2007.

3. The Annual Oscar Award ceremonies in Hollywood (still awaiting an in-depth anthropological or social-psychological study) manifest some of these polarities. On these occasions audiences and participants are treated to veritable orgies of implausible humility, outpourings of fellow-feeling, affirmations of devotion to family, as well as gratitude and love of mankind—all this against a background of the fierce competitiveness, envy, backbiting, unrelenting ambition, and status-seeking prevalent in these circles.

4. Daniel Boorstin's reflections on celebrities remain unsurpassed after almost half a century. See *The Image: A Guide to Pseudo-Events in America* (New York: Harper & Row, 1961). For a recent instructive summation of the phenomenon, see Joseph Epstein, "The Culture of Celebrity," *Weekly Standard*, October 17, 2005.

5. For some chilling examples and examination of this rhetoric see Daniel Jonah Goldhagen, "The New Threat: Radical Politics of Islamic Fundamentalism," *New Republic*, March 13, 2006.

6. Mark Steyn, "Islam *Does* Incubate Terrorism," *Daily Telegraph*, July 12, 2005.
7. Ian Fisher, "Women, Secret Hamas Strength, Win Votes at Polls and New Role," *New York Times*, February 3, 2006, 1.
8. Brenda Goodman, "Defendant Offers Details of Jeep Attack at University," *New York Times*, March 8, 2006.
9. Slavoj Zizek, "Defenders of the Faith," op-ed, *New York Times*, March 12, 2006.
10. David Brooks, "Trading Cricket for Jihad," *New York Times*, August 4, 2005.
11. Suha Maayeh, "Gunmen Kills British Man and Wounds 6 in Jordan," *New York Times*, September 5, 2006. As to the belief in killing and redemption, an Arab suicide bomber candidate explained, "by pressing the detonator, you can immediately open the door to Paradise—it is the shortest path to Heaven." In a training video for suicide bombers the trainer asked, "Are you ready? Tomorrow you will be in Paradise." (Nasra Hassan, "An Arsenal of Believers," *New Yorker*, November 19, 2001, 36, 37; see also pp. 39, 40, 41). Young suicide bombers proudly display their "martyr pictures" taken before the appropriate action. See, for example, Jeffrey Goldberg, "The Forgotten War," *New Yorker*, September 11, 2006, 45. Further illustration of this mentality may be found in the distribution of a half a million "small plastic keys" by the Iranian authorities during the Iraq-Iran war to the young, including children of twelve, who were used to clear minefields with their bodies. "Before each mission one of [these] keys would be hung around each child's neck. It was supposed to open the gates to paradise. . . ." (Matthias Kuntzel, "Ahmadinejad's Demons," *New Republic*, April 14, 2006, 15).
12. The gist of the root cause argument is that Islamic terrorism has been a product of the dire conditions in the Arab world for which the United States or Western countries are responsible. Gore Vidal (among many others) subscribed to this idea and even suggested that "our ruling junta might have seriously provoked" *both* the Oklahoma City bombing in 1995 and 9/11 attacks. See his *Perpetual War for Perpetual Peace* (New York: Nation Books, 2002), x. For a critical discussion of the root cause theory, see "Walter Reich: The Poverty Myth," *Wilson Quarterly* (Winter 2008). See also Adam Garfinkle, "How We Misunderstood Terrorism," *Orbis* (Summer 2008).
13. Brooks, "Trading Cricket for Jihad."
14. I discovered subsequently that Francis Fukuyama made the same observation: "Radical Islamism is a by-product of modernization itself, arising from the loss of identity that accompanies the transition to a modern, pluralist society." "After Neoconservativism," *New York Times Magazine*, February 19, 2006, 67. The resistance to assimilation to modern Western societies (on the part of Islamic populations) is illustrated by "imans petitioning National Health Service hospitals [in Britain] insisting that patient's beds be turned to Mecca five times a day . . . [and] female Muslim surgeons refusing to scrub their bare arms" (Michael Burleigh, "Some European Perspectives on Terrorism," Foreign Policy Research Institute, Philadelphia, May 22, 2008, available online).
15. Pankaj Mishra, *An End to Suffering* (New York: MacMillan, 2004), 394.
16. Aldous Huxley provided a classic analysis of these processes in political propaganda. See his "Words and Behavior" in his *Collected Essays* (New York: Harper, 1959).

17. Quoted in Alvaro Vargas Llosa, "The Killing Machine," *New Republic*, July 11 and 18, 2005, 26, 25, 29.

18. "With all the shirts adorned with the solemn face of . . . Che Guevara being sold in the city's souvenir shops, one would think he had once adopted New York and not Cuba as his home. . . . More than 45 years later . . . Che is all over as fashion statement." (David Gonzales, "A Cuban Revolution, Forged in the Reading Room," *New York Times*, February 22, 2005.) At an auction in Dallas, Texas, an admirer paid $100,000 for a lock of Che Guevara's hair (Mark Lacey, "Lone Bidder Buys Strands of Che's Hair at U.S. Auction," *New York Times*, October 26, 2007). Another idealized presentation of Che Guevara was the movie "Che" by Steven Soderberg that "sought to preserve the romantic notion of Guevara as a martyr and an iconic figure, an idealistic champion of the poor and oppressed" ("Cannes Journal," Entertainment Section, *New York Times*, May 23, 2008).

19. Juan Forero, "Indians in Bolivia Celebrate Swearing In of One of Their Own," *New York Times*, January 23, 2006, A5.

20. Duncan Campbell, "U.S. Bases in Britain," *Sanity* [London], May 1984, 16.

21. George F. Kennan, *Sketches from a Life* (New York: Pantheon, 1989), 49–50.

22. Martin F. Herz, ed., *Decline of the West? George Kennan and His Critics* (Washington, D.C.: Ethics and Public Policy Center, 1978), 32. For a far more balanced view of American culture see Salman Rushdie, "Rethinking the War on American Culture," *New York Times*, op-ed, March 5, 1999.

23. For a further discussion of the apparent sources of the resurgence of anti-Americanism, see the introduction in Paul Hollander, ed., *Understanding Anti-Americanism: Its Origins and Impact at Home and Abroad* (Chicago: Ivan R. Dee, 2004). For massive quantitative evidence of this resurgence, see Andrew Kohut and Bruce Stokes, *America against the World: How We Are Different and Why We Are Disliked* (New York: Times Books, 2006).

24. Josef Joffe wrote, "Between Vietnam and Iraq, America's cultural presence has expanded into ubiquity, and so has the resentment of America's soft power. . . . These American products shape images, not sympathies, and there is little, if any relationship between artifact and affection. . . . The relationship is . . . one of repulsion rather than attraction . . ." ("The Perils of Soft Power," *New York Times Magazine*, May 14, 2006, 15–16).

25. Daniel Johnson, "America and the America-Haters," *Commentary*, June 2006, 29, 30. See also Andrei Markovits, *Uncouth Nation: Why Europe Dislikes America* (Princeton, N.J.: Princeton University Press, 2007).

26. Sarah Lyall, "Playwright Takes a Prize and a Jab at U.S.," *New York Times*, December 8, 2005.

27. Noam Chomsky, "Some Thoughts on Intellectuals and the Schools," *Harvard Educational Review*, no. 4 (Fall 1966): 485.

28. Vidal, *Perpetual War for Perpetual Peace*, 20–21, 25.

29. Quoted in Alexander Cockburn, *The Golden Age Is in Us: Journeys and Encounters* (London: Verso, 1995), 149.

30. Lewis H. Lapham, "We Now Live in an Fascist State," *Harper's Magazine*, October 2005, 7–9.

31. Daniel Johnson, "America and the America-Haters," 28.

32. Paul A. Trout, "How Countless Your Sins: Anti-American Rhetoric and the Prophetic Tradition," *Texas Review* (Fall/Winter 2005): 97, 99.

33. Quoted in Alvin Rosenfeld, "Modern Jewish Intellectual Failure," *Society* (November–December 2005): 16. An outstanding example of these anti-Israeli sentiments has been the much discussed piece "The Israel Lobby and U.S. Foreign Policy" by John Mearsheimer and Stephen Walt (*London Review of Books,* March 23, 2006). For three critical discussions of the article in the *New Republic,* see Benny Morris, "And Now for Some Facts" (May 8, 2006), Martin Peretz, "Oil and Vinegar" (April 10, 2006), and Michael B. Oren, "Quiet Riot" (April 10, 2006). For a defense of the Mearsheimer/Walt argument, see Tony Judt, "A Lobby, Not a Conspiracy," op-ed, *New York Times,* April 19, 2006. For a comprehensive rebuttal, see Ben Fishman, "The 'Israel Lobby': A Realistic Assessment," *Orbis* (Winter 2008).

34. "World Briefing: Britain: Journalists Vote to Boycott Israeli Goods," *New York Times,* April 17, 2007; and Alan Cowell, "Largest Labor Union in Britain Joins Call for a Boycott of Israel," *New York Times,* June 1, 2007.

35. Rosenfeld cited, p. 21. For an outstanding example of the rejection of Israel by a prominent Israeli politician/intellectual (Avraham Burg), see Hillel Halkin, "A Wicked Son," *Commentary,* September 2007.

36. Quoted in Emily Eakin, "The Theory of Everything, R.I.P.," Week in Review, *New York Times,* October 17, 2004. More recently (further repudiating his earlier positions), Fish proposed that "academics should teach not proselytize" and declared "the invasion of political agendas into the classroom . . . extremely dangerous." (Rachel Donadio, "Revisiting the Canon Wars," *New York Times Book Review,* September 16, 2007, 17.)

37. Susan Shell, review, "Richard Wolin: The Seduction of Unreason: The Intellectual Romance with Fascism from Nietzsche to Postmodernism," *Society* (January–February 2006): 95.

38. "The Restaurant Mogul's Retreat," *New York Times Magazine,* February 11, 2007.

39. Michael Wilson: "A Stolen Love Is Found, 37 Years Down the Road," *New York Times,* January 17, 2006. The editors considered the story so important that they put it on the front page, with a photo of the vehicle. Its continuation on page 19 had two more photos of the happy owner as a young man and at the present time. The three television networks each had the story as the last item on the evening news intended as the heartwarming "human interest" conclusion.

40. Carol Ianone, "Reading Literature: Decline and Fall?" *Academic Question* (Summer 2005): 14. A study in 2004 found that 53 percent of Americans surveyed had not read in the previous year a single novel, play, or poem (Steve Wasserman, "Goodbye to All That," *Columbia Journalism Review* [September–October 2007]: 20). For a recent book-length discussion of such trends, see Susan Jacoby, *The Age of American Unreason* (New York: Pantheon, 2008). See also "To Read or Not to Read: Symposium," *Academic Questions* (Spring 2008).

41. Michiko Kakutani, "Bending the Truth in a Million Little Ways," *New York Times,* Arts Section, January 17, 2006, 8. In another similar literary fraud, author Mar-

garet Seltzer invented her "life as a foster child in gang-infested South-Central Los Angeles." See Motoko Rich, "Lies and Consequences: Tracking the Fallout of (Another) Literary Fraud," *New York Times*, March 5, 2008.

42. Daniel Mendelsohn, "Stolen Suffering," op-ed, *New York Times*, March 9, 2008.

43. Anne Applebaum, "The Blog of War," *New Republic*, May 28, 2008, 42.

44. Deborrah Solomon, "Questions for Jean Baudrillard," *New York Times Magazine*, November 20, 2005, 22; "Men of Letters: Baudrillard On Tour," *New Yorker*, November 28, 2005, 62.

45. Alan Cowell, "Britain Is Watching 'Big Brother,' for an Eccentric Politician's On-Screen Escapades," *New York Times*, January 14, 2006, A6.

46. For an illuminating examination of "the Hollywood foreign policy establishment," see Richard Grenier, "Hollywood's Foreign Policy: Utopianism Tempered by Greed," *National Interest* (Summer 1991).

47. Leon Wieseltier, "The African Queen," *New Republic*, October 24, 2005, 34. For a remarkable report on the excesses of the celebrity cult and the media see David Samuels, "Shooting Brittney," *The Atlantic*, April 2008.

48. Jerold S. Auerbach, "Means and Ends in the 1960s," *Society* (September–October 2005): 13. Ross Douthat, "The Return of the Paranoid Style," *The Atlantic*, April 2008. Wendy Kaminer, *Sleeping with Extra-Terrestrials* (New York: Pantheon 1999), 13.

49. Quoted in Ronald Radosh, "Don't Need a Weatherman: The Clouded Mind of Bill Ayers," *Weekly Standard*, October 8, 2001, 38. More surprisingly, Barack Obama could not bring himself to renounce his friendly relationship to him: "Asked about his friendly relationship with the former Weather Underground anarchist William Ayers . . . Obama defended him with a line that only eggheads orbiting his campaign could appreciate. Ayers, he said, was 'a professor of English in Chicago.'" (Maureen Dowd, "Brush It Off," *New York Times*, April 20, 2008.) Ayers is closely examined in my book *The End of Commitment: Intellectuals, Revolutionaries, and Political Morality* (Chicago: Ivan R. Dee, 2006).

50. Joseph Rago, "Rosenberg Reruns," *Wall Street Journal*, January 27, 2006.

51. Benedict Carey, "Psychotherapy on the Road to . . . Where?" Science Section, *New York Times*, December 17, 2005.

52. Ariel Dorfman, "It's No Joke Anymore," *Los Angeles Times*, January 15, 2006, M3.

53. Christopher Hitchens, "Taking Sides," *Nation*, October 14, 2002, 9.

54. Anne Applebaum, "I Am Victim," *Washington Post*, February 25, 2004.

55. Charles Murray, "The Inequality Taboo," *Commentary*, September 2005. See also Linda Chavez, "Let Us by All Means Have an Honest Conversation about Race," *Commentary*, June 2008; and John McWhorter, "Against Reparations," *New Republic*, July 23, 2001.

56. See, for example, Martin Peretz, "Summer's End," *New Republic*, March 6, 2006.

57. Alan Finder, "High Schools Avoid Class Ranking, Vexing Colleges," *New York Times*, March 5, 2006.

58. Max Hocutt, "Black Teachers for Black Studies? A Philosophical Critique of Multiculturalist Pedagogy," *Independent Review* (Summer 2004): 130, 131. For a cognate discussion of "therapeutic alienation" see John McWhorter, "Americans without Americannes," *National Review*, April 16, 2007.

59. Diana Jean Schemo, "Turmoil at Gallaudet Reflects Broader Debate over Deaf Culture," *New York Times*, October 21, 2006.

60. "National Briefing," *New York Times*, October 7, 2006.

61. Diana Jean Schemo, "At Gallaudet Trustees Relent on Leadership," *New York Times*, November 30, 2006.

62. Damien Cave, "No Change in Definition of Gender," *New York Times*, December 6, 2006.

63. Lawrence F. Kaplan, "Mall Rats," *New Republic*, October 10, 2005, 10.

64. T. A. Frank, "Washington Diarist: Left Out," *New Republic*, February 7, 2005.

65. Michelle York, "After Hung Jury, 4 Who Poured Blood at Army Center Face Federal Trial," *New York Times*, September 18, 2005; Clyde Haberman, "Carnage There but Not Much Happens Here," *New York Times*, March 21, 2006.

66. "Antiwar Campaigner Speaks on Chavez Broadcast," *New York Times*, January 29, 2006. See also Juan Forero, "Visitors Seek a Taste of Revolution in Venezuela," *New York Times*, March 21, 2006; Ian Buruma, "Thank You, My Foolish Friends in the West," *Sunday Times* [London], May 15, 2006; and Franklin Foer, "The Talented Mr. Chavez," *The Atlantic*, May 2006. Tariq Ali, the aging British "new leftist," also joined the admirers of Chavez (see his "Diary" in the *London Review of Books*, June 21, 2007) as have the Hollywood celebrities Sean Penn, Danny Glover, and Harry Belafonte ("Celebrity Fans," *Newsweek*, September 3, 2007).

67. Quoted in Buruma, "Thank You, My Foolish Friends in the West."

68. Deborah Orin, "Harvard Loves a Thug," *New York Post* (online edition), May 1, 2006.

69. See, for example, Kanan Makiya, *Republic of Fear: The Politics of Modern Iraq* (Berkeley: University Press of California, 1989).

70. For an example of thoughtful soul-searching regarding Iraq, see Michael Ignatieff, "Getting Iraq Wrong," *New York Times Magazine*, August 5, 2007. For a critique of what has been often been called "triumphalism" and its contribution to American involvement in Iraq see the introduction and chapter 22 in Tony Judt, *Reappraisals* (New York: Penguin Press, 2008).

71. "Why a Truck? And Not Just Any Truck," Alix Browne "On the Cult of the Toyota Land Cruiser," *New York Times*, *Style*, February 20, 2005.

72. Daphne Markin, "What's So Hot About 50? Sex and the Female Boomer Is NOT Booming," *New York Times Magazine*, February 12, 2006, 17.

73. Eric Cohen and Leon R. Kass, "'Cast Me Not off in Old Age,'" *Commentary*, January 2006, 34.

I

THE NEW ANTI-AMERICANISM

Chapter One

Anti-Americanism and a World-Class Hate Crime

The September 11, 2001, suicide attacks on the United States were the purest hate crime imaginable, and the vast majority of Americans have responded to them with unalloyed pain and anger. But among a significant minority, another response has made an appearance. Conditioned by a venerable anti-American impulse, it seeks not only to find explanations for the terrorists' actions but to make the United States responsible for its own misfortune. And it is especially in evidence on the campuses of American colleges and universities, and in the communities that surround them—the very places, ironically, that routinely promote the idea that hate crimes belong to a special category of offense that deserves no sympathetic understanding and the strictest punishment.

At Harvard, students hoist a sign that declares "War Is Also Terrorism." One of my colleagues at the University of Massachusetts sends out an e-mail pleading that we find "ways to reduce those alienating actions whereby we create our own enemies." In a widely circulated e-mail, feminist poet Robin Morgan excuses the attacks as not just the work of madmen or monsters, but as tactics that "come from a complex set of circumstances, including despair over not being heard."

Unfortunately, it is not true, as writer George Packer recently argued in the *New York Times* magazine, that September 11 destroyed "the notion . . . that to be stirred by national identity, carry a flag and feel grateful toward someone in uniform ought to be a source of embarrassment." Far from it. Writing only days after the attacks, the *Nation*'s Katha Pollitt, for example, declared her conviction that the American flag "stands for jingoism and vengeance."

The champions of global peace and social justice readily rise to moral indignation and anger against the United States but appear incapable of similar sentiments against the terrorists. Concern for the unintended victims of American action against the terrorists and the nations that harbor them greatly outweighs compassion toward the actual and wholly intentional victims of September 11. Historian Eric Foner, writing in the *London Review of Books*, cannot decide "which is more frightening: the horror that engulfed New York City or the apocalyptic rhetoric emanating daily from the White House."

At the core of these attitudes is anti-Americanism, which I define as a historically specific expression of a universal scapegoating impulse, a type of bias similar to racism, sexism, or anti-Semitism, and a largely irrational, often visceral aversion to the United States and its government, domestic institutions, prevailing values, culture, and people fueled by a variety of frustrations and grievances. It culminates in the feeling, memorably expressed by a Hamas leader, that "America is the problem that lies behind all other problems." Those within our shores who harbor these sentiments have seized on the events of September 11 to express renewed hostility toward our society.

America's homegrown critics hold the peculiar conviction that if hatred of the sort that led to the destruction of the World Trade Center is directed at the United States, there must be good and justifiable reason for it. Yet these same critics never seem to take such a position in regard to victims of other hate crimes. Many of those habitually critical of this society (and claiming a desire to "understand" why it is hated while simultaneously believing that such hatred is fully justified) support severe punishment for hate crimes without seeking to understand the grievances and resentments that produce them. They do not ask what battered women have done to justify their mistreatment, or what it is in the behavior of homosexuals or blacks that stimulates virulent hatred. Nor do they seek to "understand" or to plumb the "root causes" behind the actions of the wife beater or those who assault or murder gays.

These critics take for granted that certain groups of people are hated and assaulted for no good (that is, moral or ethical) reason, that consuming hatred culminating in violent actions is not necessarily something justified by weighty, extenuating social causes. It is only when people have some sympathy with the violent act and its perpetrator that they start looking for root causes, to "understand" the aggressor and something in the behavior or attitude of the victim that shifts at least some of the responsibility from victimizer to victim.

It is an unhappy fact that some groups and individuals thrive on hatred, on holding others responsible for their grievances, whatever they may be. Most people have such tendencies in moderation: It is far more satisfactory to find the source of our problems outside ourselves. In most instances such inclinations do not culminate in obsessive hatred and violence against the alleged or imagined source of the grievances. But they did in the case of the attacks on the United States. Those attacks (as well as recent suicide bombings in Israel) originate in intense, irrational anti-Americanism and in the hatred of Israel and Jews. What inspires these hatreds is modernity. The United States has become a symbol of and scapegoat for modernity—which is at once liberating and destabilizing.

The problems modernity creates are not primarily those of poverty (which it more often alleviates than aggravates) but loss of meaning, the erosion of a coherent worldview, and the anxieties created by personal freedom. Traditional societies, though poor, used to be capable of providing their members with a stable, religiously grounded worldview. Modernity undermines this worldview and the sense of certainty and community associated with it. The cultural relativism and moral uncertainty that modernity unwittingly stimulates lie at the heart of the protest against globalization, the West, and the United States. In the Arab world, Israel is hated as much for being an outpost of modernity and Western values as it is for occupying lands claimed by Palestinians.

It is an interesting question as to why the anger and resentment over these developments have been particularly intense in Islamic societies. Clearly, the expectation of suicide bombers and pilots that great otherworldly rewards await them has a connection with their religious beliefs. But it is also true that history abounds with examples of ruthless assault on the targets of murderous hatred inspired by other kinds of perverted idealism, from Stalin's purges to the Holocaust.

The pathology of such hate crimes does require a better understanding—but not a new round of self-flagellation. To help us determine how to combat the terrorists who attacked us, it is certainly worthwhile to learn what they have in common in regard to motivation, personality type, life experience, education, social class, and so on. We already know that many of these individuals come from settings where violence is glorified and legitimated, where suicide bombing is seen as a sacred mission and people dance in the streets at the news of mass murders (such as those committed in New York and Washington), where individual killers joyously show their bloody hands on television (as did the killers of two Israeli soldiers on the West Bank), celebrating violence against their enemies unembarrassed.

These and other socio-historical conditions do not provide moral license or mitigation for indiscriminate mass murder by individuals who, from all indications, choose their actions freely, with utmost deliberation and under no compulsion other than the prodding of their beliefs. Hard as it may be to accept, the recent suicide attacks are the purest expression of a pathological hatred, fanaticism, and irrationality that deserves no sympathetic understanding.

Chapter Two

Anti-Americanism: Murderous and Rhetorical

I was in Budapest, Hungary, on September 11, 2001, and learned about the attacks in a new shopping center where TV sets were tuned to CNN. I was, of course, unprepared for the news and thought that this was some kind of docudrama using the title "Attack on America."

Once more a major historical event was totally unanticipated. Other forms of terrorism had been discussed over the years, but not the use of hijacked planes against buildings. The actual devastation was less disturbing than the easy triumph of evil. As a social scientist, I am not supposed to think of "evil" as an acceptable concept. We know that desirable and undesirable traits are part of all human beings, that a sharp delineation between good and evil is a primitive notion. Yet I could not help thinking of evil, even though the use of such an archaic concept without underlying religious beliefs is problematic. But some phenomena compel its use, for instance, the gas chambers, torture to extract false confessions (as in the Communist show trial), the Gulag, the lynching of blacks in the United States, as well as nonpolitical crimes involving gratuitous brutality and the apparent pleasure in its display. Surely the deliberate, carefully planned mass murder of civilians whose only "crime" was being Americans qualifies as an act of evil.

In contrast to the moral outrages of the past century, the latest was not the product of some impersonal design committed in the spirit of "obedience to authority" by people indifferently playing their roles in an elaborate division of labor. These were a handful of highly motivated individuals under no compulsion except their beliefs and hatreds, inspired by a mixture of religious-political ideas and a willingness to destroy themselves for the sake of destroying thousands of others. They were moved by a consuming hatred and determination to deal a staggering blow to their perceived enemies and their material incarnation.

This was a classic hate crime against the United States and all that it symbolizes: modernity, global power, Western values, and support for Israel. Such intense hatred can only be appeased by murderous violence, and those consumed by it do not mind destroying themselves. That is what distinguishes this act from other acts of terror. Members of the Red Brigades, the Baader-Meinhof gang, the IRA, the Basque terrorists, the Weathermen, and the Black Liberation Army were not animated by religious beliefs promising generous otherworldly rewards. By contrast, the suicide pilots (and suicide bombers in Israel) expected paradise to await them for their good works of killing.

Religious beliefs, although powerful, are only a part of the explanation; there is also a political culture of murderous hatred that Arab countries produce and maintain. In Palestinian refugee camps and religious schools, children are taught to hate Israel and its supporters; the mass media routinely disseminate this hatred—blessed by religious authorities—even in more moderate Arab countries like Egypt and Saudi Arabia.

In these political cultures violence is glorified, suicide bombing is a sacred mission, and people dance in the streets at the news of mass murders such as those committed at the World Trade Center. A good visual representation of this political culture may be found in pictures (often seen on television) of Arab crowds demonstrating with faces contorted with hatred, wildly gesticulating and screaming for the blood of their enemies.

In Hungary, a former communist country, it was especially tempting to speculate on the connections between "theory and practice," that is, Islamic beliefs and the violence they seemingly inspire. I think there is a similarity between the relationship of Marxism to communist states and Islamic religious teachings' relationship to the political violence they apparently inspire and legitimize. To be sure, Marx cannot be held responsible for Stalin, the KGB, the purges, and the Gulag. But there was *some* connection between the great ideals he articulated and the ruthlessness employed on their behalf by the communist leaders seeking to implement them. Likewise, Islamic beliefs may not explicitly demand or justify the indiscriminate killing of noncombatants, but they certainly encourage crusades, merciless struggles against the numerous incarnations of the enemy. They certainly do not encourage tolerance toward the infidel. Furthermore, the allure of sacred martyrdom is a religious notion, not one invented by the individuals in question. Moreover, the families of suicide bombers are very well taken care of by various Arab states and organizations and enjoy a privileged status in their community. Thus, both moral and material incentives are in place to motivate terrorists.

In the days following September 11 I spent much time watching CNN and Hungarian television, reading the whole spectrum of newspapers, and reflecting on the disturbing questions these events raised. After my return to the

United States on September 22 I continued to ponder both the Hungarian and American responses.

In Hungary, as in this country, the vast majority condemned the atrocities without reservations. There was astonishment that this powerful country could have proven to be so vulnerable. Some intellectuals could not resist the notion that if the United States inspired such murderous hatred there must have been sound reasons for it. One Hungarian columnist wrote,

> We must reflect on the causes. Behind the irrational, unrestrained evil there must be rational reasons. . . . It is impossible to overlook that this world is unjust and lacking in solidarity; that there are intolerable differences between the free and rich world and the starving millions who live like pariahs. . . .
>
> When someone is impoverished for years and decades, his children dying of hunger or the diseases of poverty, in despair he can reach for violence looking for scapegoats. . . .
>
> We must scrutinize our evil, our selfishness. The civilized world also destroys, both people and nature. . . .

Not unlike some of his American colleagues, this author makes an exceedingly dubious connection between destitution and the suicide pilots (and their organizers) who were in fact well-educated, prosperous individuals of middle- or upper-middle-class backgrounds. Their hatred had little discernible connection with the bitterness that poverty generates.

The most determined attribution of American responsibility for the terrorist acts came from the radical right-wing party MIEP (the Hungarian Party of Justice and Life) and its leader Istvan Csurka who said "this [event] was not unexpected, it had to happen. The oppressed people of the world could not tolerate without a counterblow the humiliations, the exploitation and the purposeful genocide taking place in Palestine." This same politician also had suggested that Israeli capitalists investing in shopping malls in Hungary were not merely interested in profit but wished to inject alien cultural influences into Hungarian life.

Another Hungarian commentator put his finger on the anti-American sentiments and ambivalence coloring the responses of some of his fellow countrymen: "Those who believe that this was the day when justice was done cry with one eye and laugh with the other. . . . This was payment for Hollywood, for chewing gum, Vietnam and the malls. For globalization that equals America. All those who demonized the International Currency Fund, the World Bank, McDonalds and Uncle Sam are now content. . . ."

Upon returning to America, I also found that this horrendous atrocity could provide an occasion for giving new expression to a long simmering, intense, and gnawing hostility toward this society and everything it stands for. This unprecedented outrage was seized upon by some to vent hostility not seen since the Vietnam War. Predictably these sentiments and attitudes were most pronounced on campuses and among academic intellectuals.

The question most frequently—and almost gleefully—asked and all too readily answered (by critics of the United States) was "Why do they hate us?" It was taken for granted that if people hated the United States they had to have sound, justifiable reasons that led to the regrettable, but fully understandable mass murders. Often the same people were the staunchest advocates of hate crime legislation (when the victims were women, homosexuals, or other minorities) with no questions asked about the "root causes" of such despicable behavior or about the ways the victims might have brought these misfortunes upon themselves. In such instances it was either tacitly acknowledged or vocally asserted that hate crimes are pathologies that need to be punished without mercy and without any consideration of extenuating social circumstances.

Not so when it came to the events of September 11. In its aftermath the search was on for "root causes," for "understanding" the terrorists and their actions. Attention and responsibility was shifted from victimizer to victim.

The common thread running through the critiques of the United States was the notion of moral equivalence many of the same people used earlier in comparisons of the United States and the Soviet Union. Russell Mead, the Native American activist, compared the American responses to "what I used to see when I was behind the so called [*sic*] Iron Curtain touring Eastern Europe. . . . [These responses] increased the fear I've always had of the ongoing deprivation of individual liberties . . . by the federal government. My concern is that the government has . . . become an outlaw." Michael Mandel, a law professor, declared that "the bombing of Afghanistan is the legal and moral equivalent of what was done to Americans on September 11."

Another major theme, as expressed by Vivian Gornick, was that "Force will get us nowhere. It is reparations that are owing, not retribution." Richard Gere, the actor, advised people to look upon the terrorists "as a relative who's dangerously sick and we have to give them medicine, and the medicine is love and compassion." The general secretary of the American Friends Service Committee proclaimed that "Our grief is not a cry for retaliation. Terrorism must be stopped at its root cause. . . ."

It soon became apparent that the "root causes" were American foreign policy, domestic social injustice, global insensitivity, arrogance, and greed. A correspondent for the British newspaper the *Guardian* wrote, "During my lifetime, America has been constantly waging war against much of humanity: impoverished people mostly. . . . It is this record of unabashed national egotism and arrogance that drives anti-Americanism. . . ." Edward Said made clear on the pages of an Egyptian newspaper that the United States is a genocidal power with a "history of reducing whole peoples, countries, and even continents to ruin by nothing short of holocaust."

It is no mystery why the embittered domestic critics of the United States have been so preoccupied with the question of "why they hate us." The better and more abundant reasons they find the more they rest assured that their own hostility and alienation are well founded.

Chapter Three

The Politics of Envy

Until recently, anti-Americanism attracted little serious attention among social scientists and intellectuals. Apparently it was not considered worthy of study or close scrutiny, because it was rarely seen as a pathology that required better understanding. Unlike other more researched, consensually reprehensible attitudes and prejudices, such as racism, sexism, anti-Semitism, and homophobia, anti-Americanism was regarded among the intelligentsia as a more or less natural phenomenon, perhaps regrettable but easy to explain and largely justified.

Admittedly, anti-Americanism is not easy to study given its diffuseness, varieties, endless sources, and the difficulty in locating it on the spectrum of political attitudes and positions. Anti-Americanism may be associated with radical revolutionaries or with the guardians of traditional moralities and social orders. There is anti-Americanism on the left as well as the right. Intense anti-Americanism sometimes makes the extreme right and extreme left hard to distinguish from one another.

Anti-Americanism can be found in both highly developed, complex Western societies and in the most backward ones of the Third World; it can be found in the remaining communist states as well as the postcommunist ones. Identification and analysis are complicated by their tendencies to shade into ambivalence.

Anti-American rhetoric often denigrates the United States by comparing and equating it with something self-evidently worse, such as Nazi Germany, the former Soviet Union, or apartheid-era South Africa. During the Cold War, anti-Americanism found expression in the moral-equivalence thesis that held there was little to choose from, morally speaking, between the United States and the Soviet Union. Even in this comparative framework, the United States was, as a rule, savaged with far greater relish and specificity while critiques of the Soviet system were few and perfunctory.

Paradoxically, anti-Americanism has always coexisted with a fervent desire of vast numbers of people around the world to come and live in this much-maligned country; to this day it remains difficult to keep them out. Even those who harbor no such aspirations widely imitate American fashions, fads, and patterns of consumption and look to American mass culture for entertainment. In light of these observations it is tempting to suggest that anti-Americanism is mainly the malaise of intellectuals, quasi-intellectuals, and those influenced by them. Still, even ordinary people with little education are susceptible to it when blaming the United States becomes a readily available, soothing alternative to confronting the real sources of their distress and taking responsibility for them.

The major dimensions or types of anti-Americanism include the longstanding historical/theoretical version (currently intertwined with "postmodernism" and "multiculturalism") rooted in the rejection of universalistic values and especially the rationalism associated with the Enlightenment. This form of anti-Americanism shades into a broad anti-Western disposition.

There is an anti-Americanism that is barely distinguishable from anticapitalism (a tributary of Marxism), viewing the United States as both the pillar of capitalism around the world and its most repugnant embodiment.

There is a cultural anti-Americanism that focuses on American mass culture (correctly) seen as an integral part of American society. And there is a conservative anti-Americanism that suspects all that is new and lacking in traditional legitimation.

Anti-Americanism as a by-product of nationalistic grievances, resentments, and competitive disadvantage is among its most prominent incarnations. Weakness is a major stimulant of anti-Americanism.

In my study of the phenomenon a decade ago, I defined anti-Americanism as a hostile predisposition that may range from distaste and aversion to intense hostility, rooted in conditions and circumstances that are often largely unrelated to the actual qualities or attributes of American society, institutions, values, or foreign policy. I compared anti-Americanism to other hostile predispositions such as racism, anti-Semitism, sexism, or various kinds of ethnic prejudice. Stereotyping that involves exaggeration, distortion, and contempt is an integral part of anti-Americanism, especially as regards (what is seen as) the American national character, cultural norms, tastes, manners, and ways of life.

In my original definition I failed to note that anti-American sentiments may culminate in political violence; at the time most forms of anti-Americanism appeared largely rhetorical or otherwise expressed in ways short of mass murder.

The scapegoating impulse is central to anti-Americanism, followed by envy and ambivalence. It is not difficult to explain why the United States has become a symbol, the entity upon which a wide range of grievances and resentments can be projected. Not only has the United States been powerful and wealthy, it has also generated high expectations both at home and abroad, promises of opportunity and fulfillment that cannot be fully realized.

From the sociological and historical points of view, anti-Americanism may best be understood as a diffuse, ongoing protest against modernity—its major components and unintended consequences. These include secularization, industrialization, urbanization, bureaucratization, mobility (both social and spatial), and the decline of community and social-cultural cohesion. Less obvious is how and why modernity nurtures anti-Americanism even in societies that are stable, democratic, wealthy, and thoroughly modernized—as opposed to those societies that are in the throes of uneasy and ineffectual modernization that undermines old certainties and social organizations while yielding few tangible material benefits.

The most obvious and clear link between anti-Americanism and modernization is encountered in Islamic countries and other traditional societies where modernization clashes head on with entrenched traditional beliefs, institutions, and patterns of behavior and where it challenges the very meaning of life, social relations, and religious verities. What becomes of the world when women can go to work and show large surfaces of skin to men they are not related to? In a recent case, the indignant male members of a Kurdish family in Sweden were "provoked" by the transgressing female of their family who had the temerity to have a job and a boyfriend and dress in Western ways. She was finally killed by her father. According to the *New York Times* correspondent reporting the matter, "[her] desire for independence . . . turn[ed] her into the tragic emblem of a European society's failure to bridge the gap . . . between its own culture and those of its newer arrivals." These comments also exemplify the guilty, antimodernist impulse of the journalist seeking to implicate a Western society in the kind of criminality traditional morality sometimes sanctions.

In Arab countries and among Muslim populations, anti-Americanism is not only the monopoly of intellectuals but also a widespread disposition of the masses. In these areas, traditional religion, radical politics, and economic backwardness combine to make anti-Americanism an exceptionally widespread, virulent, and reflexive response to a wide range of collective and personal frustrations and grievances—and a welcome alternative to any collective or individual self-examination or stock-taking.

More generally, it is the rise of alternatives, ushered in by modernization, that threatens traditional societies and generates anti-American reaction. The stability of traditional society (like that of modern totalitarian systems) rests on the lack of alternatives, on the lack of choice. Choice is deeply subversive—culturally, politically, psychologically.

The recent outburst of murderous anti-Americanism has added a new dimension to the phenomenon, or, at any rate, throws into relief the intense hatred it may encapsulate. The violence of September 11 shows that when anti-Americanism is nurtured by the kind of indignation and resentment that is stimulated and sanctioned by religious convictions, it can become spectacularly destructive. Suicide killings have not been unknown in history, but usually they were directed at important military and political targets—not at symbolic ones (such as buildings) or at undifferentiated noncombatants who, like other victims of political mass murders in recent history, have been killed for what they are (Americans, or Jews), not for what they did. Anti-Israeli, anti-Jewish violence has become intertwined with anti-Americanism; in the minds of Islamic fanatics, Israel, Jews, and the United States are a closely linked evil entity.

A new stage has been reached in the development and history of anti-Americanism when the United States and all things American are identified with a religiously defined, transcendent Evil and not merely with social injustice, moral corruption, economic exploitation, or the abuse of power as used to be the case until recently.

One would expect anti-Americanism to be mainly a phenomenon outside the United States, but this also is not the case. Domestic anti-Americanism has for a long time been as vigorous as its foreign varieties, although it is largely limited to the intelligentsia. Even the events of September 11 became for them an occasion for vilifying the United States and for taking a new, expanded inventory of its numberless misdeeds, past and present. Hostile critics claim that the attacks originated in "root causes" (all of which had something to do with the folly or evil of American society and U.S. policies) and that these attacks were fully understandable responses to the many wrongheaded, selfish, irresponsible, and corrupt American policies and postures. These include U.S. support for Israel and repression of Palestinians, for upholding global inequality, for exploiting the poor, for plundering the resources of the world, for conducting militaristic policies, and for erecting provocatively tall buildings that symbolize American capitalistic greed. The preeminent French anti-American intellectual Jean Baudrillard found these buildings no less horrific than the terrorist attacks on them: "In terms of collective drama we can say that the horror for the 4,000 [sic] victims of dying in those towers was inseparable from the horror of living and working in sarcophagi of concrete and steel." Noam Chomsky, never prey to such uncertainties, has long been convinced that the United States is the "leading terrorist state." This is a conviction he shares with Gore Vidal, who wanted "readers seriously to consider that the Oklahoma City bombing was a conspiracy by federal agents ... to justify further strengthening of the American terror-police state."

Domestic or native anti-Americanism is a more mysterious and puzzling phenomenon than the foreign varieties, but it too can be linked to the problems and afflictions of modernity, and especially to the spiritual emptiness and social isolation associated with it.

"Inauthenticity" is a key component of the criticism directed at American society and culture both at home and abroad. It is linked both to spiritual emptiness and more specifically to mass culture, the consumer ethos, the fraudulence associated with commerce, the pursuit of profit, and capitalist competitiveness. German poet Rainer Maria Rilke captured these sentiments in the early twentieth century, speaking of

> the American way of life in which all products have lost their connection with anything real or human. ... [F]or our grandparents ... a house, a well, a familiar tower, even their own pieces of clothing [were] something intimate and meaningful. ... Now is emerging from out of America pure undifferentiated things, mere things of appearance, sham articles. ... A house, in the American understanding, an American apple, or an American vine has nothing in common with the house, the fruit, or the grape that had been adopted in the hopes and thoughts of our forefathers.

In our times, similar anti-American sentiments generate protests against McDonald's and Wal-Mart, "ticky tacky" houses in the suburbs, the omnipresence of plastics, or the difficulty of finding organic produce in the nearest supermarket.

Complaints about inauthenticity and standardization illuminate the romantic, individualistic components of what (I call) cultural anti-Americanism found in the United States and other Western societies. Romantic anti-Americanism has much in common with romantic anticapitalism, which in turn is an integral part of the aversion to the rationalistic ethos of the French Enlightenment.

Another remarkable convergence may be discerned between the Marxist critiques of capitalist modernity and those emanating in our times from traditionalist societies and their spokesmen who attack Americanization—that is to say, the power of American capitalism to erode, degrade, and demystify all that is sacred, unique, and time honored:

> uninterrupted disturbance of all social conditions, everlasting uncertainty and agitation distinguish the bourgeois epoch from all earlier ones. All fixed, fast-frozen relations, with their train of ancient and venerable prejudices and opinions are swept away, all new-formed ones become antiquated. ... All that is solid melts into air all that is holy is profaned and man is at last compelled to face with sober

senses, his real conditions of life, and his relations with his kind. (from the *Communist Manifesto* [1848])

Anti-Americanism was also a centerpiece in the vast propaganda campaigns of communist systems, especially in the former Soviet Union. These states sought (some still do) to capitalize on spontaneous anti-Americanism, and they devoted substantial resources to stimulate it wherever possible. As far as their own peoples were concerned these campaigns were quite ineffectual, since citizens of communist countries mistrusted official propaganda and often had alternative sources of information about the world outside. The official anti-Americanism—like much of the official propaganda in general—backfired: what the authorities denounced, the populace approached with sympathetic curiosity.

The communist campaigns of anti-American disinformation probably had more of an impact outside these countries. For example, Soviet allegations that the United States created and disseminated the AIDS virus to decimate third-world populations were not rejected out of hand in these countries, and a good deal of antinuclear propaganda seeking to disarm the West had some influence in Western Europe.

It might have been plausible to expect a decline of global as well as domestic anti-Americanism in the wake of the collapse of Soviet communism. On the one hand, a major source of anti-American propaganda ceased to exist; on the other, at least in theory, the juxtaposition of the fall of state socialism with the survival of vigorous democratic capitalism could have conclusively discredited the apparent and alleged alternatives to Western democracy and capitalism the United States has represented. This, however, did not happen. Anti-Americanism has persisted and, arguably, increased in Western Europe, in postcommunist Russia, and, above all, in the Islamic world.

The "last remaining superpower" status doubtlessly contributed to the recent upsurges of anti-Americanism, making it more plausible to blame the United States for a wide variety of problems all over the world. Its ability and willingness to intervene in conflicts abroad (in Afghanistan, Kosovo, and Iraq) lent more plausibility to the image of the United States as a reckless, irresponsible, militarist superpower throwing its weight around. There have also been trade disputes between the European Union and the United States that suggest that the current administration sometimes prefers to support American farmers and steelmakers at the expense of upholding the principles of free trade. These are matters that invite reasonable criticism but at the same time also feed anti-Americanism, which by (my) definition has a large irrational component.

The personality and qualifications of our current president have also contributed to recent manifestations of anti-Americanism; like Reagan, George

W. Bush invites stereotypes of the "cowboy," the "airhead," and, with better justification, the critique that he is an all-too-eager supporter of big business. His environmental policies and indifference to conservation to a more prudent use of energy, appear to derive from an excessively pro-business mentality that he and much of his cabinet share.

Dwelling on aspects of American society that invite criticism of a more rational kind almost inevitably leads to some somber reflections about American mass culture. No friend of America, domestic or foreign, can easily dispute that mass culture enshrines mindlessness, triviality, the cult of violence, a shallow sentimentality, and a pervasive entertainment orientation that has had discernible effect on the whole society including its political, educational, artistic, and religious institutions. I am well aware that American mass culture is popular all over the world and that it does not represent a coercive imposition upon the masses yearning for cheaper CDs of Bach cantatas or Beethoven string quartets. Nonetheless its existence and influence make a substantial contribution not only to anti-Americanism but also to more informed critiques of American society.

Much of what people fear or dislike about American society and culture is synonymous with modernity, or aspects thereof. Americanization is the major, perhaps the only, widespread form of modernization. The process—as we all know—involves gains as well as losses. The anti-American reaction dwells on the losses and ignores the gains. Anti-Americanism is a reaction against the same process of modernization most people yearn for, but that when advanced or attained leads to second thoughts, to doubts, and to reservations and irreconcilable desires and demands that cannot be met or, when they are, create disappointment. I am reminded here of what Daniel Boorstin wrote almost half a century ago about Americans and their attitude toward vacation travel:

> We expect our two week vacation to be romantic, exotic, cheap and effortless. We expect a faraway atmosphere if we go to a nearby place; and we expect everything to be relaxing, sanitary and Americanized if we go to a faraway place. We expect the contradictory and the impossible. . . . Never have people been more the masters of their environment yet never has a people felt more deceived and disappointed. For never has a people expected so much more than the world can offer.

The attitude sketched above is not confined to Americans and vacation travel, but it is most conspicuous in this society given the high expectations American culture and history have always generated and encouraged. It is these high expectations and their recurring frustration that best explain domestic anti-Americanism, that is to say, alienation, the adversary culture, embittered social criticism, the reflexive rejection of the whole social system, and its supporting values. The frustration of these high expectations also explains the often-voiced feeling that America failed to live up to its promises and potentials.

Wherever it appears, anti-Americanism is a response—however indirect—to the burdens and conflicts of choice and freedom and to living in a world that no longer provides the cushion of community and the web of taken-for-granted beliefs that protect against the specters of meaninglessness and spiritual void.

Chapter Four

Anti-Americanism and Moral Equivalence

In the second half of the past century, a new intellectual-polemical phenomenon appeared making it more difficult to distinguish between what is humane or inhumane, politically acceptable or repugnant. It is the willful and often ignorant equation of different political phenomena, the attribution of similarity, that is to say, of moral equivalence, to political practices, systems, movements, or institutions that are in fact quite different and far from equivalent morally.

A book recently published by the University of California Press is a case in point. It is entitled *American Gulag*—a title that obviously seeks to convey that the American prison system is as bad as, and the moral equivalent of, the former Soviet one that came to be known as the Gulag. The moral equivalence is created by associating the Gulag—widely recognized as cruel, inhuman, and unjust—with American prisons, thereby automatically denigrating the latter and by extension American society as a whole.

Mark Dow, the author, was not the only one to reach for the concept of gulag to discredit American society. Bruce Cumings, a historian, suggested that conditions in the labor camps of communist North Korea should be assessed in light of the "longstanding, never-ending gulag full of black men in our prisons," which ought to disqualify us from "pointing a finger." Even Al Gore, discussing Guantanamo and Abu Ghraib, could not resist invoking the gulag metaphor, as reported in *The New Yorker*.

Could these authors be truly unaware of the profound differences between the American and Soviet or North Korean prison systems? Or do they dismiss the differences in the belief that they are insignificant and insufficient to set apart the two systems? Bruce Cumings and Mark Dow doubtless would also support the idea (widespread in the 1960s and 1970s and still surviving) that all black prison inmates in the United States are by definition political prisoners. It was a belief upheld by the late George Jackson, who considered himself one of them and who preferred to compare American prisons to Dachau and Buchenwald.

Since the late 1960s, the attribution of moral equivalence between the United States and some self-evidently noxious political entity, force, or system (often opposed to it) has become the most favored form of denigration of the United States and American society. The practice began during the Cold War and was used most widely in comparisons of the United States and the Soviet Union. (Jeane Kirkpatrick was in the forefront of those criticizing these attributions.) It was memorably conveyed in what might be considered the definitive text on moral equivalence, Richard Barnett's *The Giants*:

> The CIA and the KGB have the same conspiratorial worldview. . . . In both countries leading military bureaucrats constitute a potent political force. . . . The military establishments of the United States and the Soviet Union are . . . each other's best allies. . . . Khrushchev and Dulles were perfect partners. . . . Both sides have a professional interest in the nostalgic illusions of victory through secret weapons. Both societies were suffering a crisis of legitimacy. . . . Military bureaucracies are developing in the Soviet Union that are mirror images of American bureaucracies. . . . The madness of one bureaucracy sustains the other. . . . Each [country] is a prisoner of a sixty-year-old obsession.

In turn, E. L. Doctorow wrote:

> We and the Soviets have actually created an unholy alliance, a gargantuan intimacy, in which, by now, our ideological differences are less important than the fact that we think the same thoughts, mirror each other's responses, heft the same bombs, and take turns committing crimes and deploring them.

In Noam Chomsky's version of moral equivalence, the United States and the Soviet Union were "the world's two great propaganda states." Furthermore, for the Americans, "association of socialism with the Soviet Union . . . serves as a powerful ideological weapon to enforce conformity and obedience to the State capitalist institutions . . . the only alternative to the 'socialist' dungeon. The Soviet leadership . . . portrays itself as socialist to protect its right to wield the club, and Western ideologists adopt the same pretense in order to forestall the threat of a more free and just society."

Moral equivalence was widely embraced by the peace movement, the protest movements of the 1960s (and their descendants), and by all critics of American society who came to constitute the adversary culture. The gist of the argument was (and remains) that the United States cannot claim any moral high ground in comparison to the Soviet Union (or most other societies) and, if so, its leaders should not self-righteously lecture, chide, or oppose the Soviet system and by doing so risk nuclear war. The argument emerged at a time when the domestic denigrations of American society peaked and gradually became conventional wisdom: American society was not to be contrasted favorably to any other, least of all those claiming socialist credentials. To this day President Reagan is showered with scorn for calling the Soviet Union an "evil empire."

The idea of moral equivalence also gained support from the old, discredited notion of a "convergence" between the United States and the Soviet Union or between capitalist and state socialist societies. The idea of the "two superpowers" further bolstered the notion of moral equivalence; the shared superpower status was supposed to determine many of the social and political practices, structures, and policies of these systems. Those who believed that such a convergence between the social, economic, political, and cultural institutions and policies of these countries was taking place inclined to diminish or dismiss the moral-ethical differences between them. Thus Lewis Lapham could write, "Like communism, capitalism is a materialist and utopian faith; also like communism it has shown itself empty of a moral imperative or a spiritual meaning. To the questions likely to be asked by the next century, the sayings of the late Malcolm Forbes will seem as useless as the maxims of Lenin."

Another form of moral equivalence, which arose during the 1960s, was the comparison and equation of the United States with Nazi Germany—not as widespread as the Soviet-American equation, but not uncommon, either; it even found its way into high school texts, as Sandra Stotsky has shown in her study "Moral Equivalence in Education" in *Understanding Anti-Americanism*, which I edited. Spelling America as it would be in German ("Amerika") was an expression of these sentiments, as were comparisons of the FBI to the Gestapo and the internment of Japanese-Americans during World War II to the Nazi concentration camps.

More recently, Carlos Fuentes considered the United States comparable to both Nazi Germany and the Soviet Union under Stalin (but more dangerous than either) and President Bush comparable to Hitler and Stalin. A statement made of late by Attorney General John Ashcroft reminded George Soros "of Germany under the Nazis. . . . It was the kind of talk that Goebbels used to use to line the Germans up." Moral equivalence even crept into a study by David Chandler of Pol Pot's terror state: "Dehumanization of the prisoners [in Cambodia] was immediate and total. Just as Lon Nol [the previous anticommunist leader] had seen his opponents as nonbelievers . . . and just as [!] the U.S. Congress until recently regarded indigenous Communists as 'un-American' Pol Pot and his colleagues thought of Cambodia's internal enemies as intrinsically foreign and impure." This example of a reflexive and casual attribution of moral equivalence probably intended to suggest that delving into the horrors of Pol Pot's Cambodia did not divert the author from an awareness of supposedly similar evils in the United States, that his heart was still in the right place from the politically correct point of view.

Ramsey Clark's comparison of the United States to Saddam Hussein's Iraq went beyond moral equivalence. Discussing the Iraq war, he wrote that "the United States, a technologically advanced superpower, has created weapons systems and executed plans to devastate a small, defenseless country . . . first by direct assault by fire, then with . . . enforced isolation, malnutrition, impoverishment. . . . [It was] a deliberate, systematic genocide of a defenseless population."

The most recent attributions of moral equivalence link the United States to Islamic terrorists. It began with 9/11, which created unease among many critics of America by casting the United States into the role of innocent victim, morally vindicated. These critics felt compelled to find some way to implicate and hold her responsible for the outrage. This was accomplished by the "root cause" theory: the terrorists were products of profound grievances (the root causes) in the Arab world for which, in the final analysis, the United States was responsible by supporting Israel, promoting globalism (and the attendant global inequalities), exploiting poor third-world countries, and destabilizing traditional societies with its tawdry mass culture and consumer goods.

Robert Jay Lifton wrote about a "malignant synergy" between the United States and Al Qaeda "when in their mutual zealotry, Islamist and American leaders seem to act in concert." As for Chalmers Johnson, a professor at Berkeley, "It is not at all obvious which is the greater threat to the safety and integrity of the citizens of the United States: the possibility of a terrorist attack using weapons of mass destruction or an out-of-control military intent on displacing elected officials who stand in their way." Professor Thomas Laqueur, also of Berkeley, suggested that the scale of evil 9/11 represents was not "so extraordinary and our government has been responsible for many that are probably worse." Gore Vidal wrote that "bin Laden was merely responding to U.S. foreign policy." Susan Sontag believed that 9/11 was "a consequence of specific American alliances and actions."

Closer examination of the comparative critiques embedded in moral equivalence reveals that the disparagement of the United States (or American society) has been, as a rule, far more vehement and impassioned than corresponding critiques of the USSR (or any other political entity involved in the equation), which tend to be mild and perfunctory. Critiques of Soviet misbehavior were also tempered by frequently ascribing the latter to provocative American policies; responsibility for the Cold War too increasingly rested with the United States as the Cold War revisionists saw it; Soviet aggression (if any) was defensive and as such had to be "understood"; it was also rooted in the misfortunes of Russian history. Even George Kennan came to adopt this position, as his disenchantment with American society grew during the 1960s and 1970s. Soviet aggression too had "root causes."

Moral equivalence has also been associated with what Richard Niebuhr called "perfectionist pacifism." The latter holds that "all things not utterly perfect . . . are equally imperfect, and therefore morally equivalent" as for example "the flawed good that is America" and "the pathological evil of those who attack civilians at their work" as happened on 9/11.

There has always been a tension between the relativizing impulse associated with the attribution of moral equivalence and the judgmental, partisan disposition at its hidden core. (Similar contradictions lurk in multiculturalism and political correctness.) That is to say, moral relativism and the often associated social determinism are rarely consistent; they are selectively applied to mitigate the misconduct of political entities the critics favor but not to entities and actors the critics abhor: the policies or conduct of the latter are never mitigated or excused by some deterministic force, they always have a choice to do the right thing.

It should also be noted here that certain attributions of moral equivalence have been strenuously resisted on the left. Many academic intellectuals have rejected the concept of totalitarianism largely because it proposes moral equivalence between the Soviet Union and Nazi Germany—a form of moral equivalence that was politically incorrect.

The most obvious source of the attribution of moral equivalence to morally and ethically disparate societies has been the wish to discredit American society by equating it with others generally considered far worse. Norman Mailer "declared his support for Mr. Rushdie because if he were not supported fundamentalist groups in America . . . will know how to apply the same methods to American writers." Mailer could not bring himself to condemn fundamentalist Islamic censorship and death threats against Rushdie without suggesting that morally equivalent trends were also to be found in American society.

A similar inhibition to make moral distinctions and judgments discourages radical feminists from vocally protesting the mistreatment of women in Islamic countries, or, when they do, compels them to discern similarities between such mistreatment and that which allegedly exists in the United States. Joan Jacobs Brumberg and Jacqueline Jackson succeeded in finding moral equivalence between "the burka and the bikini"; that is to say, between the "constraints" placed on what women can wear in the United States and in Afghanistan ruled by the Taliban.

It is likely that moral equivalence is a tactical concession on the part of those convinced that the United States is in fact much inferior to the societies it is equated with, that it is a historically unique incarnation of evil and corruption rather than just morally equivalent to other brutal and inhumane political systems.

The phenomenon has another less ideological and polemical source, namely the decline in the capacity to make moral, cultural, political, or historical distinctions. The intention to discredit the United States may thus be bolstered by a genuine inability to recognize differences, to make important distinctions, say, between McCarthyism and the Soviet purges or American prisons and the Gulag. This trend has been encouraged and nurtured by our educational institutions, mass media, and popular culture. It can be traced back to the 1960s and its embrace of egalitarianism, hostility to elitism, "judgmentalism," and rejection of almost any kind of differentiation since the latter was branded as discriminatory and linked to the propagation of inequality.

Moral equivalence may also be compared to aesthetic equivalence that permeates "multiculturalism," resting on the idea that nobody can or should rank cultures or cultural products; or, as UNESCO at one point declared, "All cultures are equal." Again, as in the case of moral equivalence, closer inspection reveals that there is at least one major exception to this proposition: Western culture, produced by dead, white males, can be denounced and devalued.

The tendency to designate as "genocidal" almost any indignity or injustice found in the United States (or in Western societies) is another manifestation of a diminished capacity to make important distinctions; it also tends to be motivated by the intention to raise levels of moral indignation: labeling something as "genocidal" is expected and hoped to legitimize and maximize moral revulsion.

Richard Pipes suggested another cultural and social psychological source of the unease many Americans experience when facing the task of making important distinctions:

> Americans feel uncomfortable when told that other people are "different" . . . because it is a basic premise of American culture . . . that people are everywhere the same. . . . This belief in the identity of human nature and human interests and the view that conflict is rooted in ignorance, prejudice and misunderstanding is the source of the belief that if the American and Soviet leaders only got together they could solve all the problems dividing their countries.

At last, many people who have no political ideological axe to grind are drawn to moral equivalence because it suggests even-handedness and rejection of self-righteousness. These commendable attitudes often shade into (and are prompted by) a collective self-doubt, unease, and sense of guilt over the shortcomings (real or imagined) of Western and especially American society. Intellectuals on the left and representatives of the liberal churches are especially prone to this disposition.

The questionable attribution of moral equivalence may also be associated with a generalizing impulse, often displayed by intellectuals, with their desire to "unmask" and show that "apparent" differences conceal underlying similarities.

In concluding, it must be reasserted that not all social-political systems (or human beings) are equally flawed; it is possible and necessary to differentiate among them. A measure of moral clarity—the opposite of moral equivalence—need not be simplistic, arrogant, or self-righteous. We can and should be aware and critical of the flaws of American society without succumbing to the groundless belief that it is no better than communist totalitarianism or Islamic fundamentalism.

II

AMERICANA

Chapter Five

Our Society and Its Celebrities

An article in the *New Yorker* (published September 9, 2002) chronicled the Paris visit of Puff Daddy (Sean Combs), the renowned rap singer and fashion entrepreneur. It was written by a reporter who accompanied him to provide a detailed account of virtually every moment of the four-day trip. The reader could learn a great deal about Puff Daddy, a bona fide celebrity of our times— his way of life, beliefs, and favored forms of entertainment, consumption, and socializing. He was introduced as "the 32 year old rap impresario, restaurateur, clothing entrepreneur, bon vivant, actor and Page Six regular." His claim to fame also rests on having been nominated by the Council of Fashion Designers of America as "the menswear designer of the year." He was urgently summoned to fly to Paris (via Concorde, First Class) to lend glamour to a Versace fashion show:

> With his hip-hop credentials and his love of the spotlight, not to mention a past that includes highly public moments of violence, Combs provided exactly what the fashion crowd craves. . . . He wore fur and leather and draped himself in enough diamonds to rival Princess Caroline of Monaco. . . . Donatella Versace . . . was counting on Combs' presence to add some adrenaline to her show. . . . [His accessories included] a silver tie, smoke-colored sunglasses, diamond-and-platinum earrings, a bracelet or two, a couple of diamond rings the size of cherry tomatoes, and a watch covered with jewels and worth nearly a million dollars.

The article also noted (without a hint of disapproval) that his "career has been punctuated by violence. . . . In 1999 he and two others were arrested for beating a rival record-company executive. . . . [He] was [also] involved in an incident at a Manhattan night club in which three people were shot."

On his trip to Paris "he was traveling with a trainer, a stylist and at least two personal assistants." In his Paris hotel suite "there were several garment racks in the living room, with more than a dozen suits, scores of shirts, leather jackets . . . enough shoes to last a lifetime . . . flown over from New York. . . . Sunglasses had been arranged in three rows on a high table. . . . There were about ten pairs in each row; each pair in its original case, with the top flipped up."

The elevation of Puff Daddy to celebrity status illustrates a phenomenon that will be of interest to future social historians seeking to understand the sources and manifestations of American cultural decline in the late twentieth and early twenty-first centuries. It may be argued that the rise and veneration of celebrities has been a characteristic expression of this decline. Almost half a century ago, Daniel Boorstin, the social historian, wrote:

> Our age has produced a new kind of eminence. . . . This new kind of eminence is "celebrity.". . . He has been fabricated . . . to satisfy our exaggerated expectations of human greatness. He is morally neutral. . . . The hero was distinguished by his achievement; the celebrity by his image or trademark. The hero created himself; the celebrity is created by the media. . . .
>
> The celebrity is always a contemporary. The hero is made by folklore, sacred texts and history books but the celebrity is the creature of gossip . . . of magazines, newspapers and the ephemeral images of movie and television screen. . . .
>
> Celebrities are differentiated mainly by trivia of personality. . . . Entertainers are best qualified to become celebrities because they are skilled in the marginal differentiation of their personalities. . . . Anyone can become a celebrity if only he can get into the news and stay there.

As Boorstin suggests, several forces sustain the phenomenon. The existence of the mass media is a fundamental precondition since it creates, disseminates, and dwells on the images of celebrities; it assures that the celebrity will be known, however superficially, to millions of people. The celebrities have been created by the media (and their own PR people) because there are millions interested in such fantasy figures upon whom they can project transitory admiration and perhaps a spurious identification.

The second precondition for the phenomenon is a moral, cultural, and aesthetic relativism that allows and stimulates the admiration of people of no genuine distinction—moral, artistic, or intellectual. Genuine heroes, people of great accomplishments, are few and far between. If fame based on some impressive accomplishment is in short supply, notoriety will do. Celebrities are the readily available substitutes for true greatness. It is also quite likely that the attacks on "elitism" nurture this relativism and the cult of mediocre and amoral celebrities. Arguably the populist and egalitarian strains in American history provide further support and legitimation for the rise and proliferation of celebrities. Anybody can become a celebrity, no special qualifications are required, only adequate publicity, a certain degree of egomania, and some attention-getting trait or activity.

The celebrity phenomenon also feeds on the enlarged, democratic individualism of our times. A growing number of people feel that they are entitled to fame, attention, wealth, power, and special treatment; countless people take themselves far more seriously than is warranted. People wish and can actually become widely known for odd, dubious, or absurd reasons, including colorful criminal acts.

Figures of entertainment and fashion fill most of the celebrity ranks, in part because they have at their disposal a well-lubricated publicity machine; their fame and fortune is tied to the financial success of the enterprises associated with the celebrities and sustained by popular culture. There is a financial incentive for creating celebrities: movies, TV programs, and popular music revolve around them; the advertising industry regularly avails itself of their services and endorsements to sell a wide range of products. Most celebrities come from the world of entertainment because the entertainment industries occupy such a prominent place in American life.

As the *New Yorker* article makes clear, celebrities are handsomely rewarded for the functions they perform. These rewards in turn reinforce their bloated and unrealistic self-conceptions.

The *New Yorker*'s treatment of Puff Daddy is but one of countless examples of a totally uncritical and unreflective view of the phenomenon of celebrity worship. Another telling indication of the trend has been the gradual transformation of the *New York Times Magazine* from a serious publication focusing on major political and social events or problems into one that devotes, more often than not, more than half of its space to profiling assorted celebrities from the world of entertainment, sports, and fashion.

The celebrity worship and the moral-aesthetic-intellectual relativism it enshrines are symptoms of cultural decline and confusion—time will tell how serious a decline. As the *New Yorker* article pointed out about other celebrities, "Ralph Lauren and Martha Stewart are more than brands; they offer visions of the world." Hopefully these visions will not become dominant.

Chapter Six

Watching Celebrities

Time and again, reading travel magazines I come upon the promise that the destination described will provide great opportunities for "celebrity watching." Writers of these articles take it for granted that readers get excited by the possibility of spotting celebrities.

In a recent issue of the *New York Times* Travel Section, readers were assured that in St. Moritz (Switzerland) "despite the scent of exclusivity . . . you are free to mingle" with celebrities such as "supermodels, business tycoons, former heads of state . . . the rich, the very rich, the royals and those who want to marry a royal." A nightclub in the same location was described as a "celebrity haunt" providing "your opportunity to rub shoulders" with these important individuals. Another recent article in the *Times* entitled "Feeling at Home Among the Elite" was intended to encourage ordinary readers that they could fit into the rarified playground of Punta del Este, Uruguay, "despite its jet set reputation."

I would like to ask people who enjoy "celebrity watching" (or those who write articles suggesting that they do) to explain why such ogling, mingling, or rubbing shoulders is a source of pleasure and self-fulfillment? Should we believe that people thrive on fantasized ersatz relationships by laying eyes on celebrities?

It is possible that those who rejoice in "rubbing shoulders" harbor a hope that sharing temporarily the same space as celebrities elevates their own social standing. As the *New York Times* article on St. Moritz put it, "You can attend their events, eat in their restaurants, walk among them, wear their clothes, sleep on the same luscious sheets." So what?

Daniel Boorstin grasped the essentials of the celebrity cult half a century ago: "Our age has produced a new kind of eminence. . . . He is the human pseudo-event... a substitute for the hero who is the celebrity and whose main characteristic is well-knownness.... Anyone can become a celebrity if only he can get into the news and stay there. Figures from the world of entertainment and sports [and fashion industry] are most apt to be well known.... The hero was distinguished by his achievement; the celebrity by his image or trademark."

Many highly talented, knowledgeable, and creative people are not widely known and are not celebrities. Great scientists are not celebrities. They don't provide entertainment, and their skills and accomplishments are hard to emulate; nor are they uniformly good-looking. Looks are very important for becoming a celebrity; most of them are good-looking and cultivate some aspect of physical appearance that can become a "trademark." Vast amounts of publicity, a degree of egomania, and some attention-getting trait or activity are the prerequisites of becoming a celebrity. And of course we would not have celebrities without the mass media of communications that disseminate their images and activities.

The celebrity cult is a form of vicarious gratification, an attempt at identification with those who possess attributes missing from the lives of ordinary human beings: fame, wealth, vast amounts of attention, and often adulation as well. In a populist, anti-elitist, socially mobile society, a growing number of individuals feel entitled to fame, fortune, attention, power, and special treatment. They also believe that each individual has limitless potential and there are no exclusive, hard-to-enter elites of the gifted. Many unlikely individuals ascend to celebrity status when they succeed in drawing attention to themselves by some means, becoming widely known for odd, dubious, or absurd reasons, including spectacular criminal acts. Kidnappers, bank robbers, and murderers often demand the opportunity to make statements on television or radio before they surrender. Like the rest of us, they want to transcend anonymity.

Celebrity worship is a reflection of moral and aesthetic relativism and the insecurity many feel about their social status in a highly competitive society. The celebrity phenomenon reflects an American (or modern?) uncertainty as to what kinds of accomplishments truly deserve respect or admiration.

Why is Paris Hilton a celebrity? She is rich, good-looking, a prominent socialite, a playgirl, successful at getting publicity; one of her partners made public a video of their sexual activities; notoriety enhances celebrity status.

Aside from their exciting and scandalous sex and social lives, the most widely publicized thing about celebrities is their tastes and possessions. Celebrities are also good for business and enthusiastically participate in lucrative advertising campaigns endorsing products and services. Becoming a celebrity is an obvious avenue for personal enrichment: if you are famous enough, sooner or later you will also become rich because fame sells.

Less obvious among the preconditions of celebrity worship is the decline of community and the rise of social isolation that leads to fantasies of having something in common with or relating to the rich and famous. "Celebrity watching" expresses and exemplifies "false consciousness"; it is an attempt to find meaning and fulfillment in the life and the attributes of others far removed from one's own far more circumscribed circumstances.

Chapter Seven

Michael Moore: The New Political Celebrity

Michael Moore embodies the fusion of the realms of entertainment and social criticism, each enhanced by his celebrity status. Even among politically active celebrity entertainers, Moore stands out by virtue of his determination to influence domestic politics by tirelessly disseminating his messages through movies, television, books, and personal appearances of every kind. His popularity—both in the United States and abroad—exceeds that of all other detractors of the United States (except Che Guevara and Osama bin Laden, whose images also appear on T-shirts). It is difficult to think of any other individual in this line of work whose message has reached comparable numbers.

In 2004 at the Cannes Film Festival in France, his *Fahrenheit 9/11* was given the highest award and was "greeted with a 20-minute standing ovation."[1] At home the same film "has broken the record of the highest grossing documentary of all time. . . ."[2] During the 2004 presidential campaign, prominent Democratic politicians embraced Moore (literally and figuratively) hoping that this movie would help them to prevail in the elections. Among the appeal of the film, as one reviewer put it, is that it "offers the thrill of a coherent explanation of everything. . . ."[3] His books were similarly successful:

> *Stupid White Men* (2001), a diatribe against rich people, white people, dumb people, men . . . was on the *Times* best-seller list for forty-nine weeks and sold more than four million copies worldwide. *Dude. Where's My Country* (2003) . . . a diatribe against rich people, white people and the Iraq war . . . started out at No. 1. His first book, *Downsize This!* was also a best-seller. . . . Everywhere Moore went on a recent forty-eight city book tour through America and Europe, thousands of people showed up to see him. . . .[4]

In his capacity as both a producer and product of mass culture, Moore personifies the pervasive entertainment orientation of our society that requires everything to be entertaining, from social criticism to the weather report, from warnings about lung cancer to the teaching of mathematics (if any) in the schools.

More unusual, given his animating hatred of American society, is Moore's working-class social background, albeit of a rather prosperous working class without memories of deprivations conducive to lifelong bitterness. Even in the notable absence of such memories, Moore has cultivated an intense moral indignation and resentfulness on behalf of this working class, although it is impossible to locate any objective factor, personal injury, or grievance that would account for the embittered stance he has taken. By the time Moore had come of age, autoworkers, such as his father, were virtually part of the middle class:

> his father, as a member of the United Auto Workers, was entitled to free medical care, free dental care and four weeks of paid vacation. If he needed legal help the union provided a lawyer free. He had two cars and owned his house outright. He lived not in the city of Flint . . . but in Davison, a white middle class community. . . . His family took nice vacations and sent his three children to college. . . . He worked the first shift, from six until two, then played golf. . . . He retired with a full pension . . . at the age of fifty-three . . . and did volunteer work at the church.[5]

This background notwithstanding (or because of it?) Moore assiduously cultivated a working class identity (or at any rate appearance), generally dressing down, wearing baseball caps, sporting a beer belly, and trying to talk like the common man. In the film *Roger and Me*, he seemed to make a special point of being disheveled and dressed down on the occasions of seeking to interview Roger Smith, the CEO of General Motors.

It is not unlikely that Moore—by all accounts, including his own, a rebellious youngster—found the middle-class trappings of his youth boring and irritating. This is all the more plausible since his adolescence and youth coincided with the 1960s. In the fourth grade he started an underground school paper.[6] His parents sent him to a Catholic school and "after 8th grade he enrolled in a seminary: He admired the Berrigan brothers and thought the priesthood was the way to effect social change." It is not clear what precisely led to these ideas. After the tenth grade he returned to the secular world of the public high school. Subsequently he attended the Flint campus of the University of Michigan for one year, then dropped out. Moore became a hippie and produced a weekly radio show called "Radio Free Flint." He was often on the evening news "leading a rally or antinuclear protest or . . . criticizing the police. He started a crisis center for teenagers . . . that somehow mutated into a small alternative newspaper called *Flint Voice*."[7]

In 1986 Moore left Flint for San Francisco to become editor of *Mother Jones*, but within weeks he was fired. Staff members said that "he was impossible to work with." Part of the problem was that "his employees expected him to be the ideal boss—after all he was the defender of the little guy. . . . But as the staff of *Mother Jones* discovered, Moore wasn't the ideal boss. . . . He disliked sharing credit with his writers. He would often come in late. . . . If someone said something he didn't like . . . he would simply not invite that person to the next meeting, or the person would be fired. . . ."[8] As is often the case, the personal and the political did not converge.

Moore claimed that *Mother Jones* fired him because he opposed the publication of an article by Paul Berman that was critical of the Sandinistas (Moore was not). He "accused Berman . . . of being a traitor to the left and giving aid and comfort to Reagan." After *Mother Jones*, he worked briefly for Ralph Nader whom he had admired since high school.[9]

Moore visited Sandinista Nicaragua and also thought well of Castro's Cuba. In his "Letter of Apology to Elian Gonzales" (published on his website) he deplored Gonzales's "kidnapping" from a country providing "free health care whenever you needed it [and] an excellent education, one of the few countries that has 100% literacy and lower infant mortality than the United States." He suggested that Gonzales's mother (who took him with her to the United States), as most other Cubans, only left Cuba because "they simply wanted to make more money." Moore further suggested that Cuban exiles in Miami interested in fighting for freedom should have stayed in Cuba to fight rather than "turn tail and [run] to Miami. . . . These very ex-Cubans . . . were afraid to stand and fight Castro. . . ."[10] The last remark illustrates Moore's grasp of the realities of life in a totalitarian police state and the opportunities it allows its citizens to express their opposition.

Moore's political views have much in common with Noam Chomsky's— including the visceral rejection of American society and the conviction that it is (alongside much of the rest of the world) relentlessly manipulated by unscrupulous, greedy elites. The cardinal message of Moore's *Fahrenheit 9/11* is identical with the verities of Chomsky: "America is not a democracy. . . . [It is] an oligarchy in which the wealthy pull the strings behind a facade of manufactured democratic consent."[11] Moore takes the notion of conspiracy quite personally and employs security guards to protect him. He "seems to feel . . . that people are out to get him and that there are few people he can trust."[12]

Like most skilled propagandists, Moore prefers selectivity and misrepresentation to outright falsehood. As a critic wrote, "Moore as a rule only conveys enough information to arouse suspicion, not nearly enough to make a case."[13] In *Fahrenheit 9/11* there is no reference to "Islamic fundamentalism, . . . obsessive anti-Americanism or suicide terrorists and the difficulty of guarding against them. . . . There are apparently no justifiable fears, only hysterical fears manipulated by the authorities, whose every act is purposive and conspiratorial."[14] What Moore chose to show in this movie about Sadam Hussein's Iraq is an example of heavy-handed selectivity in service of a transparent political agenda: ". . . a peaceable kingdom . . . children flying kites, shoppers . . . smiling in the sunshine . . . the gentle rhythms of life undisturbed. . . ." That is, until the American bombardments and invasion.[15]

Moore also shares with Chomsky, and other similarly disposed social critics, the conviction that the American public has been brainwashed and suffers from false consciousness, thanks to the manipulations of their amoral rulers and the media they control: "we live in a system of enforced ignorance. The way the media works, the way our education system works, it's all about keeping us stupid. . . ."[16] He is apparently among the few who was able to resist these manipulations. He regards these rulers as more dangerous than any terrorists: "'just because there are a few terrorists doesn't mean that we are in some exaggerated state of danger,' he said, except that is from 'our multi-millionaire, corporate terrorists. . . .'"[17]

A vitriolic hatred of the rich suffuses Moore's writings and movies, all the more peculiar since he has become one of them. Evidently he senses no "cognitive dissonance" between such hatred and the fact that—as he notes in passing—"I live on the island of Manhattan . . . that is luxury home and corporate suite to America's elite. Much of the suffering you experience as an American emanates from this piece of platinum real estate. . . . Those who run your lives live in my neighborhood. I walk the streets with them each day."[18] Why did he choose to share a neighborhood with such deplorable human beings instead of living in some wholesome working-class district? He does not explain. Reportedly his apartment cost $1.9 million, many years ago. He also owns a beachfront summer house in Michigan that cost $1.2 million. On the college lecture circuit, his fees range from $10,000 to $30,000.[19] Notwithstanding such circumstances, his condemnation of the rich is relentless:

> The rich and powerful make it their mission to destroy our air, poison our water, rip us off. . . . I've decided that the only hope we have in this country to bring aid to the sick . . . and a better life to those who suffer is to pray like crazy that those in power are afflicted with the worst possible diseases, tragedies and circumstances in life. . . .
>
> With that in mind I've written a prayer to speed the recovery of all those in need by asking God to smite every political leader and corporate executive with

some form of deadly disease.... So I've written "A Prayer to Afflict the Comfortable with as Many Afflictions as Possible."[20]

Whether or not Moore intended these lines to be humorous, they illuminate a bottomless hatred the origins of which remain unclear.

In contrast to this hatred of the heartless rich, Moore overflows with love for the poor, especially if black. Unlike most of the white working-class people he claims to be a self-appointed spokesman of, Moore seems burdened by a guilt complex about black Americans and displays great solicitousness toward them. He avers that "every mean word, every cruel act, every bit of pain and suffering in my life has had a Caucasian face attached to it." Black crime is an invention of white racists and the media, he tells his readers. He firmly believes (or so he says) that the white race is responsible for "this planet [becoming] such a pitiful, scary place to inhabit," afflicted with nuclear weapons, environmental degradation, slavery, the Holocaust, and unemployment, among other evils. To sum it up: "You name a problem ... or the abject misery visited upon millions and I'll bet you ... I can put a white face on it." This is Moore's version of Susan Sontag's famous proposition about the white race being the cancer of humanity. Moore also insists that there has been no genuine improvement in the conditions of the black population; racism has just become more subtle; the system remains "rigged." He proclaims that he will only hire blacks and advocates intermarriage and the production of babies of such marriages[21] — advice he himself did not follow.

Moore's critiques of American society are comprehensive, extreme, unqualified, and apocalyptic; they incorporate every variety of denunciation. He wholeheartedly subscribes to the view that the United States is the evil empire having observed, in connection with the demise of the Soviet Union, "one evil empire down, one to go."[22]

It is hard to know how much exactly Moore believes of his own words, as for example that "millions of Americans ... are off-balance, unsure, upset, unglued. The rest are in prison."[23] Or is it possible that this is the way *he* feels? (off-balance, unsure, unglued). He also writes: "So I'm stuck with a car that doesn't run, in a country where nothing works, and it is every man, woman and state-tested child for themselves. Survival of the richest—no more lifeboats for you...."[24] Again, an unlikely characterization of his personal circumstances.

Moore is among the many critics of this society who reaped considerable material rewards for their critical messages as well as personal popularity. He is a perfect example of the compatibility of vocal alienation with great material and popular success and celebrity status.

ACKNOWLEDGMENTS

I thank Mr. Alan Edelstein for his comments about this essay.

NOTES

1. Pascal Bruckner, "Tour de Farce," *New Republic*, July 19, 2004, 19.
2. Jason Zengerle, "Crashing the Party," *New Republic*, July 19, 2004, 110.
3. David Denby, "George and Me," *New Yorker*, June 28, 2004, 110.
4. Larissa MacFarquhar, "The Populist," *New Yorker*, February 16 and 23, 2004, 134.
5. MacFarquhar, "The Populist," 137.
6. *Stupid White Men—and Other Sorry Excuses for the State of the Nation* (New York: ReganBooks, 2001), 96.
7. MacFarquhar, "The Populist," 135, 136.
8. MacFarquhar, "The Populist," 140, 142, 143, 144.
9. MacFarquhar, "The Populist," 141, 142.
10. See his website: michaelmoore.com/words/message/index.php7message Date=2000-03-31.
11. Denby, "George and Me," 110.
12. MacFarquhar, "The Populist," 138.
13. Geoffrey O'Brien, "Is It All Just a Dream?" *New York Review of Books*, August 12, 2004, 17.
14. Denby, "George and Me," 110.
15. Christopher Hitchens, *Love, Poverty, and War: Journeys and Essays* (New York: Nation Books, 2004), 293.
16. Moore, *Stupid White Men*.
17. Quoted in O'Brien, "Is It All Just a Dream?" 19.
18. Moore, *Stupid White Men*, 51.
19. David T. Hardy and Jason Clarke, *Michael Moore Is a Big Fat Stupid White Man* (New York: ReganBooks, 2004), 117–18.
20. Moore, *Stupid White Men*, 231–33
21. Moore, *Stupid White Men*, 57, 58, 62–63, 70, 72.
22. *Playboy*, July 1999, 155.
23. Moore, *Stupid White Men*, xviii.
24. Moore, *Stupid White Men*, xx.

Chapter Eight

SUVs and Americans

"Common Ground on the Environment" (*Daily Hampshire Gazette*, January 9, 2003, written by an employee of a skiing company in Aspen, Colorado) puts a highly unconvincing, Pollyannaish gloss on SUV use. Most implausibly the article claims that people drive SUVs "because there are no comparably priced options with better gas mileage that offer equivalent safety, convenience, performance and comfort." There are in fact many such options.

SUV safety is a myth except in collisions with smaller cars; SUV rollovers have been notorious. As to performance, one may ask what "performance" is required by most SUV drivers who rarely if ever leave a paved road, let alone penetrate the roadless areas pictured in SUV commercials. And what is "convenient" about a car that barely fits into a regular parking space and has trouble turning a tight corner? As to the comfort SUVs offer, most regular sedans and family vans offer comparable comfort and space for luggage. The only rational claim that can be made for SUVs is that people sit higher and see better. But as competing SUV models get bigger, even that advantage diminishes. In any event, this small benefit is bought at a high price.

A major source of the popularity of SUVs is the (false) sense of security owners seem to derive from being encased in these large and heavy vehicles equipped with four-wheel drive (they rarely need or use). SUVs are supposed to be "rugged" and are invariably portrayed in advertisements in remote, roadless, scenic settings. The promise of security is thus linked with fantasies of adventure that appeal to sedentary, urban, and suburban middle-class Americans. A recent ad for the Mercedes SUV (published in the *New Yorker*) was openly cynical about such appeals: "Autobahn [the German superhighway] meets Audubon. . . . There is nothing like the great outdoors. Especially when it is whipping past at 147 mph on the autobahn." Even during the camping season you will see more SUVs at suburban malls than at remote campgrounds. One may doubt that "many of those who drive SUVs . . . see themselves as outdoor people." But even if they do so, such pleasant fantasies merely distract from the impact of their SUV on the outdoors.

Since these vehicles are not cheap to buy and run, being authentic gas guzzlers, and offer only marginal or questionable benefits, it is all the more puzzling why they are so popular. It is likely that the possession of these ungainly vehicles is connected with a sense of power, self-assertion, and (sometimes) aggression. As Keith Bradhser (who wrote a book on the subject) put it, SUVs have been "designed to intimidate other motorists." Tanklike, they can go anywhere (not that people want them to) and in a collision they will crush smaller vehicles. And they keep getting bigger. The civilian version of the army vehicle, the Hummer is the latest status symbol among Hollywood celebrities.

SUVs have become a prominent item of conspicuous consumption suggesting excess and abundance—they have more power, weight, and space than most people need. Such excess is the essence of display, like "McMansions" with five bathrooms and immense unused spaces. In offering excessive amounts of weight and space, SUVs also resemble limos, which are even more impractical, more wasteful of space, and more obviously intended to "make a statement" divorced from any discernible need other than showing off.

It is another possibility that the expansion of the size of vehicles represented by SUVs is associated with the corresponding expansion of the size of Americans. SUVs are likely to have a special appeal to those who are overweight on account of the comfort they promise. But for the most part people drive SUVs because they have become (mistakenly) identified with safety, freedom, adventure, self-sufficiency, and ruggedness and because they offer marginal advantages like sitting higher and more comfortably than in some regular cars. But these preferences have costly unintended consequences: air pollution, congestion, and aggravating the dependence on imported oil. The largely imaginary benefits of these vehicles are greatly outweighed by their damage to the environment and public health and the increased economic-political dependence on oil-producing countries.

While it is always risky to pronounce on what people "truly need," I believe that few people truly need SUVs since they do not live on dirt roads and do not have to move around huge families. Life without SUVs should not be a hardship or sacrifice for most people and is compatible with safety, comfort, and performance.

Chapter Nine

The Chronic Ailments of Television News

A few years ago Jim Maceda, a reporter on *NBC Evening News*, informed viewers that based on interviews he had conducted on the streets of Baghdad he had reached the conclusion that Saddam Hussein enjoyed broad and strong support among the people of Iraq. Disturbed by the ignorance and journalistic irresponsibility these comments reflected, I wrote a letter to the producer of *NBC Evening News* asking "does Mr. Maceda truly believe that in an exceptionally brutal police state such as present day Iraq any critic of the ruling dictator will come forward and unburden himself or herself in public to an American TV reporter? Did he ever hear about the treatment of the critics of the system? ... How did he select his informants and who did the translations ... ?" I received no reply from NBC.

A recent article in the *New Republic* helps to explain the attitude of Maceda and many of his fellow reporters in Iraq. Foreign journalists in Iraq are tightly controlled by the government and its ubiquitous "minders" who accompany them everywhere; if they displease the authorities they get kicked out or are refused visas. As the *New Republic* article pointed out, "broadcasting his [Hussein's] propaganda is simply the only way they can continue to work in Iraq.... The networks make these concessions because the alternative is no access."

We do not know what proportion of American reporters are aware that "like their Sovietbloc predecessors, the Iraqis have become masters of the Orwellian pantomime—the state-orchestrated anti-American rally, the state-led tours of alleged chemical weapons sites that turn out to be baby milk factories ..." and other deceptions they are exposed to and expected to report. Whatever their level of awareness of the latter, these reporters faithfully report what they are allowed to see. An exception was the excellent *Frontline*/World program on public television entitled *Truth and Lies in Baghdad*. It was made by a British reporter who was expelled well before his visa expired and who probably does not expect to return soon, if ever, in view of his findings.

It is no mystery why the Iraqi government is intent on denying free access to foreign reporters and why it manipulates and shapes what they report. The mystery is why American news organizations and especially TV networks "mindlessly recite Baghdad's spin" and why they are convinced that under these conditions having reporters in Iraq serves a useful purpose. A CNN executive (interviewed for the *New Republic* article) insists that these manipulated reports are "newsworthy" and it is essential for CNN to be able to report from Iraq; being there "is an end in itself," the *New Republic* concluded.

But why this obsession with "being there" when it not only precludes the gathering of reliable and informative news but actually assures the opposite: the steady, abundant flow of misinformation, amounting to Iraqi government propaganda?

An attempt to understand this peculiar policy leads to further reflections about the chronic and broader flaws of television news. The striving for a spurious authenticity is a major explanation, and one that is not limited to the misleading reports from Iraq. It is this quest for "authenticity" that prompts network executives and reporters to believe that "being on the spot" is in and of itself valuable, that thrusting a microphone in the face of a docile and intimidated pedestrian in Baghdad is a notable accomplishment.

But the presumed benefits of "being on the spot" have become an obsolete journalistic article of faith in our age of resourceful police states, mass manipulation, organized spontaneity, and model institutions created for propaganda purposes and especially for the benefit of foreign visitors. In a book of mine (*Political Pilgrims*) I referred to some of these efforts as the "techniques of hospitality" authorities in communist systems devised for the explicit purpose of deceiving visitors from abroad; these techniques have not been limited to communist states as the case of Iraq shows.

The pursuit of authenticity is not the only explanation of the problems here discussed. There is also genuine ignorance on the part of many American journalists about repressive political systems abroad—quite similar to past ignorance about communist states that led to purveying similarly misleading information about them. These journalists and their employers find it particularly difficult to grasp that public opinion in repressive police states cannot be easily, if at all, assessed, sampled, or measured, because in these societies people wear a tightly fitting mask of conformity.

Asking people on the streets of Baghdad what they think of their government or of the United States has certain parallels in domestic television news, not that the Americans queried are intimidated and hence cannot respond truthfully. The similarity lies in the compulsion to solicit the views of ordinary people more or less randomly selected, who have no particular expertise or qualifications for offering enlightening comments on the subjects in question, only semiarticulate gut reactions. In spite of this, no newscast passes without reporters earnestly extracting some such snippet of banality from these randomly picked "ordinary people," usually on the street, in shopping malls, or at other public places. Their opinions or reactions are compulsively solicited about major events deemed newsworthy, whether it is war with Iraq, the state of the economy, the price of drugs, airport check-ins, or disasters of one kind or another. A handful of interviews, regardless of their minimal substance, are not meaningful samples of public opinion.

I suggest two explanations for this phenomenon. One is the motivation to pay lip service to egalitarianism by conveying that the networks care for the opinions of ordinary folks and not only the experts; we are to believe that it is enlightening and important to learn what these handful of anonymous, interchangeable "regular" people opine on various issues in the seconds allotted to them. Such people must come from all walks of life — an approach also dear to advertisers who like to illustrate the wonders of their products through "regular" but "diverse" people — bus drivers, nurses, farmers, old-age pensioners, firefighters, and police officers, preferably of different skin color and ethnicity.

Inserting the snippets by ordinary people into a newscast serves a second purpose: to avoid dreaded abstractions or more complicated ideas; presumably it would tax the intelligence of the viewers to be informed, say, that a certain percentage of old-age pensioners cannot afford to pay for their drugs instead of showing an actual old-age pensioner who cannot afford them and says so. Likewise information about the rising gasoline prices cannot be dispensed without showing a human being pumping gas and muttering something about the changing prices.

Since the news has to be lively and, if possible, dramatic and entertaining, whatever is abstract, dry, analytical, and lacking in entertainment value is strenuously avoided. This, of course, is the obvious explanation of the fondness for reporting violence and disasters of every kind, as well as tearful personal responses to loss and suffering. As of this writing, every network provided on several occasions an extended and identical coverage of an earthquake in a small town in Italy, doubtless because the victims were children. Here was a juicy disaster with a particularly sad toll. The Italians portrayed met (without intending) the network requirements for stereotypical emotional display: they sobbed, gesticulated wildly, ran around; they were authentically and spectacularly grief-stricken.

It should also be noted here that while photogenic catastrophes in different parts of the world are given eager and detailed coverage, in the normal course of events approximately 90 percent of the world remains shrouded in obscurity and is never referred to. News coverage is trapped between a resolute parochialism (the overwhelming majority of news being domestic) and the pursuit of the odd, exotic, and disastrous elsewhere whenever it occurs. In order to deflect critiques of dwelling on the morbid or pathological, the evening news usually ends with an uplifting, feel-good, human-interest story, often quite trivial.

Television news will only become informative and honest if and when its makers decide that providing entertainment to maximize the audience is not its first obligation, when criteria other than photogenic suffering or banal feel-good snippets govern news selection, and when the producers of the news acquire a better understanding of the world outside the United States, including the kind of political repression that has no precedent and parallel in American experience.

At the time when the United States is approaching the possibility of war with Iraq, it is particularly important that the American public be well informed. This includes information about the character of the prevailing Iraqi political system, its exceptionally repressive nature, and its pathologically brutal leader. The media does not have to "demonize" Saddam Hussein, since the facts speak for themselves. Most Americans have no idea how he came to power and how he stays in power. There are plenty of Iraqi exiles in the United States who can provide chilling "human interest" stories about the system that could be a revealing counterpoint to supervised, sham interviews on the streets of Baghdad.

A thorough examination of political conditions in Iraq on television could contribute to the kind of moral clarity that would help the public to decide whether or not regime change in Iraq would or would not constitute a "just war."

Chapter Ten

Stereotyping and the Decline of Common Sense

According to a textbook in my possession entitled *Modern Geography* ("simplified and adapted to the capacity of Youth") published in 1830 in Hartford, Connecticut, "The Afghans are a brave, fierce and warlike people . . . distinguished for their hospitality. . . ." By contrast, "the French are polite, gay, active and industrious and celebrated for their proficiency in the arts and sciences." In turn, "the Dutch are honest, patient and persevering and remarkable for their industry, frugality and neatness," whereas "the Italians are affable and polite and excel in music, painting and sculpture . . . they are effeminate, superstitious, slavish and revengeful." The Russians are "hardy, vigorous and patient of labor but extremely rude, ignorant and barbarous."

As these examples make clear, Americans in those days were not apprehensive about heavy-handed stereotyping. It was not considered impossible or offensive to offer brief generalizations about attributes that groups or nationalities had in common or were supposed to have in common. Deep in his or her heart, even the most enlightened present-day reader may admit that these characterizations were not wholly without foundation. It is almost as clear today as it was in the early nineteenth century that the Dutch, in many respects, are quite unlike the Afghans, and a comparison of the French and Russians, or Swedes and Italians, would also yield some obvious and highly patterned differences. Stereotyping fell into bad repute because of the hate-filled racial-ethnic labeling that justified the mistreatment and persecution in our times of groups including Jews, blacks, Native Americans, Armenians, gypsies—you name it.

Group differences are not limited to those rooted in nationality: social class and levels of education too are associated with identifiable group differences.

Truck drivers share traits found far less frequently among mathematicians and stockbrokers; the latter in turn would be difficult to confuse with professional musicians. I read once that there used to be a high concentration of individuals of Scandinavian origin among tugboat captains in New York harbor but not of those with a Jewish background. Asian Americans excel in the sciences and engineering, African Americans in sports—scandalous as it has become to say so in public. Of course each and every one of these and other groups shares a common humanity that is the point of departure for a wide range of admissible differences, as multiculturalists proudly emphasize.

Are shared group attributes vicious, degrading stereotypes or commonsense observations about certain traits, propensities, talents, or interests some groups have in common for reasons both known and unknown? Stereotypes are widely held generalizations about groups; some are accurate, some are not; they often exaggerate certain attributes and ignore others. Such generalizations do not mean that every individual in a particular group possesses the widely perceived characteristics ascribed to the group but a greater probability that he will have them. Such generalizations are basic to human cognition: we tend to classify and group all kinds of phenomena—few things in this world, animate or inanimate, are totally unique or singular.

None of this is a uniquely modern phenomenon: aversion toward the stranger, the outsider, variously defined (and often associated with the negative stereotypes) is as old as human beings living in groups. But only in the past few decades has the practice become strongly condemned, indeed outlawed (for the most part only in the West, one must hasten to add). Stereotyping in much of the non-Western world remains a time-honored, taken-for-granted practice; the suggestion that Indians and Pakistanis or the Chinese and Japanese, Chechens and Russians or Arabs and Israelis are fundamentally alike would prompt incomprehension or a good laugh in those parts of the world.

At the same time it has been largely overlooked that a recently prominent trend in American society—multiculturalism—thrives on stereotyping. It insists that there are ineradicable differences among groups (or the sexes) that are the sources of group identity and identity politics, of ethnic, feminist, or gay pride. It is politically correct and praiseworthy to claim that certain groups have unique needs and attributes (which, for example, educational institutions should respect and cater to) but totally inadmissible to suggest that certain groups may also share, along with their particular religious-political convictions, different propensities to commit violent acts of terrorism.

It is thus important to point out that the ban on stereotyping—central to political correctness—has been highly selective. White heterosexual males, corporate executives, evangelical Christians, housewives not interested in feminism, anti-abortionists, and others can be openly stereotyped in highly unfavorable ways. Racism, sexism, homophobia, elitism, and ethnocentrism have been freely and sweepingly attributed to such groups. These too are stereotypes, and especially venomous ones given the frequent claim that they are inherent and ineradicable.

Profiling or racial profiling is a form of stereotyping that rests on the assumption that members of some groups are more likely than others to commit crimes or acts of political violence. Such profiling has become a particularly pressing issue in the wake of 9/11 and the preventive measures it has inspired. Is it fair or reasonable to pay more attention at airports and elsewhere to people who belong to groups known to have a greater propensity, statistically speaking, to commit acts of terrorism than others, that is, young males of Arab or Middle Eastern background and often of darker complexion? How many native-born American old-age pensioners, suburban mothers, or members of symphony orchestras have been among the known suicide pilots or bombers? Why pretend that old ladies in wheelchairs have the same potential to blow up planes than physically fit, young males from Islamic countries?

The current procedure at airports and elsewhere is based on the ludicrous premise and pretense that the propensity and capability to carry out acts of terrorism are randomly distributed in the American population, although everybody knows that this is not the case. This is why we see women with babies frisked and octogenarians' luggage carefully examined. Random searches of this kind are a colossal waste of time and resources. They are necessary only insofar as not everybody can be searched thoroughly, thus some people have to be singled out. But the latter should not be a random procedure. What we need are intelligent forms of profiling that take into account the largest number of probable variables associated with acts of terrorism and the beliefs underpinning them.

The precipitous decline of common sense in our times, associated with a politically correct solicitousness toward some minorities, was also revealed in the recent case of a Muslim woman in Florida who insisted on her right to wear a veil (hijab) that covered her entire face except her eyes in the photograph used in her driver's license. Such a photo, needless to say, is completely useless for the purpose it is supposed to serve, namely the visual identification of the driver. Upon the request of the Florida Department of Motor Vehicles to provide a photo showing her entire face, she and her lawyers argued (as reported in the *New York Times* on June 27, 2002) that "her religious beliefs dictate that she not reveal her face to strangers or men outside her family" and the demand that she submit an unveiled photo "is subjective, unreasonable and violates her religious freedom as well as her right to privacy and due process." The demand that Muslim women be exempt from rules that apply to the rest of the population (such as being allowed not to have photos on their drivers' licenses and presumably in other documents that reveal their faces) illuminates the sharp conflict between politically correct multiculturalism and public safety and the routine, rational procedures of life in a modern, secular society. Presumably in an Islamic theocracy the problem would not arise since women are not allowed to drive.

Acceding to the request of this woman and her lawyers would be an unambiguous declaration of the supremacy of religious values over secular ones that would legitimate the special treatment of certain groups at the expense of public safety and equality before the law. Perhaps the time will come when some other religious believers will demand that women be altogether deprived of a driver's license, perceiving such privilege a violation of *their* religious beliefs. And of course many Islamic groups find other practices and liberties prevailing in modern secular societies offensive, distasteful, and irksome and would gladly take legal or other action to get rid of them.

The Florida case makes clear that multiculturalism carried to its logical, politically correct conclusion is incompatible with the existence of a modem secular society in which the laws apply equally to everybody regardless of their religious beliefs. By the same token the pretense that everybody who gets on a plane or hangs around a nuclear power plant has an equal likelihood of committing acts of terrorism is as absurd as to insist that no differences exist among human groups or that members of particular social, national, or ethnic groups have nothing in common. At the root of these beliefs we find the type of multiculturalism that harbors relentless hostility toward American society and Western values and extends sympathy to every group that questions or rejects these values.

Chapter Eleven

Tawana Brawley and the "Exotic Dancer" at Duke

The recent case of the lacrosse players at Duke University accused of raping a young black woman brings to mind the case of Tawana Brawley, the black teenager who in 1988 made similar charges against a group of white men in Wappinger Falls, New York.

In both cases, what turned out to be unfounded charges were widely given credit and generated immense publicity; celebrities and politicians rallied to the cause of the alleged victims, lengthy and costly legal investigations followed, and at last it emerged that the accusations were groundless. In both incidents, the charges were seized upon as self-evident, incontrovertible proof of the incorrigible and ineradicable racism that continues to permeate and infect every pore of American society.

On the Duke campus, the incident was seen, at least initially, as proof not only of the ingrained racism of American society but of other evils as well, such as sexism and "classism." Rallies, demonstrations, protest marches, and candlelight vigils were held and demands were made on the administration of the university to combat racism with greater determination. "On a single day in March 550 news outlets featured some version of the story."[1] The incident was said to be a "wake-up call against sexual assault," and "enraged students raised questions about their safety on campus."[2] Members of the faculty were in the forefront of those denouncing American society and its endemic racism. Eighty-eight members of the faculty "issued a statement in April saying 'thank you' to the protesters who had branded the players rapists."[3]

Protestations of the presumed innocence of the accused were often brushed aside; they were, after all, white, upper-middle-class males accused by a poor black female. The black female in question worked for an escort service and attended the lacrosse players' social gathering as an "exotic dancer." It is doubtful that similar attention would have been generated if the alleged rape victim had been white since being black and female has, for some time, been a quintessential defining attribute of authentic victimhood. The long and indisputable legacy of mistreatment and discrimination black people have suffered helps to explain the continued, ready acceptance of claims of victimization also enshrined in compensatory legislation, known as affirmative action. White guilt has been an understandable, but increasingly questionable, response to this historical record.

According to the president of Duke, "the lacrosse episode . . . put into high relief deep structures of inequality in our society—inequalities of wealth, privilege and opportunity . . . and the attitudes of superiority these inequalities breed." The vice provost said that "whatever we have been doing to address these problems [race, class, sex, and privilege] has been insufficient and needs to be redoubled and tripled." A law professor who was also the chair of the academic council asked, "Have we tolerated behavior that would cause people to believe that they can treat other people without respect?"[4] The *Raleigh News and Observer* concluded that the situation "has exposed serious issues of race, gender, and class division."[5]

An article in the *New Yorker* reported that

> much of the bitterest vitriol came from members of the Duke faculty who were willing to assume not only the players' guilt but the university's. At a session of the Academic Council Brodhead, [the president] was roundly assailed for not taking decisive action against the team and one professor . . . urged him to confess publicly that Duke was a racist and misogynist institution. Houston Baker, an English professor . . . asserted in a letter (he subsequently made public) to . . . the Provost, that at Duke, white male athletes were "veritably given license to rape, maraud, deploy hate speech" and excoriated the university for its complicity in the "sexual assault, verbal racial violence and drunken white male privilege loosed amongst us."[6]

Duke faculty were not unanimous in harboring such sentiments. There were some willing to remind the public of presumptions of innocence, and James Coleman, in particular, another law professor, was highly critical of the handling of the case by the district attorney who characterized the accused as "a bunch of hooligans."[7]

While the Duke case is not yet officially closed, the charges of rape have been dropped (but not those of sexual assault and kidnapping). The accuser has expressed a new uncertainty about the nature of the incident, and DNA tests have indicated that the lacrosse players had no sexual contact (that could be defined as rape) with the accuser but that she had such contact with others prior to the time of the alleged rape.[8]

Unlike in the Tawana Brawley case, in North Carolina the district attorney gave every indication of a politically motivated urge to indict the accused, and he pursued his case with an ethically dubious zeal (which included withholding information from the defense and using questionable methods for identifying the alleged wrongdoers). He was running in an election and appeared to seize the opportunity to display his antiracist credentials for the benefit of black and liberal voters. It worked, and he won reelection.

After several decades of compensatory legislation, widespread reverse discrimination (known as "affirmative action"), and numerous indicators suggesting that both official and unofficial racism have greatly diminished, demagogues like Al Sharpton continue to make lifelong careers out of mining white guilt, and this guilt shows little decline, as the Duke incident also suggests. Why should this be the case?

It is reasonable to suspect that when the dust settles and it becomes widely known and fully acknowledged that the accusations against the lacrosse players were questionable and probably altogether groundless, those who had been convinced of the truthfulness of the charges will fall back on the reasoning that was offered by professor Stanley Diamond in 1988 in the aftermath of the Tawana Brawley incident: "The case cannot be measured by legal canons, official justice or received morality. . . . The grand jury has responded to the technical questions of the case, weighing the evidence but necessarily blind to its deeper meanings. In cultural perspective, if not in fact, it doesn't matter whether the crime occurred or not. . . . What is most remarkable about this faked crime is that traditional victims have re-created themselves as victims in a dreadfully plausible situation."[9]

This point of view is likely to originate in deep reservoirs of sympathy and guilt for the past sufferings of the "traditional victims" that resist being drained by the evidence of substantial social and cultural change. This resistance may be linked to sentiments of enlightened moral superiority that manifest themselves in the eager and profuse admissions of guilt. To feel guilty for the sins of one's ancestors (or fellow citizens) and to dwell on this guilt in public is a lofty and attractive moral position not easily abandoned.

Many academic intellectuals' senses of identity rest on the role of the virtuous social critic, on "conspicuous compassion," and the associated readiness to renounce society for a variety of sins. But wallowing in guilt is not necessarily the best guide to action, or policy, or even to self-esteem. Overwhelming feelings of guilt led to the policies of reverse discrimination and new injustices in a variety of competitive situations when a middle- or upper-class black individual is given automatic preference over a similarly (or better) qualified poor or lower-class white one on account of the color of his skin and the sufferings of his ancestors.

White guilt is complemented and validated by the self-appointed spokesmen of the black population who thrive on and make abundant use of what Shelby Steele called "the victim-focused identity." The image of the innocent victim fortifies, morally and psychologically, the righteous critic of society broadcasting collective guilt—it provides a self-evident, unchallengeable moral high ground. At the same time, considerable material and social status benefits follow from the legally certified and institutionalized victim identity.

When white guilt converges with the attachment to the victim identity there is an enlarged, reflexive receptivity to the claims of the likes of Tawana Brawley and "the exotic dancer" at Duke University. It may be time for the emotionally satisfying white guilt to give way to more careful considerations of right and wrong that are not automatically determined by the skin color of either the wrongdoer or his victim.[10]

NOTES

1. *Duke Magazine*, May/June 2006.
2. *Duke Chronicle* online, March 29, 2006.
3. "At Law," *Wall Street Journal*, December 27, 2006.
4. *Duke Magazine*, May/June 2006.
5. Quoted in the *New Yorker*, September 4, 2006.
6. Peter S. Boyer, "Letter from Durham," *New Yorker*, September 4, 2006.
7. *Raleigh News Observer*, March 29, 2006.
8. *New York Times*, December 23 and 24, 2006.
9. Stanley Diamond, "Reversing Brawley," *The Nation*, October 31, 1988.
10. In the end the total groundlessness of the charges was fully and legally established and the prosecutor, Michael Nifong, became the subject of investigation for ethical misconduct. (See "Duke Prosecutor Throws out Case against Players," *New York Times*, April 12, 2007; see also "After Duke Prosecution Began to Collapse, Demonizing Continued," *New York Times*, April 15, 2007.)

Chapter Twelve

An Islamic Requirement on Campus

Requiring incoming freshmen at the University of North Carolina to read a partial and incomplete interpretation of the Koran has been a triumph of political correctness and the double standards often associated with it. One may ask, to begin with, if the goal is purely educational, as the university authorities claimed, why should such a requirement exclude other major world religions? Why not also require students to read something about Buddhism, Judaism, and the major varieties of Christianity of which they are also ignorant? Surely Catholics and Protestant know little of each others' beliefs and religious teachings and many misconceptions of Judaism still flourish waiting to be dispelled.

The educational authorities at Chapel Hill argue that there is at the present time a particularly pressing need for a better understanding of Islam and dispelling misconceptions about it. There would be little to object to if the program at North Carolina represented a serious attempt to understand Islam even to the exclusion of other religions. But the claim that this requirement was introduced merely to foster a better understanding of Islam and Islamic cultures is not credible. If that were the case, students would have been required to read not merely the early chapters of the Koran; they would also have been assigned various interpretations of Islam, including critical ones, and those that probe the affinities between the professed beliefs and behavior of Islamic terrorists and aspects of the Koran that apparently lend themselves to such uses.

Instead the university authorities intended to expose students to an uncritical, partial, and selective treatment of the Koran, one that bypasses the attempt to understand the connection between Islamic beliefs and the savagery and fanaticism of terrorists who insistently proclaim being motivated by such values and beliefs. There is every indication that the book the students were required to read avoids reference to the militant, intolerant, dogmatic, conflict-oriented, and self-righteous aspects of Islamic beliefs that have an affinity with the mindset, motivation, and behavior of Islamic terrorists.

If the academic authorities wished students "to understand a culture we don't know anything about"—as chancellor of North Carolina University Moeser said in an interview reported in the *New York Times* (August 20, 2002)—students should have been given the opportunity to learn something about the Sharia Laws too, which legitimate discrimination against women and the most brutal ways of punishing criminals such as stoning, flogging, amputation, and beheading for reasons American students would find barely comprehensible let alone justified.

Will the newly assigned volume and the teachers discussing it explain (in search of a better understanding of a different culture) why these exceptionally gruesome forms of punishments persist only in Islamic cultures and countries? Do such punishments represent a misinterpretation or misunderstanding of Islamic values, and if so why have they persisted for centuries? Evidently a discussion of these and other unsavory practices and attitudes are not part of the educational efforts the University of North Carolina—perhaps they are considered harmless items of "cultural diversity" students need not be familiar with, let alone be judgmental of.

Even if it were true (which it is not) that there is nothing in the Koran and Islamic religious teachings that could possibly justify, legitimate, motivate, or inspire the actions of terrorists, it would still have to be asked why, and on what grounds, do they claim the opposite? What makes it possible for the terrorists to find legitimation and encouragement in these allegedly misunderstood religious beliefs? Even if the Koran does not outright advocate the indiscriminate slaughter of civilian "infidels," how is it possible that the terrorists find in it legitimation for such actions? What aspect of these religious doctrines help terrorists to fantasize about Paradise awaiting them as a reward for killing the infidel?

These are exactly the kinds of questions that have been raised in connection with the relationship between Marxist theory and the practices of communist states and movements. People seeking to defend the purity and high moral tone of Marxism insisted that there was nothing in it to justify or legitimate the murderous, repressive policies of communist systems, that theory and practice were wholly unrelated. By contrast communist leaders constantly invoked Marxist theory and ideals to justify their actions and claimed to be deeply committed disciples of Marx and authoritative interpreters of his thought. Nor was it difficult to find affinities, if not explicit connections, between Marxist ideas and the policies of communist states. What precisely was the nature of the connections, of the affinity? Why did these ideas lend themselves to misapplication or distortion, if indeed that what the case?

These are precisely the questions that should be raised regarding Islam and the political violence many of its adherents practice with notable zest. But this is not part of the educational program at the campuses of the University of North Carolina; rather, it appears that an effort is underway to erase and divert attention from the possible connections between Islamic beliefs and Islamic political behavior, including terrorism.

Why this urgency to absolve Islam of any responsibility for what has been done in its name? Why expose students to a book that will leave them with an uncritical interpretation of Islam? Why the reluctance to embark on a serious educational effort that would help students grasp the essentials of this religion and culture and their impact on the political beliefs and behavior of those molded by them?

The answer lies in the attributes of the politically correct mindset and the adversary culture that continue to dominate our institutions of higher education. The educators in charge of this program in North Carolina would prefer their students to believe that the source of all current social, political, economic, or spiritual problems and conflicts is located in the United States or the Western world. Blaming Islam, or Islamic fanatics, for terrorism is inadmissible and politically incorrect because it lets the United States off the hook. If people in other countries hate the United States, there must be good reasons for it. We must look for "root causes"—which always end up being U.S. foreign policy and the nature of American society. We must always be self-critical, never critical of others—that is, those outside the United States or outside the Western world. We must not be judgmental of religious or other beliefs—unless they happen to be American or Western.

The University of North Carolina seeks to encourage a positive, or at least nonjudgmental, view of a religion that has numerous less than appealing features and of those who believe in it. Political correctness and "multiculturalism" (which as a rule entails a reflexive aversion to all things Western) hold the key to the determination at the University of North Carolina to impose a selective and flawed understanding of Islam on its freshmen.

Chapter Thirteen

Rehabilitating the Great Books: Literature and Life

It is hardly a secret that what used to be considered the great works of Western literature no longer inspire the kind of respect and admiration they once did. We live at a time when artistic and literary merit has become relativized in much of academic thinking and teaching—a relativization compatible with the admiration of and demand for books endowed with certain putative political-ideological virtues. Departments of English have increasingly been shifting from teaching to advocacy and to courses more sociological than literary. Many teachers in these departments apparently have lost interest in literature and found other topics and source materials more congenial and useful to support their worldview and educational objectives. As Harold Bloom observed, "students of literature have become amateur political scientists, uninformed sociologists, incompetent anthropologists, mediocre philosophers and over-determined cultural historians."[1]

Many among those who are supposed to interpret and elucidate the meaning of great literary works are at great pains to demonstrate that there is little if any qualitative difference between them and the products of popular culture. Terry Eagelton, a prominent representative of such beliefs, suggested that the teaching of literature be abandoned in favor of what he called "discourse studies" allowing instructors "to teach Shakespeare, television scripts, government memoranda, comic books, and advertising copy in a single program. . . ."[2] Such sentiments prompted Alvin Kernan to observe that

> few things are stranger than the violence and hatred with which the old literature was deconstructed by those who earn their living teaching and writing about it. . . . The most popular subjects of criticism and undergraduate and graduate courses are . . . those that demonstrate how meaningless, or . . . how wicked and

anti-progressive, the old literature has been . . . how badly it has treated those who are not white, how regularly it has voiced an aristocratic jackbooted ethos or propagandized for a brutally materialistic capitalism.³

Another critic of these trends, John Ellis, wrote, "professors of literature now argue against the Western tradition in thought and literature. They argue . . . that such study can be positively harmful. High culture is full of pernicious ideas and influences—even Shakespeare's plays reflect reactionary attitudes: jingoistic imperialism, racism, sexism, homophobia. . . . High culture is part of the ruling elite's apparatus for social control."⁴

The demotion of classics also came to be justified by the dubious argument that the important thing in higher education is not the teaching of any "great" books but the teaching of critical thinking: "The truth is that a fluency with the Great Books is no longer a prerequisite for professional or social success. Critical thinking skills arguably are."⁵ Regrettably, the educational philosophy that led to the antagonism toward the "great books" is not exactly the hotbed of critical thinking, inspired as it has been by the new orthodoxies subsumed under the concept of political correctness.

The late twentieth century was a period when new theories of literature associated with "deconstructionism" and postmodernity proclaimed that literary works have no inherent meaning or message but are subject to the diverse, changing, and arbitrary interpretations of the readers, their meaning determined by their sense of identity and group or individual interests—racial, ethnic, gender, or class.

In the same period, reading habits changed for the worse and students' attention spans shrank (probably because of habitual television watching from an early age) to a degree that makes it difficult for them to read longer and more demanding works. Academic interest in the humanities has generally declined as reflected in enrollments, majors chosen, and course offerings. These developments coincided with the removal of many classics from courses of literature and their replacement by works written by contemporary authors whose reputation was often decisively bolstered by being female or belonging to a designated "minority." The idea of "minority" itself has become narrow and arbitrary, based largely on skin color. For political and ideological reasons blacks, Hispanics (but not Cuban Americans), American Indians (or Native Americans), and women have become the officially designated minorities in the United States during the last four decades of the past century. Women, of course, are not a minority at all since they form over half of the population; Asian Americans are usually excluded since their inclusion undermines the conventional wisdom of equating minority status with underachievement and low social status. Jews have never been included, presumably for the same reason.

The recollections of a recent "literature major" illustrate current trends in the teaching of literature. She was a beneficiary of "a rarified diet of semiotics and deconstruction . . . [and met her] degree requirements by taking 'Feminist Literary Criticism' and 'Women and the Avant-Garde' as well as two courses devoted principally to film. . . ." She graduated "without having read for credit 'The Odyssey,' 'Paradise Lost,' and a single play by Shakespeare or a single novel by Jane Austen, George Eliot or Henry James."[6] She was, moreover, serenely convinced—as were other supposed authorities on the teaching of English quoted in the same article—that this state of affairs did no harm to her education,

The policies leading to such changes in the curriculum were also described as a form of a "cultural populism" representing "attempts of women, ethnic and racial minorities to achieve cultural enfranchisement. . . ."[7] Such "representativeness" often came to outweigh aesthetic or intellectual criteria. Harold Bloom wrote, "if you believe that all value ascribed to poems or plays or novels and stories is only a mystification in the service of the ruling class, then why should you read at all . . . ? The idea that you benefit the insulted and injured by reading someone of their own origins rather than reading Shakespeare is one of the oddest illusions ever promoted by or in our schools."[8]

All in all, the closing decades of the past century were not auspicious for the teaching and appreciation of the more demanding works of fiction often written by those labeled as "dead white males." On the other hand, the new policies and trends did go a long way to satisfy the prevailing notions of social justice and group representation.

This essay registers strong disagreement with the trends outlined above. It should not be necessary to remind readers that many works of fiction, classics and others, provide intellectual and emotional nourishment greatly superior to the offerings of mass culture or to much of the currently embraced politically correct readings. Good fiction (the "great books") is a source of guidance for confronting the profound and timeless problems of life that are not dependent on particular social settings or historical conditions. Great writers are unusually gifted human beings who, for reasons far from clear, possess powers of insight, understanding, and expressive talent that distinguish them from most of their readers and critics. Mario Vargas Llosa believes that writers "plunge into the innermost universe of memory, nostalgia, secret desires, intuition and instinct . . . that nourish the creative imagination," that they incorporate into their writing "the element that rushes out spontaneously from the most secret corner of one's personality" and they dwell "on the vertiginous complexity of human nature." Poetic and somewhat vague as these notions may be, they do suggest a special, indefinable talent that, for instance, enabled Shakespeare to "sketch . . . certain images in which men of every era discover their own faces."[9]

Audrey Borenstein designated the distinctive contribution of literature as its capacity to help us to grasp how others experience life; paraphrasing Carlos Fuentes, she suggests that "we are in need of many experiences and this is what literature offers us."[10] Novels provide examples of how individuals solve (or fail to solve) problems the readers also confront, or some more exotic ones they do not, but wonder about them from a distance, as it were. Literary characters (like readers) grapple with matters such as love, death, success and failure, control over one's life, and personal aspirations and expectations and their problematic fulfillment.

Harold Bloom advocates reading "not only because we cannot know enough people but because friendship is so vulnerable, so likely to diminish, to disappear . . . [because] we cannot know enough people, profoundly enough . . . [because] we need to know ourselves better" as well as for what he calls a "secular transcendence" he likens to "falling in love."[11] A Hungarian writer recalled the views of an unusually articulate Soviet soldier upon learning that he was a writer: "He thought for a moment and then said: 'That's good [being a writer] because if you are one you can tell us what we really are thinking.' . . . The Russian soldier regarded 'the literary trade' tantamount to having access to some general truths. . . . The writer [was seen] as a magician, whose powers originated in some distant realm. . . . The soldier expected truth to be articulated by writers, above all."[12] Like the views of Vargas Llosa quoted earlier this too had a mythical, mysterious element to it, crediting the writer with great, unfathomable powers.

It is not easy to propose precise criteria as to what qualities must be present in order to assign greatness to a work of literature. Even educated tastes vary and cultural elites can be divided in their judgment as to what constitutes a great work of art, literary and other. Sometimes the greatness of a work of art is recognized at the time of its creation, sometimes well after the passing of its creator. At the present time museums are increasingly filled with objects artists and their patrons of earlier times would have contemplated with bewilderment and revulsion. The Guggenheim Museum in New York in recent years featured an exhibit of motor bicycles and garments by the fashion designer Versace. The new Tate Gallery in London in 2002 displayed "cans of excrement" produced by Piero Manzoni who said that "he produced these artifacts with the express purpose of showing the gullibility of art buyers. But the Tate defended its purchase . . . on the grounds that he was an 'incredibly important international artist' and his cans were 'a seminal work.'" The recent Holocaust exhibition at the Jewish Museum in New York featured "a trick photograph of a well-fed young man holding a Diet

Coke, surrounded by the emaciated Jews of Buchenwald . . . [as well as] a work . . . portraying cans of Zyklon B gas stamped with Chanel and Hermes labels." One of the contributing "artists" said, "I am using the iconography of the Holocaust to bring attention to fashion. . . . Fashion like fascism is about a loss of identity."[13]

According to one opinion, "A great writer is like a great scientist: through his work something vital becomes known which wasn't known before." For example, "it was Dostoevsky's discovery . . . that the most destructive and dangerous of all religions was the new-found faith in the power of reason, science, industry, revolution and the perfectibility of man."[14] Harold Bloom singles out "strangeness, a mode of originality" as the major criterion of greatness and, more elusively, the writer's capacity "to augment one's growing inner self," or "to enlarge a solitary existence."[15] John Aldridge suggests that "the novel will be most influential at those moments when it is able to explore areas of experience that are not yet completely familiar to the reading public, thus functioning in its classic role as literally a bringer of the news, a discoverer of what is indeed novel." Novelists make a lasting impact when they "express for the first time hitherto unknown or unexplored modes of feeling."[16] John Updike observed that "fiction seeks to concoct imaginary lives more clearly significant than our own. . . ."[17]

At a time when cultural relativism combines with political correctness, it is especially difficult to reach agreement as to what constitutes great literature. Much of what used to be regarded as such is often dismissed as irrelevant, obsolete, and hopelessly "Eurocentric," that is, influenced by allegedly dated European traditions and standards. The rise of the demand for "role models" in fiction (as in popular culture) adds a new dimension to these difficulties. When a novel is praised for providing role models (or dismissed for not providing them), we are certainly in the presence of sociological or political criteria rather than aesthetic or intellectual. It is an approach reminiscent of the socialist realist literature of the former Soviet Union and other communist systems that too was supposed to provide politically appropriate role models and for which doing so was the major criterion of literary merit.

There used to be a far greater consensus, at any rate, among academic specialists and the educated public as to what constitutes good literature or what works may be considered classics. Certainly sheer survival and a truly multicultural appeal are useful criteria. A work of fiction that is read and enjoyed around the world, over long periods of time, even in countries and cultures other than those of its origin, speaks to human needs and concerns that transcend particular historical settings and periods. Once more Harold Bloom observed "Shakespeare for hundreds of millions who are not white Europeans is a signifier for their own pathos, their own sense of identity. . . . For them his universality is not historical but fundamental; he puts their lives upon his stage. In his characters they behold and confront their own anguish and their own fantasies. . . ."[18] Italo Calvino defines the classic as "a book which with each reading offers as much of a sense of discovery as the first reading . . . which even when we read it first time gives the sense of rereading something we have read before."[19] One may add, obvious as it may seem, that the classics are a bridge to the past. Of course, this assumes that knowing about the past is important, an assumption not self-evident to present-day readers and especially the younger generations. Recognizing the influence and significance of the past is especially challenging for Americans inclined to believe that everything can be changed, fixed, or reinvented, including their innermost selves.

Besides addressing the timeless concerns and dilemmas of human existence, novels are also enlightening (without in the least distracting from their literary-artistic merit) about social arrangements and institutions and the problematic relationship between personal autonomy and social pressures, or individual and society. They show how the social realm influences, if not determines, the personal one, how social or cultural norms regulate, or fail to regulate, individual behavior and how our behavior and freedom of choice is impinged upon and curtailed by social forces and institutions; they also show the degree to which we are "products" of our class, society, and culture, and the extent to which our behavior and social position can or cannot be explained satisfactorily by relying exclusively upon conscious motives and goals pursued by the individual.

In turn the literature of a period and a society, its major topics, schools, and styles, is influenced by the broader social setting. An all too obvious example of the social-political determination of literary topics and styles can be found in the era of socialist-realism in the former Soviet Union. Soviet writers were explicitly instructed by the cultural-ideological authorities as to the topics to address, the spirit in which to approach them, and the types of characters they had to create. These writers steered clear of matters sexual for reasons that were to be found outside the literary realm, in the neo-Victorian official morality and its institutional imposition by censorship and self-censorship, the rewards and punishments meted out, and by the very doctrine of socialist realism. By the same token the singular preoccupation of large numbers of American writers in the second half of the twentieth century with matters sexual cannot be explained purely as a matter of personal taste (or lack of it) but it points to broader social-cultural influences and preoccupations also attested to by the mass media, sex manuals, fashions, and other nonliterary phenomena.

Even when writers seek to remove their topic from the familiar reaches of their society by fleeing into the past or future, or to settings unknown to their readers, when they cater to the escapist impulse rather than to the disposition to identify with the familiar—even under these circumstances they tend to anchor their work in some experience familiar to them and their readers, or they project into the future or past such experiences in a modified form. In Chateaubriand's *Atala and Renee*, the unfamiliar, exotic setting of late-eighteenth-century North American wilderness (which the author visited in 1791) is populated by characters who resemble more closely idle French aristocrats tormented by "weltschmerz" (a malaise combining alienation, identity problems, and lack of purpose) than its actual inhabitants preoccupied with survival in a harsh physical environment and the necessities of life obtained by physical exertion. Chateaubriand knew little about the character and way of life of American Indians but knew a lot about members of the French aristocracy (to which he belonged), and he projected aspects of their character upon the Indians in conformity with the requirements of romantic storytelling and character portrayal.

Such escapist literature appeals to readers because it does not reflect realities and settings familiar to them but transports them into realms they can only fantasize about and thereby offers vicarious gratifications. This applies most obviously at the present time to best-selling novels including those redolent with sex and violence, books which have in common a "primitivist revolt against social controls, especially those on sexual and aggressive impulses. . . . The success of this kind of fiction depends precisely on its not being a reflection of contemporary reality. . . . Such works must . . . be regarded as the particular modern embodiments of the age-old and almost universal tendency to enjoy imaginative gratifications of impulses which are largely denied in social life."[20]

Whatever the needs they meet, wittingly or unwittingly, novels provide information about matters social or social historical in ways not available to the social sciences. They may be the only source of information about the past, incomplete and subjective as they might be. Thomas Mann's *Magic Mountain* offered "a loving vision of a reality now vanished, of a European high culture now forever gone, the culture of Goethe and Freud."[21] Similar examples of "realities now vanished" captured in novels can be readily multiplied.

Fiction offers a partially reliable mirror of matters social through the self-conscious effort of writers who wish to describe and record particular societies, social settings, or institutions—self-appointed social historians of a period. Several well-known nineteenth-century authors such as Balzac, Dickens, Flaubert, Stendhal, Thackeray, and Tolstoy exemplify this approach—not that their work reduces to the social-historical description. Balzac, in the spirit of a zoologist, "wanted to analyze the social species of which French society consisted and to write a true history of morals which the historians ... usually forgot to write."[22] More broadly speaking, "realists and naturalists, such as Flaubert, Zola, Frank Norris and Theodore Dreiser saw their fiction as objective reports on human behavior."[23] More recently Tom Wolfe insisted that writers go "beyond the confines of their own personal experience to get novelistic material"—by which he meant that they should observe and describe the details of social and material existence including what and how people consume, down to brand names of clothing and footwear—an approach in which he himself excelled.[24] Elsewhere he wrote, "the realistic novel—[is] a form that wallows enthusiastically in the dirt of everyday life and the dirty secrets of class envy. . . . A highly detailed realism [is] based on reporting . . . that would portray the individual in intimate and inextricable relation to the society around him . . . [including] . . . the demonstration of the influence of society on even the most personal aspects of the life of the individual. . . ."[25]

Unfortunately, as one of his critics pointed out, this is an approach that can lead to "a portrayal of human beings entirely subsumed under their external aspects, such as their favorite objects, clothing, physical appearance—beyond that there is—nothing."[26]

There is more profound and authentic sociological information to be found in the unintended revelations of writers, in their reference to matters they take for granted rather than self-consciously and purposefully address and elaborate. As Ian Watt wrote, even "literature which makes no pretense whatever at reflecting social reality always does so in some form. . . . Literature reflects society, but it usually does so with various degrees of indirectness and selectivity."[27] Novels are full of such unintended revelations about particular societies and the prevailing cultural assumptions in the settings the writer dealt with. For instance, in most nineteenth-century novels servants and the subservience of servants are taken for granted (as for instance in those of Edith Wharton) while their feelings or personalities are infrequently, if ever, probed. By contrast, in a late-twentieth-century novel such as Ishiguro's *The Remains of the Day*, it is the social role and function of the main character and narrator, a head butler, that is a key ingredient of the narrative and of the character of the protagonist. Being a faithful, unreflecting servant is far from taken for granted here; it is the role and mindset of the servant that is at the center of the narrative and its unresolved conflict. Taking servants for granted is, of course, part of taking for granted spectacular social inequalities, as was the case in nineteenth-century novels and life. In *Robinson Crusoe*, slave trading is a commonplace commercial activity that does not inspire moral indignation or reflection. In contemporary American fiction, it is geographic and social mobility that is taken for granted as people move around matter-of-factly and effortlessly for a wide range of motives.

Another equally obvious example of unintended literary reflections or revelations of social realities is social role differentiation based on sex, more specifically the social-occupational status of women in novels throughout much of the entire existence of the genre (until the twentieth century). Few of these writers wasted words, questions, or moral reflections on the condition of women or commented on the fact that their vast majority had little formal education and no work or power outside the home. On the other hand, and somewhat startling for the present-day reader, eighteenth- and nineteenth-century writers often portrayed men shedding copious tears (as for example in *Robinson Crusoe*, *Atala and Renee*, and *Werther*), as if such behavior were as natural and usual for men as for women. That this, too, was taken for granted is all the more remarkable since in most other respects men and women were portrayed as if they had fundamentally different natures (including expressive behavior) and hence different social roles and places in the division of labor. The profusion of tears in the eyes of both sexes may be explained by the romantic sensibility embraced by Chateaubriand and Goethe, though not by Defoe.

Social-historical information can also be gleaned from the reception accorded to books and the treatment of their authors. When a writer is taken to court because his novel is alleged to harm the prevailing conceptions of morality (as happened to Flaubert because of *Madame Bovary*), we learn a great deal about cultural, moral, and political conditions in a given society. When the ruler of a country reads the manuscripts of major novelists before they can be published—as Stalin often did—much is revealed about the relationship between literature and society, or rather writers and rulers.

Censorship is, needless to say, the most telling indicator of the relationship between the power-holders and writers (or artists) and the reigning conceptions of the relationship between literature and social behavior, between ideas and reality—the most obvious reflection of the belief that ideas matter and may strongly influence, and even corrupt, behavior. Conversely, social honors bestowed on writers—awards, prizes, official appointments—also tell us about prevailing social values, tastes, and political-cultural currents.

Further light is shed on the relationship between fiction and reality when people model their lives on fictional characters, when "they have made love, committed crimes and suicide according to the book."[28] The minor epidemic of suicide sparked by *The Sorrows of Young Werther* (who commits suicide at the end of the story) is one such example. In more recent times it has been the mass media, and television in particular, rather than books, that provides such models and motivates some to imitate forms of behavior portrayed.

In seeking parallels between social existence and its literary reflections, it is especially informative to observe how much personal autonomy literary characters possess, to what degree their personal decisions and wishes shape their lives, or, to the contrary, what part is played by identifiable social-historical forces, including the social norms and expectations prevailing in their times. How important in the literary presentation of individual choice are class, age, sex, race, ethnicity, or even physical attributes and appearance (the latter rarely a matter of interest to sociologists)? The sociological approach here outlined must be distinguished from a Marxist analysis that attributes everything to class and class interest (or social position defined by class and material interest). The novel, contrary to the belief of Marxist critics, does not reduce to "an epic of bourgeois life." If the principal bourgeois values are "acquisitiveness, belief in material progress, disciplined social behavior, sobriety, dedication to family, patriotism and boosterism, one must conclude that major figures in the canon of the 19th century novel—Stendhal, Flaubert, Dostoyevsky, Melville, even Balzac—radically subvert these values or vehemently spurn them in their fiction."[29] Marx's belief (expressed most succinctly in *The German Ideology*) that the "ruling ideas" of a period (those of its ruling class) dominate all cultural, intellectual, or artistic endeavors is empirically incorrect, or at least vastly oversimplified, certainly as regards complex, pluralistic, and modern societies. As Levin Schucking pointed out, "there is no such thing as a spirit of the age; there are only . . . a series of Spirits of the Age." He also noted that "in earlier times the sociological soil is most plainly to see, the influence of people of social eminence is manifest, and there are only a few obvious centers from which the sustenance of the arts proceeds."[30] However in modern, pluralistic societies it has become increasingly difficult to specify which "class" rules, and which ideas "dominate" and whom they dominate. Even if the identity of such a ruling class can be specified, it is far from clear what its ideas are and impossible to prove that they dominate society and culture. Works of literature, especially the great ones, rarely express class or group "interest," although they may reflect the influence of the social background and various affiliations of the author.

Although fiction enshrines the subjective and the unique, dealing as it does with particular individuals, not with classes or categories of people, at its best literature combines the uniquely personal with the universally human. It does so by addressing all the key human concerns and preoccupations: conceptions of good and evil, death and violence, love and hate, the great variety of human relationships, the cultural and individual definitions of and responses to both success and failure, the varieties of social and personal conflict, the entire range of human desires and aspirations, both attainable and unattainable. Novels also address the major preoccupations of sociologists and other social scientists: questions of social order and change, the relationship between individual and society, the impact of particular social institutions on personal behavior, the many forms of inequality, the striving for status and power, social mobility, family life, the attributes of various social groups, and the norms and values that govern most behavior, among others.

Literature is particularly informative in grasping and revealing details of social existence that elude social scientific inquiry that is not equipped to penetrate the sphere of private (but socially relevant) feelings, motives, and values. Novels are capable of depicting the quality of human interactions and relationships and expectations governed by unwritten, informal norms, conventions, or customs. Literary portrayals also help to unearth the social determinants of personal problems and predicaments, the ways in which the social impinges on the personal as well as the extent to which the patterns and demands of social existence clash with the personal, the unique, the accidental, or idiosyncratic—a clash that makes the prediction of both individual and group behavior such a difficult enterprise for social scientists.

There are some parallels between the literary and sociological endeavors. Audrey Borenstein's summation is that "social scientists and writers alike are . . . engaged in an unending search for the reasons why people act and think and feel as they do."[31] Morroe Berger observed that "the novel and social science are two ways of commenting on human behavior and social institutions. . . . Both sought to explain life on the basis of institutions created by men and women rather than by appealing to immutable absolutes and divine powers."[32] Sociology itself "has oscillated between a scientific orientation which has led it to ape the natural sciences and a hermeneutic attitude which has shifted the discipline toward the realm of literature." The same author also described sociology "as a kind of third culture between the natural sciences on the one hand and literature and the humanities on the other."[33] He further argues that "from the moment of its inception sociology became both a competitor and a counterpart of literature"[34]—a somewhat questionable proposition in light of the actual practices of most sociologists. The latter, and especially those of a scientific bent, unlike writers of fiction, have little interest in the less predictable and more idiosyncratic aspects of human motivation and behavior. Instead they strive to capture and systematize (and quantify) broad and observable patterns and regularities of human behavior and interaction and their enduring, institutional results. This is not to deny that there are some similarities between the realistic-literary impulse to gather descriptive information about social settings and circumstances and the sociological data-gathering impulse.

Many sociologists and writers also share a desire "to see through" social arrangements, institutions, and practices, to demystify, unmask, unravel, or expose. These writers and sociologists are animated by a keen, stimulating awareness of the numerous recurring differences between appearance and reality. Hypocrisy, deception, and self-deception have been a favorite target of writers—unintended consequences or latent functions of sociologists. The impulse to probe beneath the surface often merges into full-blown social criticism, on the part of both writers and sociologists. For example, "the more one studies Flaubert, the clearer it becomes how much insight into the problematic nature and the hollowness of 19th century bourgeois culture is contained in his realistic works. . . ."[35]

One may also entertain some reservations about the apparently taken-for-granted benefits of "unmasking" or "demystifying"—literary or social scientific. The mistrust, cynicism, or skepticism that underlies these frames of mind can be carried too far, it can become all too standardized, stale, and reflexive. There is a danger that an overpowering awareness of the discrepancies between ideal and actual, theory and practice, appearance and reality might lead to a malignant obsession with concealment that cannot allow for any degree of idealism or truth seeking. Eugene Goodheart asked, "Why as a matter of principle, should we trust the hidden rather than the evident sense of an intellectual or cultural product? Why couldn't we apply the demystifying procedure to the reductionist method and . . . expose the will to discover the hidden truth as a mask for the will to power. The habit of ideological suspicion *when it become systematic and totalizing* tends to produce an insensitivity to 'higher' values, an inclination to associate truth with a cynical view of motive."[36]

Dwelling on the similarities between literature and sociology should not be overdone. Sociologists are not interested in what is unique but rather in what certain groups of people have in common: the married or unmarried, educated or uneducated, criminal or law-abiding, the rich, the poor, members of different religions denominations, ethnic groups, generations. Even more important, most sociologists professionally disbelieve in the ineffable uniqueness of human beings; instead they see them as products of social circumstance, displaying highly patterned behavior.

There are also profound methodological differences between literature and sociology; writers rely on observation and intuition, sociologists (while not rejecting them completely) prefer explicit hypotheses, rational measurement, quantification, elaborate data-gathering techniques. In the nineteenth century when the prestige and impact of the natural sciences were rapidly rising, it was tempting for sociologists, and to a lesser degree for writers, to believe that they too could attain a measure of scientific certainty in their respective endeavors.

Even more important is the fact that writers rely on and prize imagination, unlike sociologists except perhaps in their research design or development of hypotheses. The latter seek to describe and understand a reality that is external to them, for the most part, whereas writers wish to create a reality of their own that blends in some fashion with objective, external reality. Writers also wish to entertain, whereas few reputable sociologists or other social scientists have such aspirations.

Novels—regardless of their reliability as witnesses to the facts of social life and human behavior—appeal to our interests for a variety of reasons, not all of them compatible. On the one hand readers rely on them in order "to be different, [and] to be elsewhere...."[37] On the other, they also wish to make contact with what is reassuringly familiar and confirms their experience. We also look for simple diversion, for entertainment, including the childlike pleasure of following a story and finding out what happens to its characters. And if all this can be combined with some moral insight or instruction, that too will be acceptable, or welcome, as the case may be.

NOTES

1. Harold Bloom, *The Western Canon* (New York: Harcourt, Brace 1994), 521.
2. Quoted in Robert Alter, *The Pleasures of Reading in an Ideological Age* (New York: Simon & Schuster, 1989), 13.
3. Alvin Kernan, *The Death of Literature* (New Haven, Conn.: Yale University Press, 1990), 70.
4. John M. Ellis, *Literature Lost: Social Agendas and the Corruption of the Humanities* (New Haven, Conn.: Yale University Press, 1977), 5.
5. Emily Eakin, "More Ado (Yawn) about Great Books," *New York Times, Education Life*, April 8, 2001, 41.
6. Eakin, "More Ado," 24.
7. Eugene Goodheart, *The Reign of Ideology* (New York: Columbia University Press, 1997), 91.
8. Bloom, *The Western Canon*, 522.
9. Mario Vargas Llosa, "Literature and Freedom," *Chronicles*, April 1992, 15, 16.
10. Audrey Borenstein, *Redeeming Sin: Social Science and Literature* (New York: Columbia University Press, 1978), 68, 214, 179.
11. Harold Bloom, *How to Read and Why* (New York: Scribner, 2000), 29.
12 DraganVelkic, "A Lehetetlen Valosaga" [The reality of the impossible], *Elet es Irodalom*, [Budapest], August 13, 1999.
13. Robert Conquest, *The Dragons of Expectation* (New York: Norton, 2005), 195; Stefan Kanfer, "How to Trivialize the Holocaust," *City Journal*, Spring 2002, 10.
14. Stephen Vizinczey, *Truth and Lies in Literature* (London: Hamish Hamilton, 1986), 227, 232.
15. Bloom, *The Western Canon*, 3, 30, 518.
16. John W. Alridge, *The American Novel and the Way We Live Now* (New York: Oxford University Press, 1983), 3, 4.

17. John Updike, "Medieval Superheroes," *New York Times Book Review*, January 28, 2001, 27.

18. Bloom, *The Western Canon*, 38–39.

19. Italo Calvino, *Why Read the Classics?* (New York: Pantheon, 1999), 5.

20. Ian Watt, "Literature and Society," in *The Arts in Society*, ed. Robert N. Wilson (Englewood Cliffs, N.J.: Prentice Hall, 1964), 310.

21. Bloom, *How to Read and Why*, 189.

22. Wolf Lepenies, *Between Literature and Science: The Rise of Sociology* (New York: Cambridge University Press, 1988), 4.

23. Morroe Berger, *Real and Imagined Worlds: The Novel and Social Science* (Cambridge, Mass.: Harvard University Press, 1977), 5–6.

24. Tom Wolfe, *Hooking Up* (New York: Farrar, Straus, Giroux, 2000), 159, 161.

25. Tom Wolfe, "Stalking the Billion-Footed Beast: A Literary Manifesto for the New Social Novel," *Harpers*, November 1989, 47, 50, 51.

26. Jonathan Raban, *For Love and Money* (New York: Harper & Row, 1989), 150.

27. Watt, "Literature and Society," 308.

28. Rene Wellek and Austin Warren, *Theory of Literature* (New York: Harcourt, Brace & World, 1956), 102.

29. Alter, *The Pleasures of Reading*, 31.

30. Levin L. Schucking, *The Sociology of Literary Taste* (Chicago: University of Chicago Press, 1961), 8, 19.

31. Borenstein, *Redeeming Sin*, 148.

32. Berger, *Real and Imagined Worlds*, 215, 126.

33. Lepenies, *Between Literature and Science*, 1, 7.

34. Lepenies, *Between Literature and Science*, 12.

35. Erich Auerbach, *Mimesis: The Representation of Reality in Western Literature* (New York: Doubleday, 1957), 433.

36. Goodheart, *The Reign of Ideology*, 18.

37. Bloom, *The Western Canon*, 523.

Chapter Fourteen

The Counterculture of the Heart

According to a *New York Times* report (Style Section, November 24, 2002) "16.6 million people visited matchmaking Web sites in September alone—a figure [that] has made Internet dating seem almost stigma free. . . ." Internet dating is not the only unconventional approach to matchmaking: there are also computer dating services and "personals" in printed publications offering new ways to initiate romantic and other relationships. It all adds up to a massive social phenomenon, yet its meaning and ramifications remain largely unexplored.

"Personals" (online or printed) are a new departure in the pursuit of serious and important relationships; their rise reflects doubt over the efficacy of the conventional methods or inability to make use of them. The communication of intimate personal needs via terse advertisements may promise to be a more rational and effective approach to mate-selection than those that used to prevail in modern Western societies. The innovative "rationality" of the personals lies in the notion that the specification of attributes and interests possessed and looked for can be a shortcut to finding a compatible person. It would make it possible to bypass the haphazard and often frustrating contacts based on introductions or the advice of others or initiated on the basis of superficial personal impressions, appearances, and chance. If you specify what kind of a person you are and what kind of a person you are looking for, make clear, for instance, that the centerpiece of your recreational interests are Bach cantatas and vacations in Mediterranean fishing villages rather than country music and bowling, there may be a better chance of meeting kindred spirits.

As will be shown below, the content of these messages conflicts with the presumed rationality of the method—the attempt to gratify intimate emotional needs on the basis of written specifications subverts the romantic impulse and its veneration of unpredictability and spontaneity while the attempted rational specification of personal needs is permeated by nonrational, romantic notions.

The phenomenon being discussed suggests that in the second half of the twentieth century conventional ways of meeting people for romantic purposes, or other serious relationships, has been abandoned in the United States by large numbers of people including many apparently successful, attractive, and well-educated ones—if their self-assessments are to be believed. It is a development that sheds further light on the characteristics and problems of modernity, including the decline of community, the growth of social isolation (especially in major urban settings), and the tension between the demands of professional work and those of emotionally gratifying intimate personal relationships.

The conventional methods of matchmaking being abandoned include introductions by friends or relatives (arranged marriages at this point in time need not be included, although they may persist in some ethnic enclaves) and meetings in school or college, at places of work, or in recreational or special interest organizations. Less orthodox methods of our times are the "pickups" of strangers in public places of entertainment (bars, nightclubs, etc.), museums, parks, and even the streets. In some subcultures, professional matchmakers may still be at work competing with dating services.

Dating services have in common with the printed personals that they too rely on explicit specifications of what is being offered and what is sought after. But they also involve an impartial intermediary who makes some judgments about the presumed compatibility of the interested parties based on the information presented. In theory such services could be quite successful if they could benefit from the insights psychological theories offer about the sources of human compatibility (if such insights or theories were available).

THE EMOTIONAL ASPIRATIONS OF AN ELITE GROUP

To better understand the new phenomenon of organized matchmaking, I took a closer look at one particular manifestation of it that has been in existence for over three decades—the "personals" in the *New York Review of Books* (the *Review* below). In these advertisements, anonymous individuals specify both their own attractions and the attributes they look for in others. The relationships sought range from marriage, unmarried long-term relationships, affairs, and dating, to friendship and afternoon trysts.

To the best of my knowledge, except for the *London Review*, no other comparable highbrow publication (for example, the *Atlantic, Commentary, Harpers,*

Nation, *National Review*, *New Republic*, *New York Times Book Review*, *Weekly Standard*, and so on) publishes such personals. Why and how these personals became a regular feature of the *Review* I was unable to determine.

The *Review* has been a leading intellectual biweekly journal publishing mostly long book reviews or review essays, political opinion pieces, and occasional movie reviews. Contributors tend to be prominent academics, well-known writers, and journalists, mostly American with a steady British contingent. In its earlier incarnation the *Review* closely reflected the radical trends and sentiments of the 1960s; over time this orientation has moderated. The *Review* remains liberal or left-of-center but no longer shrill, and occasionally it publishes articles critical of political correctness and radical left-wing views, movements, or political systems.

The total circulation of the *Review* is close to 140,000; the average age of its readers is 56; 73 percent are males and 27 percent are females. Ninety-seven percent of *Review* readers are college graduates; 70 percent have graduate degrees or have attended professional schools. Sixty-eight percent are classified as professionals or are in managerial occupations. The median income of readers is $71,000, the average is $123,000. (The preceding data and others to follow were kindly provided by Raymond Shapiro, business manager of the *Review* for several decades.) Clearly, this is a highly educated and affluent group of Americans.

The personals published in the *Review* provide an abundance of information for the sociologist or social historian interested in cultural values, sexual morality, tastes, ego-ideals, aspirations, and widely shared perceptions of desirable human qualities. These messages also illuminate the contemporary difficulties in "mate selection": resorting to such advertisements is an implicit admission of the narrowness, or unsatisfactory character, of the social circles one moves in; it may also be an indication of a busy professional life that permits little socializing.

I chose the *Review* for several reasons. In the first place, it is an unusually rich source, having published regularly the personals (tens of thousands) since 1970. Second, these ads are highly specific and detailed as to the types of individuals sought and in regard to the characteristics revealed of those engaged in the search. Third, focusing on one publication reduces to manageable proportions the amount of data to be examined. Moreover readers of a particular publication are already preselected to some degree; by virtue of being readers of the same publication they have in common tastes, interests, outlook, and political preferences. Fourth, it is of further interest that the *Review is* a highbrow publication, an elite journal read by well-educated people, many of whom may be considered intellectuals, aspiring intellectuals, and trendsetters; most of them are professionals of some kind and a large proportion are academics. An important question however remains unresolved: we do not know what portion of the authors of the personals actually read the *Review*, or how much of it. But even if they do not read it, they have an idea of what kind of a publication it is and what type of reader it attracts.

Representativeness is not one of the reasons for choosing the *Review*. Its readers' tastes, cultural values, aspirations, ego ideals are likely to be different from the great majority of Americans who do not read it. Readers of the *Review* are also unrepresentative politically; most Americans, unlike readers of the *Review,* are not left-of-center; there is no reason to doubt that most readers of the *Review* share its liberal editorial worldview, as the personals also testify.

The authors of the personals in the *Review* are an atypical group for yet another obvious reason: because they rely on these communications to satisfy important personal-emotional needs. (To be sure, we cannot tell if this is the *only* method they rely on.) The apparent geographical distribution of this group is also atypical: the *Review* is published in New York City and most readily available there; the personals too suggest that most readers live in the New York metropolitan area, although many do not reveal their location. (I was unable to find out the geographic distribution of subscribers or the proportion of subscribers versus those buying it at newsstands.) Probably over half of the readers of the *Review* live in the New York metropolitan area and the rest in various other metropolitan/academic settings, mostly San Francisco, Los Angeles, Boston, and Chicago.

Finally, this is also an atypical group (as far as the whole population is concerned) because it consists largely of the middle-aged, divorced, or widowed—at any rate, that is the impression conveyed (not every writer reveals his or her age or marital status, while others provide approximations like "fortyish" or fiftyish" or "mature"). This age distribution is likely to account for the infrequent reference to the love of children or interest in parenthood. Some writers make clear that they are "unencumbered," noting that their children are grown up; others may have children in the custody of a former spouse or are uninterested in having any, given their zest for living and for a rather wide range of social, cultural, and recreational activities they engage in or aspire to engage in. With very few exceptions, also missing are indications of interest in pets or having any.

The *Review* as a whole reflects and caters to intellectual-cultural trends popular among liberal academic intellectuals and those belonging to the educated middle classes influenced by them. In turn the preferences and ideals revealed in the personals are trendy and partake of the Zeitgeist educated groups are attuned to or seek to be in touch with. These ideals and attitudes are for the most part derived from, or part of, the cultural legacy of the 1960s, a tamer echo of the counterculture of that period.

It is not known and would be hard to find out how successful these communications are: how many contacts they lead to, how many letters or phone calls are exchanged before people actually meet, what proportion of communications lead to meetings and to lasting relationships. Even the most methodologically ambitious researcher would be hard put to learn about such matters. This is a great pity since such findings could provide information about, among other things, the relationship between self-assessment (conveyed in the ads) and subsequent assessment by others. Whatever the success rate, people have been contributing to these personals for decades.

How "success" in such matters is to be defined or measured is another thorny issue; presumably some durable relationship in which both participants claim satisfaction or fulfillment. How "durable" is to be defined invites further discussion.

MAIN THEMES OF THE PERSONALS

I did not attempt a quantitative analysis of this data for several reasons. To begin with, the advertisements are totally "open-ended," that is to say unconstrained by any uniform, external criteria; people tell as much or as little about themselves as they wish. All we know about the authors of the personals is what they choose reveal and that is largely limited to personal traits possessed and sought in others. The only other readily forthcoming information is age and sex, essential for the purpose at hand. But age may be misrepresented. Perhaps for that reason sometimes a photograph is requested but the possibility cannot be excluded that the photos used are not current. (I received some anecdotal evidence supporting this possibility from a handful of veterans of "personals" and computer dating.)

It would have been possible to quantify the desirable human qualities/attributes specified—both that the writers claim to possess and those they seek in others. Of course there is no way of knowing how accurate the self-characterizations are; it is quite likely that given the goal of maximizing the favorable attention of strangers, positive attributes are overstated. As the *New York Times* noted on November 24, 2002 (in the Internet context), "the opportunity for false (or at least massaged) self-advertisement is now nearly without limit." Indeed, as will be shown below, at times the self-presentations verge on parody or fantasy. To be sure it is still interesting to learn what people consider desirable or attractive human qualities—whether or not they actually possess them. The one aspect of the personals that invites no doubt is the specification of attributes sought in others.

In light of these difficulties, I settled for an impressionistic, qualitative analysis supplemented by a generous sampling of the actual advertisements, examples of which are reproduced below. I did however range over the *Review* from its earliest days to the present, examining at least one issue for each year. I read far more than one issue per year in recent years when I was a subscriber. Altogether I probably read over a thousand personals that appeared between 1970 and the end of 2002 (numbers of personals per issue ranged from approximately ten to sixty or more).

Information about approximate age is the most readily forthcoming, as most writers feel compelled to give some indication of it in order to attract their suitable counterpart. It appears that more women than men advertise—possibly two-thirds are women, one-third men—a small minority (perhaps 5 percent) of whom are homosexual and lesbian. These are mostly people looking for new departures, a large portion divorced or widowed, but again information of this type is not always provided. Evidently these age groups face far greater difficulties in their search for new partners, which helps to explain their reliance on the personals.

It is noteworthy that many of those using abbreviations such as DWF (divorced white female) include the "W." Even in this largely liberal group it is taken for granted that specifying one's race (whiteness) is an essential piece of information that needs to be disclosed. We cannot be sure exactly what is intended: does it mean that nonwhites are discouraged, or do those specifying their own whiteness think that nonwhites too may apply but should know the racial identity of the other party? To say the least, if race was irrelevant and only the personal qualities and interests mattered, there would be no Ws.

The vast majority are over forty (possibly over fifty), probably between forty and sixty. The relatively advanced age of many writers is a likely source of the recurring effort to project a countervailing youthful image associated with being active, adventurous, intense, resourceful, enterprising, curious, and spirited and having a wide range of interests. To wit:

Blonde, slender, tall, willowy DWF very attractive (a younger Faye Dunaway) with graceful lightness of heart, refined intelligence, smiling eyes. Ph.D./academic.... Optimistic, emphatic, elegant. Physically sensual, aesthetically attuned. Lovely profile, long legs. Considered great package: head, heart, spirit. Puts people at ease. Loves exploring restaurants, architecture, performing arts, hiking, yoga, Jacuzzis, narrative history. Europe any time. Thailand some day. Seeks well-educated, attractive, kind man 5'11" plus, engaged with the world, able to laugh occasionally at himself. [9/26/2002]

Green-eyed blonde, toned, trim, and very pleasing to the eye. Adventurous, appreciative, curious life-long learner with humor that reveals a dry, sarcastic side. Progressive world view, passionate about social justice, stimulating conversation, reading, psychology, diversity. Aesthetic and unpretentious DF, professional, likes art/photography, film, travel, music, the outdoors. Favorite getaways: lakes, beaches. Enjoys leisurely biking, walking, caring relationships, yoga, Spanish. Seeking affectionate man 55–65 ready to share life. . . . [12/5/02]

Dark, beautiful DJF with a passion for music and film. Anthropology Ph.D., international human rights experience combined with playful spirit, wry humor. NYC resident. Warm spontaneous smile, physical grace, calm presence, trim figure. Keenly intelligent yet gentle, quietly affectionate, unafraid to laugh. Also enjoys a good Bourdeaux, canoeing, being near water, Marx brothers, playing pool, making amazing lemon cake, blues, live jazz, gospel, world music. . . . Seeks bright, thoughtful, secure, open man 49–65 with ability to laugh. [11/7/2002]

Inviting smile, beautiful bone structure, very pretty, slim Ph.D. with a real spark (not hiding behind academic mask). Radiant, sensual, authentic, very present, poised. Studied dance (Graham). Active in public speaking, fundraising, the arts, and lefty community work. Good networker, gentle risk-taker, accentuates the positive. Loves making people laugh. Enjoys the Vineyard anytime, Monteverdi-Mozart-Modern, blackjack, theatre, movies, champagne, just looking at nature, learning something new. Seeks bright, active man 60s–70s caring about the world, concerned about others. [12/5/02]

Objective characteristics—such as ethnicity (when indicated, mostly Jewish), marital status, levels of education (when specified, usually Ph.D.), occupation and location—are only randomly and sporadically revealed. When indicated, occupation is often academic. There are also therapists, people in publishing, some physicians, some businessmen and -women. Hardly anyone was, or admitted to being, a lawyer. No industrial workers, computer programmers, farmers, or military personnel could be found, but there were a handful of prison inmates reaching out.

Most personals do not dwell on prosaic and factual matters such as occupation or income—an interesting finding in itself. "Financially secure," "solvent," "independent," or "successful" are the concessions to such down-to-earth matters, to socioeconomic status.

Being narrowly specialized in one's work or interests is shunned by most. Abhorrence of routines combines with an artsy-artistic inclination and a touch of bohemian, sometimes whimsical nonconformity. Veritable renaissance characters abound, men and women with an amazing cultural reach, originality and breadth of aspiration—free spirits, with wide-ranging interests and accomplishments, possessed of a sparkling mind and impressive physique.

These personals led me to recall advertisements of similar purpose in newspapers published in communist Hungary during the 1970s and 1980s. They had a sober, material-existential focus and flavor. Little was said about personal attributes, favorite recreational activities and pastimes, musical tastes or artistic interests. Instead people provided factual information to potential partners about their age, height, weight, occupation, educational qualifications, assets (apartment, car, phone), and the neighborhood or town they lived in; they averred freedom from bad habits (mostly drinking) and said next to nothing about their personalities, feelings, tastes, and hobbies.

The messages here discussed are the exact opposite, reflecting the desires and needs of people who can take for granted a high level of material security and comfort (among the luxuries taken for granted is travel, including foreign travel to exotic and romantic locations). For these writers, the establishment of an important relationship has little to do with financial security but everything to do with the intangibles of supposedly unique personal needs, characteristics, tastes, and entertainments.

Many of the authors of the personals seek to establish their culture-consumer credentials by specifying highbrow tastes and interests often in combination with a complementary predilection for more simple or popular entertainments hinting at a refreshing earthiness. For example:

Are you the man I am looking for? Are you single, 57 plus, physically fit, secure, enjoy Matisse as well as Woody Allen, only missing the companionship of a warm, fun-loving, attractive, slender, blue-eyed blonde artist to share movies, museums, theatre, ballet, travel, long walks, quiet dinners. [1/17/1991]

Lover of life and laughter interested in meeting a man who values communication, spontaneity and sharing. . . . This publishing professional's interests range from the elation of discovering a first edition of Gide to the exhilaration of white water rafting. If you're not afraid of romance, intimacy and full moon this caring woman (40) may want to be by your side. [4/23/1993]

Playful spirit. Natural Beauty with great legs, warm intelligent dark eyes, long hair. Stunning, well-educated, sophisticated, fit. Feminine, sensual, unpretentious, successful DWF. Loves new adventures, interested in art, community, more. Avid reader, great Italian cook, works out, adores laughter, jazz, Mozart, Michelangelo, Italy, French/English countryside, raw beauty of the Maine coast and occasional fine Bordeaux. Seeks accomplished, interesting man 45–64 with compassion, humor. [11/20/2000]

Serene, sweet, sensitive, sexy, sophisticated, spirited, petite, very pretty DJF. (Manhattan) professional (medical research) seriously seeking divorced or widowed emotionally evolved, accomplished, financially secure, urbane, gentle male 49–60. Sense of humor essential and a (partial) passion for Puccini, pasta, Paris, Provence and balmy evening promenades. [4/6/1995]

Hardly ever is reference made to religious affiliation, belief, or preference, but far more frequently to political sympathies or outlook. Sometimes politically correct attitudes are spelled out such as "liberated man," "politically concerned" (readers are expected to know that what the appropriate concerns are), "environmentally conscious divorcee," "socially concerned jogging feminist," and so on. Most writers can take for granted a measure of political compatibility or affinity that need not be spelled out given the shared preference for reading the *Review*.

In addition to a solid majority looking for long-term heterosexual relationships and a much smaller group of homosexuals and lesbians looking for partners, there is a third group of the already married (and apparently intending to stay married) who wish to supplement an unsatisfactory (or satisfactory?) marital relationship with an affair on the side. These requests invariably come from men (unless I somehow missed the females). For example:

> Handsome Chicago area *married* [my emphasis] exec, fine background, good future, looks for down to earth engaging lady for discreet involvement finding summer's butterflies & winter dreams [6/11/1987]

> *Married*, 33 year old photographer-artist, affectionate, considerate, sometimes passionate, sincere, intelligent, well-educated, unsophisticated, athletic . . . seeks compatible woman for enduring intimate relationship. [Shared] interests . . . include movies, drawing, sculpture, music, outdoors, politics, philosophy, psychology and encounter groups, teaching children, walking, swimming and open creative conversation. [1/25/1973]

> Does Alfred Brendel, Yo-Yo Ma, Julliard Quartet, Oscar Peterson turn you on? Successful, attractive *married* [my emphasis] professional mid-forties seeks a fun-loving professional woman interested in theater, art, chamber music and stimulating conversation. [1/21/1982]

> Affectionate *married* man, 28, seeks slim, intelligent woman for mutual oral intimacies. [4/7/1975]

> *Married*, foreign-born professor and man of letters—with passion for annual pilgrimage to Caribbean—seeks woman (25–45) for discreet encounters. Special bias for Oriental woman. Must love reggae. [6/25/1998]

At a time when in liberal, feminist, and politically correct circles "lookism" is a bad word, a surprisingly large portion of the writers of these messages (and mostly the women) emphasize or boast of their physique or figure, their appealing physical characteristics (slender, slim, trim, fit, "great legs," beautiful eyes, hair, and so on). The acclaimed physical attributes almost invariably are listed in the very beginning of the ad and followed by the admirable traits of character and intellect. For instance,

> Grace Kelly good looks. Stunning blonde. Doctorate. Humanist-values. Slender 5'7" DWF. Young looking 44. Strongly values integrity. . . . Adventurous, dynamic, accessible. Loves NY, theatre, music (Chopin to Gladys Knight to gospel), film, Egyptian art, impressionists, travel, Italian food. Plays piano, sings (blues/popular). Seeks trim, accomplished, kind, non-smoking 5'10" DWM 38–52, comfortable with self, ready for permanent relationship. [4/23/1993]

A younger, dark-haired more radiant Jane Fonda. Thin, smart, stunning, 40-something. Stands out in a crowd. Graceful, gracious, DJF. Long, beautiful, wavy hair, sensual smile. Interesting and interested, quick study. Art consultant, curator. Nature-lover but can do black tie at the drop of a hat. Interests: music, philanthropy, contemporary art, wine, hiking, film. Pilates. Runs daily. Loves laughter, surprise, giving small dinner parties. Open, unafraid, passionate creative. Seeks NS, very bright man, medium-large build. 40s–50s, passionate about something in his life. [12/5/2002]

Head turning good looks evocative of Diana Rigg from THE AVENGERS. Stylish with hint of glamour and whimsy. Fun, funny, insightful, Well educated, articulate, engaging. Trim, active, divorced. Good at making ordinary tasks, gives great parties. Considered "soulful hedonist." Enduring Francophile, would live in Europe again in a minute. Interested in architecture, hardware stores, seeing how things are constructed. Adores Art Deco, Klimt, Frank Lloyd Wright, Latin music, wine, country USA, watching baseball/tennis. Seeks educated, attractive 55–youthful 60s man-interest in foreign travel and aesthetic appreciation. [9/26/2002]

Stunning, head-turning good looks with a touch of glamour and a sweet heart. Passionate, sensual Sophia Loren-type, gorgeous dark hair, standout eyes, real presence. Down-to-earth, published fiction writer. Colorful, curious, open, honest. Known for wonderful contagious laugh and very nice figure. Sunny disposition, tamed wild streak. Favorite things: films, Yankees, football, opera, pop culture, THE SOPRANOS, all jazz, folk art, Miro, bantering with friends. Dreams of one day living in Sydney or New Zealand. Seeks goodhearted, streetsmart, financially secure, attractive man 45–60. [11/7/02]

Such a wondrously attractive woman. A cross between Sigourney Weaver and JoBeth Williams: poised, sensual, warm-spirited with a shy grace that lights up a room. Slim body, exquisite face, fun humor, no artificiality. Interested in people and the world around. Easygoing good company, dazzling cook (makes divine bouillabesse), something of an oenophile. Drawn to beauty in nature, art, theatre, music. Delights in generating/exchanging ideas, playing piano, hiking, travel to unexplored places. Seeks NS, vital, successful professional (49–64) with warmth and sense of discovery. [11/7/02]

The most often recurring attributes allegedly possessed and sought may be summarized (in alphabetical order) as follows: accomplished, adventurous, affectionate, attractive, authentic, bright, creative, caring, curious, down-to-earth, earthy, easy-going, fit, funny, fun-loving, gentle, honest, intelligent, irreverent, lively, open, passionate, playful, responsive, self-aware, secure, sensitive, sensual, serious, slender, slim, smart, sophisticated, spirited, stunning, stylish, successful, tender, trim, vibrant, vital, warm, well-educated, and witty. These attributes overlap with many traditional romantic virtues noted below.

It is the powerful and pervasive cultural legacy of the 1960s that accounts for these patterns. Authors of the personals appear to be the descendants or veterans of the counterculture of earlier decades. In their communications 1960s values and attitudes combine with a taken-for-granted, old-style literary romanticism made more widespread (and cheapened) by mass culture but a romantic individualism was also a part of the counterculture of the 1960s. In this culture the ideal personality is one in touch with his or her feelings, playful, expressive, adventurous, open, permeated by the love of nature and all that is "natural"; this type of individual also harbors notions of a programmatic self-realization, believes in the uniqueness of his or her personality, and is self-consciously hedonistic (albeit in a more refined fashion). The pursuit of pleasure and self-fulfillment is often tempered by social consciousness.

It is central to the romantic sensibility to believe that there is somewhere out in the world a person who will gratify one's considerable emotional needs, who will be uniquely compatible and make one's life fulfilled and meaningful. In the case in point, this elusive individual is pursued by the somewhat unromantic device of the personal advertisement that is in conflict with the spontaneity true romantics pursue and believe in. Still, the personals are steeped in an age-old romanticism and nurtured by the cultural values of the 1960s. They are also products of the high divorce rates of past decades and the social isolation of modern, mobile urban life.

Most writers embrace and affirm the entire repertory of romantic values and virtues: sensitivity, sensuality, creativity, caring, strong feelings, warmth, vitality, exuberance, tenderness, openness, sincerity, vulnerability, honesty, spontaneity, innocence, and arresting physical beauty.

Sense of humor is another frequently mentioned desirable trait, as are "fun" and "fun loving," being relaxed and easygoing. These more typical contemporary American virtues may be associated with the entertainment orientation of our society and times. A substantial portion of the ads specify the preferred recreational or leisure time activities of the writers. Many messages hint at consumption patterns that conjure up images of advertisements in classier publications such as *The New Yorker* or the *New York Times Magazine*—more refined, stylish, spiritual, or artsy versions thereof. These messages often come complete with allusions to intimate dinner parties, luxurious hideaways, contemplative walks on the beach, pastoral retreats off the beaten path, accommodations fit for connoisseurs of the good life. There are frequent references to good wines and gourmet cooking that is good for the body and the soul.

When aggregated, the attributes possessed and sought after yield an unexpected impression of uniformity, a standardization of cultural values, tastes, and ego ideals. What is advertised as attractive and appealing and what is being sought in others turn out to be remarkably similar, as also reflected in the samples provided above. It is not easy to be a unique individual in contemporary American society: what once were considered unusual, innovative, or daring attributes of nonconformity or experimental lifestyles had become the new conventions of "nonconformity" when transformed into a trend and taken up by large numbers of people.

THE SUSPENSION OF DISBELIEF

It is hard to escape the suspicion that many ads greatly overstate the personal qualities and attractions of the individuals advertising. Time and again it is conveyed that these individuals are endowed with virtually every conceivable trait highly valued in our times in our culture. They are good-natured, easy to get along with, warm, playful, accomplished, physically attractive, highly educated and of broad interests. The women in particular seek to convey that their personality combines an appealing and authentic simplicity with great sophistication. It appears that the inflated self-presentations are more common among women than men.

In an age and culture in which a degree of skepticism and refusal to take anything at face value are deeply embedded and widespread, it is surprising to come upon a phenomenon (such as the personals) that is predicated on the truthfulness and honesty of personal communications. Ours is a culture in which few things are taken for granted, in which a sharp awareness of the gulf between appearance and reality is common, especially among people who think of themselves as sophisticated. Under these circumstances the premise of the personals is unusual: we are asked to believe without reservations what people say about themselves when the purpose of these statements is to create and maximize favorable impressions.

In effect the authors of the personals are trying to sell themselves under intense competitive pressure; their self-assessments invite the kind of skepticism any example of flamboyant salesmanship elicits. How many "stunning" women such as the following could be awaiting eager partners?

Stunning academic DWF, 55, slender, dark hair and eye, seeks S/DWM 55–63 for LTR. Me: striking, charming, intellectual, witty, serious, sophisticated, self-aware, open, cultivated. You: humane, good-looking, honest, well-educated, urbane, interested in art, classical music, films, candid conversations, travel. [9/26/02]

Exuberant, warm, witty, most attractive, intelligent, cultured, elegant woman, 40s, seeks open, sensitive, literate, affectionate, successful, urbane, unattached male counterpart 45–55. Prefer tallish, music-loving, non-smoking, "for whatever pleasures may result." [6/25/1981]

Former aristocrat-Beautiful, accomplished Manhattan woman professional. 53, beach, tennis, skiing, reading, movie, theater and travel enthusiast seeks independent, affectionate, confident, funny, irreverent, healthy, enlightened, adventurous, self-supporting man 40–55 capable of long-term partnership. [2/20/1997]

Men too are capable of a similarly sanguine view of themselves:

Responsive, gentle, reflective, genuine, bright, stable, flexible, attractive, slim, 5'6" nonsmoking professional SWM seeks serious, intimate, potentially lasting relationship with slender SWF of similar qualities. I enjoy movies, theater, dogs, humor, verbal and non-verbal communications. [4/28/1983]

Joys to be shared, sights to be explored and adventures others can only dream about. You: attractive with inner beauty, responsive, considerate, affectionate, understanding, companionable, with substance, style, multiple interests and integrity, SWR n/s over 5'4" and irresistibly lovable. Me: SWM, n/s, tall, successful, no dependents, attractive, generous, intelligent, responsive, idealistic, principled, considerate, with a passion for adventure, nature, travel. . . . [5/14/1998]

World-class professor, divorcé, elegant, attractive, vivacious, earthy, caring Manhattan resident. Seeks accomplished, well-educated, dynamic man 45–55 to share life's pleasures, travel warmth and love. [4/13/1989]

Secure, confident, generous, lively DWM 47 ready for a permanent commitment to a mature woman. If you are also a non-smoker, forties, enjoy jazz and classical music, swimming, walking in the country, candlelight romance, winter vacations in Europe, we are ready for love and laughter together. [1/21/1988]

We do not know how readers of these ads deal with the problem of overselling; they may automatically reject the outlandish claims (the hype) in toto, or may discount *some* of the extraordinary assertions; they could give the benefit of doubt even to the most implausibly alluring self-presentations or reserve judgment until further communications or personal encounter. Nor do we know how the authors reconcile their idealized self-presentation with the more realistic impressions and assessments a personal encounter is likely to create. For that matter it also remains unknown to what extent these flattering self-conceptions are sincerely held, internalized, or consciously burnished and misrepresented.

The messages cited earlier are certainly not atypical, and there is a continuity of both style and substance over time. Moreover the shorter messages are similar to the longer, more elaborate ones as shown below:

Striking Southern California woman, strawberry blonde and newly single, thrives on imaginative sex, animated conversation, controversial politics, Brahms quartets and the Moody Blues. Invites uninvolved intelligent male 40–60 similarly nourished to mutual feast. [4/14/1977]

Socially concerned, jogging feminist, rural background values depth, health, arts, people work. Loves galleries, plays, outdoors, Bach, Mozart. Desires proself, 50 plus male for growth, friendship, play. [6/28/1984]

Woman of intellect and sex appeal, literate, sophisticated, thoughtful, helpful, gentle, vulnerable very attractive 49 of European extraction. Seeks strong-minded, refined, reasonably handsome man capable of sustained friendship. [1/17/1985]

Boston SWF artist/therapist 48, attractive, passionate lover of life and nature, vegetarian seeker of wisdom, Himalaya trekker seeks authentic, spiritually aware, self-actualizing man 40+, accomplished in his field, open to new experiences, willing to explore and enjoy life's many wonders. [7/19/1990]

Winsome, creative widow 60 is witty, loving, great cook, brainy and a slender good looker seeks vibrant, adventurous widower to create a lasting love affair. [8/8/1996]

DWF Young 60s, independent, 5'7" blonde, involved in the arts, loves to travel, full of wonder of life, in search of a quality man with more questions than answers. [6/25/1998]

Hopelessly intellectual Berkshire farm-dweller, 5'6" brunette, 66. Passionate about the word written and spoken. . . . Serendipitous discovery is my principal joy on the page, in travel, in people. . . . I am interested in . . . someone who is unattached and liberal who is fifty plus, well read . . . and considers himself funny, healthy and happy. . . . [7/12/1999]

Two hours from Grand Central lives a Berkshire beauty with a great sense of humor, loves theatre, nature, adventure. If you are smart, secure, romantic mensch old enough to remember WWII and still strong enough to paddle a canoe, write please. [11/24/1999]

Adventurous, lovely, connected, fit, funny and smart Jewish woman (academic 52 NYC) seeking male counterpart to share loving and joyful aspirations. Searching for a man with good mind, deep heart, full laugh and a social conscience. [4/26/2001]

Man 40s characterized by an encounter group as creative, complex, caring, authentic, intuitive, intense, impatient, durable, wise, searching, tentative, distinguished, not paranoid, not pretentious, not cynical, in transition, sharing, open, politically concerned, effective. Would like to meet woman with some of the following: stylish, slender, elegant, sensate, spontaneous, spirited. [1/25/1979]

Los Angeles male, academic physical scientist 40 . . . youthful and very good looking, sensitive, uninhibited, with broad education and interest in the arts, politics, sociology, psychology, literature, mountaineering, tennis, is going through divorce (no children) . . . seeks an attractive, educated and intelligent woman—preferably with her own career—who is emotionally stable, at peace with herself. . . . [2/19/1976]

Intense but optimistic man, 44, 5'10", trim, attractive, clean-cut, cerebral, sagacious, lethal wit, passions for political ideas and classical music, seeks spirited, stable woman. . . . [4/6/1995]

Gentle, witty world traveler DWM, Ph.D. interested in literature, law, medicine, music, museums, nature, science. Seeks S/DWF (40–60) deep, warm, responsive. [n.d.]

Nagging questions remain, in particular, why such fine human beings must invest so much time and energy in the search for suitable partners. Are these self-presentations largely wishful fantasies, or exaggerations of traits possessed?

Presumably the implausible self-presentations are attention-getting efforts, overselling oneself is a response to keen competition for partners not easy to locate; they reflect the pressures of a competitive culture and a competitive marketplace of personal relationships, especially among older age groups and especially older women, who are even more often without partners (as statistics too indicate).

Some broader conclusions may be drawn. One is that being alone in middle age is a difficult experience that sometimes stimulates problematic and cumbersome efforts to remedy the condition. The messages examined also suggest that middle or approaching old age are to be escaped at all costs—one must try to stay "young at heart" until the bitter end. Thirdly, in an age when "diversity" is extolled, the repetitive specifications of ego-ideals and ideal partners expose the narrow and stereotyped nature of our dreams and ideals.

At last there is the problem of heightened expectations central to secular modernity. They are produced by a way of life that provides an abundance of "options" and is free of pressing material concerns but is weighted down by the imbalance between material needs easily gratified and emotional ones largely unmet. Doubtless these aspects of modernity intensify expectations and the quest for intimate relationships which, it is hoped, would compensate for the loss of community, a stable worldview, and social isolation.

Chapter Fifteen

Old and Busier Than Ever

Whenever I talk to retired friends or acquaintances they invariably tell me that they are "busier than ever." They have taken up learning (or relearning) to play musical instruments, participate in creative writing workshops, take courses in adult education programs, they jog, kayak, bird-watch, take edifying trips to ancient monuments or impoverished third-world countries. They cannot sit still. Former president Carter won't stop writing books, shaking hands of strangers on the street, traveling ceaselessly in pursuit of good causes. Advertisements for retirement communities promise a mind-boggling array of recreational, cultural, and social activities. It may indeed be true that the retired are busier than ever.

If so, the question arises why so many prosperous Americans past the prime of life and regular employment are so intent on squeezing so many activities into their lives. Does the absence of routinized commitments and obligations create a threatening void that must be filled in haste to avert the onset of a profound unease? Does the lack of "busyness" drain life of purpose and meaning? Are we so programmed that our nature abhors the vacuum in our schedules?

There is, of course, nothing wrong with attempting to become a renaissance man or woman at an advanced age, or trying to keep fit physically and mentally, to do things one had less or no opportunity to do at an earlier age. But there is an urgency and compulsiveness that color these endeavors, a veritable horror of idleness, of being left with time for reflection that might lead to the contemplation of approaching death. The frantic activism of the old and aging suggests that we are ill equipped, in this most religious of all modern societies, to face death.

A better understanding of these attitudes has to take into account the deeply entrenched, long-standing veneration of being busy in American culture that allows the benefits of busyness to go unspecified; what matters is being occupied, not what we are occupied with (an attitude somewhat similar to that of endorsing "change," no matter what kind). American optimism, youth cult, and the belief that there is a solution for every problem also play a part; at an advanced age these attitudes and beliefs seem to reappear with a new urgency and intensity.

In traditional societies, the old used to be considered repositories of wisdom and had a high social standing. Even in contemporary Europe the old have more social and familial functions and bonds and therefore fewer reasons to feel superfluous and isolated; these functions and ties make life more meaningful, and there is less pressure to find meaning in being busy. In American society the old have become more marginal, and that, too, contributes to this compulsive, meaning-seeking activism. In all probability the United States leads the world in the proportion of the old who do not live with their children and grandchildren, and often not even anywhere near them. The proportion, as well as absolute numbers, of healthy retired people is also likely to be greater here than in most other modern societies.

At the same time, American society is replete with unconvincing compensatory efforts intended to glorify old age not on account of the accumulated wisdom or important social functions but largely on account of the leisure that accrues to it. But an abundance of leisure uninformed by a philosophy of life, substantial intellectual resources, or religious belief of some kind may give rise to escapism, meaningless routines, to rushing around. It seems that human beings are not programmed to enjoy unlimited amounts of leisure without unease and difficulty.

The problem is not helped by the growing reluctance or inability of American religious institutions to dwell on the subject of death. While the various denominations have developed a commendable interest in improving life here and now, in advocating social justice or environmental awareness, and in combating various social problems, they have become reticent about advising us about the ways of ending life and confronting its irrevocable end. Death remains, by and large, a taboo topic. There is plenty of it in mass culture and popular entertainments, but its treatment is unrealistic: either violent or sentimental.

These observations are not an endorsement of idle vegetation in old (or any other) age. I am not suggesting that being inactive or less active is preferable to being active, or even hyperactive. The latter may help, temporarily, to distract from the realization that living longer does not solve the problem of death or its approach; that old age, while more prolonged, remains debilitating, mentally as well as physically, and that infirmity cannot be averted indefinitely, notwithstanding the wonders of medical science. It is understandable that as we live longer we seek to avoid confronting the end in more ingenious and imaginative ways.

III

FOREIGN MATTERS

Chapter Sixteen

American Travelers to the Soviet Union

The data for this study (comprising several hundred completed questionnaires) were collected in 1966 and reposed in cardboard boxes for exactly forty years. In 2006 I rediscovered them, so to speak, and came to the conclusion that despite their antique quality they merited tabulation and analysis. There seemed to be a wealth of information in the answers to close to one hundred questions that the two sets of questionnaires contained. This was an attempt to learn about American attitudes toward the Soviet system and of characteristics of Soviet society as seen by the same Americans. As it turned out, there was more information in the data about Americans and their political and social attitudes than about Soviet society and people.

Readers may wish to learn why there was such an uncommon gap between data collection and analysis. It was in part a matter of forgetting—out of sight, out of mind; the boxes were languishing in a corner of my office while I was occupied with other, seemingly more pressing, projects. There was probably also a Freudian aspect of this forgetfulness: completing the study required the use of methodology—quantitative analysis—that was not my forte. I preferred the kind of research and writing that did not require "number crunching."

In the 1960s when I undertook this project, the Cold War and its possible culmination in nuclear war were major concerns in the United States. One group of particularly alarmed Americans founded or joined an organization called Citizens Exchange Corps (CEC) committed to improving the relationship between the United States and the Soviet Union by establishing and cultivating grassroots contacts between their citizens. A quintessentially American organization, CEC advocated face-to-face contacts and informal, interpersonal communications to bring about such improvements and help to avert the threat of nuclear war.

It was the major premise of this organization—derived both from longstanding American cultural beliefs and the spirit of the 1960s and its therapeutic orientation—that in their essential attributes all human beings are alike no matter under what kind of political systems they live. Unfettered, informal communications between them will make them aware of these shared attributes. Given a chance to experience these basic similarities, intergroup suspicions will evaporate and friction between different countries would correspondingly vanish. The complementary assumption was that mutual understanding between ordinary citizens would translate into high-level policy. CEC members who visited the Soviet Union were the prime subject of this research project.

The second group that was sent questionnaires consisted of American mathematicians who attended the World Congress of Mathematics in Moscow in the same year (1966). I included them as a control group of sorts, individuals who had no ostensible reason to be especially interested in Soviet society or Soviet policies, to have strong feelings about Soviet-American relations, or to harbor apprehensions about nuclear war. I also expected them to be more apolitical and less informed about the Soviet Union than the CEC group. As it turned out, the major differences between these groups were demographic and educational rather than attitudinal. The mathematicians were older (no teenagers among them, while 8 percent in the CEC group were teenagers); 69 percent of the mathematicians were between 39 and 49, while only 24 percent of the CEC members were in that age group; 44 percent of the CEC group was under 40. For this reason a high proportion of the mathematicians were married—83 percent as against 55 percent of CEC members. Another major difference was that, for obvious reasons, 67 percent of the mathematicians had Ph.D.s (against only 8 percent of the CEC group).

The differences in the levels of information, opinion, and attitude between the two groups were less substantial than expected. It is possible that the mathematicians who chose to attend the Moscow congress *and* chose to respond to the questionnaire were a subgroup distinguished by a greater interest in Soviet society and international relations. Twelve of them (out of a total of eighty-two) were capable of conversing in Russian, and twenty-three reported being invited to the homes of Soviet people. A much smaller proportion of CEC participants—10 out of 230—reported being capable of conversing in Russian.

The two groups had in common—besides being educated, middle-class Americans—the more or less simultaneous experience of visiting the Soviet Union in the year of 1966. The CEC members went in order to further the goals of their organization: to meet and better understand ordinary Soviet citizens in pursuit of improving relations between the two countries; the mathematicians went mainly to attend the world congress.

Although deeply influenced by the characteristics and concerns of the period, the relevance of this study is not limited to the 1960s; this was also a more general inquiry into political attitude formation, persistence, and change. The information collected had the potential to shed light on these questions:

1. What kind of people (sociologically speaking) were particularly concerned in the 1960s with Soviet-American relations and the danger of nuclear war between these countries? (This question applies mainly to the CEC contingent.)
2. How much and what kind of information these well-educated, middle-class Americans had about the Soviet Union in the 1960s.
3. What kinds of attitudes these two groups harbored toward the Soviet Union.
4. How their views of their own society influenced the respondents' perceptions and judgments of the Soviet Union.
5. What, if any impact, the trip had on their attitudes toward the Soviet Union *and* American society. What proportions of the visitors returned with largely positive or largely negative impressions.
6. What the specifics of the travel experience were. (What did the visitors actually do and see? Whom did they meet?) Were they aware of the political controls over their experiences, of what I called (in another study, entitled *Political Pilgrims*) "the techniques of hospitality"?

It was not possible to provide answers to all these questions, given the limitations of space and the abundance of information to be tabulated or cross-tabulated.

CEC AND THE COLD WAR

The background of the founders, trustees, and advisors of the CEC suggests, for the most part, that knowledge or expertise about international relations and the Soviet Union was not an important requirement for holding such positions and hardly a defining characteristic of this organization. The president and executive director was "an advertising writer" (see Francis Sugrue, "Peace Ideas—Soviet Jobs for Americans," *Herald Tribune*, November 28, 1965); others listed on CEC stationery were mostly businessmen, members of the clergy, and college administrators. Eugene Burdick, coauthor of *The Ugly American* (a spirited critique of U.S. foreign policies) was one of the trustees.

Anatol Rapoport, an academic specialist of conflict resolution, was also on the advisory board. Overall there was a notable absence on these boards of specialists on Soviet history, politics, or society.

Thus, it seems appropriate to characterize the CEC, its founders, and officers as liberal, idealistic, and somewhat naive. It is likely that these organizers and founders were animated to some degree by the notion of moral equivalence between the two systems, especially in regard to responsibility for the Cold War. CEC pamphlets produced in the early 1960s described it as

> a nonprofit, tax-exempt organization chartered in 1962 to engage in people-to-people contact for easing international tensions. Our goal is to raise the level of contact between East and West before it is too late to reduce the danger of nuclear war through mutual understanding. . . . CEC believes that there must be a meaningful build-up in mutual understanding to produce a suitable climate for nuclear disarmament before a holocaust by accident or attack. . . . Unlike other exchange programs which are limited to members of specific professions . . . CEC exchanges include individuals of all ages and from every occupation—a true cross section of U.S. and Communist societies.

The cultural-philosophical assumptions underlying the mission of the CEC were deeply American. Central to them was the taken-for-granted conviction that ordinary citizens exert substantial influence on their government because the government is representative and responsive to their wishes and concerns, and the latter shape government policies, including foreign policies. If so, the peaceful, peace-loving attitudes of both ordinary American and Soviet citizens—if effectively communicated to their respective governments—would result in more peaceful policies and reduce or eliminate the threat of nuclear war.

A second major premise of the CEC was that since ordinary people everywhere are similar to one another in certain crucial respects, groups of different national or ethnic backgrounds could readily and rapidly develop mutual understanding and appreciation given the opportunity to meet and exchange ideas. It was a basically apolitical and optimistic conception of human nature averred, for example, by Edison Plunkett of Elmira, New York (former president of Elmira Foods), a participant in the CEC exchange:

> The Soviet people seemed as friendly, peace-loving and ambitious for their country's improvement as do people here in the United States . . . the goals and aspirations of the Russians . . . were similar to those of their American counterparts. . . . To see people going about their business . . . one can see their enthusiastic attitude toward their work, their industriousness—a puritanical ethic similar to that in our American heritage. . . . (Jack Freed, "Elmiran Visits Russians, Finds Them Like Americans," *Star-Gazette* [Elmira, New York], October 5, 1966.)

The associated or implied view of conflict between nation states was correspondingly optimistic: such conflicts resulted from misunderstanding, misperception, and miscommunication or insufficient communication. These beliefs, needless to say, did not take sufficient account of the profound differences between American and Soviet society, their respective histories and divergent political systems, and least of all, the huge difference between the degree to which citizens, or public opinion, influenced the policymakers and leaders of these two political systems.

There was a further, corresponding failure to fully grasp the important structural differences between these two societies. In the United States it was possible for ordinary citizens to create and sustain spontaneously, without government approval, permission, or assistance, a wide variety of social, cultural, political, or economic organizations (including CEC), but no such opportunities existed in the former Soviet Union in the 1960s. Hence, the Soviet "counterparts" of the Americans belonging to the CEC were hardly counterparts; they could become involved in these exchanges only with official approval. In all probability, the Soviet citizens participating in these exchanges were carefully selected by the political authorities to represent and articulate the officially approved points of views. They were not, and could not be, "ordinary" Soviet citizens, spontaneously taking certain positions or joining a social organization or movement; they could not be genuine "counterparts" of the American participants.

The Soviet official purpose in these exchanges was illustrated by a recollection of one of the American participants who noted that in the organized seminars and discussion groups the focus of Soviet interest was on "why America is making war on Vietnam and what can be done to stop the American government from its genocidal policies." Also characteristic of these exchanges was the observation of Professor Samuel Hendel (chairman at the time of the Russian area program at City College, New York, and member of the advisory board of the CEC Field Institute). While "he felt the exchange experiment was 'breaking new ground'. . . he added, 'I would be happier, frankly, if there were more opportunities for the Americans to present their side'" (quoted in Raymond H. Anderson, "Lost Soviet Visas Delay 2 U.S. Women in Moscow," *New York Times*, July 14, 1966). These asymmetries were also reflected in the striking quantitative difference between the numbers of tourists (of all kinds) of each country visiting the other. For example, in 1969, a total of 20,000 Americans visited the Soviet Union and 165 Soviet "tourists" visited the United States. In 1982 it was 50,000 Americans against a few hundred Soviet visitors (Yale Richmond, *Soviet-American Cultural Exchanges: Ripoff or Payoff?* Washington, D.C., 1984, 60).

None of this is intended to suggest that these exchanges were doomed to total futility; something useful could still be accomplished even if officially selected Soviet citizens representing their government's positions met Americans who had no similar identification with their government and its policies. Allen Kassof, for many years the head of IREX (International Research and Exchanges Board), the American organization that arranged scholarly exchanges with the Soviet Union, took an even more charitable view of the kinds of exchanges CEC sought to foster. In an April 2006 letter to me he wrote: "I knew the organizers of many of the 'amateur' exchanges . . . and it would be wrong to think that they were naive. If anyone began with the illusion that the contacts were a direct path to understanding and peace (and few did), they were quickly disabused by having to deal with Soviet bureaucracy. . . . It was a rare American who returned dewy-eyed from a sojourn in the USSR (on the contrary they were often appalled by what they saw). . . ."

While it remains difficult to establish what proportions of Americans were naive or realistic about these (nonscholarly) exchanges, there was a further, important asymmetry between participants of the exchanges the CEC fostered. Not only were the Americans free to join CEC without governmental authorization but many of them were critical of their own government and its foreign policies as well as their society and freely expressed such sentiments. (When asked "what were the major criticisms Soviet people made of American society," one CEC respondent wrote "the same ones I make.")

FACTS AND FINDINGS

Two hundred thirty pretravel questionnaires were returned by the CEC group but only eighty-three posttravel; eighty-two pretravel by the mathematicians and sixty-four post. Forty years after the questionnaires were sent out, it was impossible to establish the total number sent and how many in each group embarked on these trips. Reportedly, in 1965, 140 took the same CEC trip (M. S. Handler, "140 Fly to Soviet to Start Citizen Exchange," *New York Times*, August 28, 1965). Respondents in my survey sometimes made references to 160 people in their group, but there was also reference to a total number of 500 such visitors in the same year. There had to be more than 160 such travelers since I received 230 responses. Most likely, three such groups of 160 took the trip in 1966 and all of them were sent questionnaires.

It is more difficult to guess how many mathematicians from the United States attended the International Congress; eighty-two seems like a reasonable figure but it is possible that twice as many, or even more, attended.

Approximately a third of the CEC visitors completed the second questionnaire (as opposed to 80 percent of the mathematicians). I can only speculate about the sources of this discrepancy. It is possible that in the aftermath of the trip there was a diminished enthusiasm about and interest in the whole undertaking. There might also have been a measure of disappointment, which some of the respondents did not wish to confront or articulate, as the second questionnaire might have prompted them to do.

In any event, the first set of questionnaires provides abundant information about the sociological and attitudinal attributes of the CEC members surveyed. Unless otherwise indicated, all figures to follow refer to the CEC group: 48 percent were male, 50 percent female (of the mathematicians, 73 percent were male and only 25 percent female); 55 percent were married, 41 percent single, and only 2 percent divorced.

As regards the occupational background, teachers/academics were the largest group, 29 percent; followed by businessmen and managerial, 19 percent; students, 19 percent; housewives, 9 percent; social workers, 5 percent; lawyers and doctors, 3 percent each; and clergy, 2 percent. Eighteen percent were high school graduates; 31 percent were college graduates with first degrees; 23 percent had master's degrees, and 8 percent had Ph.D.s.

The great majority (67 percent) was from the Northeast (26 percent from New York City and 17 percent from other parts of New York state); 17 percent from the Midwest, only 5 percent from the West and 2 percent from the South. This lopsided distribution may reflect the influence of the location of CEC (in New York City) as well as the concentration of people in the greater New York City area interested in foreign affairs and especially Soviet-American relations. The area concentration and the interest expressed in Soviet anti-Semitism also suggest the likelihood that a high proportion of the respondents were Jewish.

More evenly distributed, 40 percent of the mathematicians were from the Northeast, 22 percent from the Midwest, 13 percent from the West, 5 percent from the South, and 3 percent from Canada.

There were several questions about the sources of information that these respondents had about the Soviet Union or Russia. These questions do not imply a belief that information necessarily determines attitudes or beliefs. People use information selectively and tend to favor whatever supports their predisposition or preferences. Often identical bits of information are subject to different interpretation.

Unexpectedly high proportions indicated familiarity with Russian fiction (56 percent) and Soviet fiction (33 percent). Over 60 percent read some of the works of Marx and Engels; 34 percent those of Lenin, 23 percent those of Stalin. The mathematicians' familiarity with these sources was also substantial: 43 percent read some Russian fiction, 36 percent Soviet fiction, and 42 percent some Marx, again highly atypical figures even for well-read academics, especially outside the humanities.

Soviet sources of information were not widely consulted, with 96 percent never or rarely having listened to Radio Moscow, which regularly broadcast in English. As to American sources of information about the USSR, over half relied on television, about one-third on radio, 85 percent on newspapers, and 76 percent on magazines—the latter figures probably a reflection of the greater importance of printed sources forty years ago than would be the case today.

I was also interested in the factual knowledge of these travelers in such matters as the land area of the USSR compared with that of the United States, the size of the Soviet population, estimates of Communist Party membership, and the percentage of votes the party received in the national elections under Stalin (over 90 percent) and after Stalin (74 percent) The latter estimate was wrong. The votes were in the ninetieth percentile even after the death of Stalin. The other estimates were largely correct.

The population in rural areas (as percentage of the total) was widely overestimated: 69 percent of the respondents put it between 51 percent and 75 percent; 16 percent estimated it between 26 and 50 percent (it was in fact around 20 percent). The preponderant overestimation of the rural population suggests an image of the Soviet Union as largely rural.

I also asked what the "Committee on State Security" (KGB) was (again providing options for the answer). Forty-two percent correctly chose "major coercive organ of the Soviet state" and 34 percent chose "an arm of the Secret Police." More humorously, 5 percent chose "government controlled insurance institute," 4 percent "loans and savings organization," and 1 percent "an organization concerned with the prevention of accidents."

As to the standard of living, 72 percent correctly believed that it was "much lower than in the United States;" and 26 percent that it was "somewhat lower. . . ." Very few chose "about the same. . . ." Regarding income differentials, 76 percent rightly thought that they were "considerable," 15 percent that they were "very high," and only 6 percent that they were "nonexistent" or "very small." Responses to these factual questions suggest that this was, for the most part, a fairly well-informed group.

ATTITUDES AND OPINIONS

I was also interested in the attitudes toward the exchanges CEC championed. Forty-four percent chose the statement that most accurately captures the CEC philosophy, namely that "basically people are alike all over the world; by meeting them informally we can eliminate tension and misunderstanding between countries which is always a product of ignorance and lack of communications." Twenty-five percent averred that "meeting people of other countries helps to destroy national stereotypes . . ."; 19 percent agreed that such meetings were not sufficient by themselves to improve international relations; and only 11 percent supported the proposition that "it matters little how the average citizens of different countries feel about each other . . . because hostility between countries is produced by clashing ideologies, or economic and political interests."

To sum up, two-thirds adhered to what may be seen as the more naive, personalized view of international relations and one-third supported the more realistic one.

The mathematicians' attitudes were more realistic; only 24 percent agreed with the statement that the informal get-togethers eliminate misunderstanding and tension, as opposed to the 44 percent of the CEC members. Twenty-seven percent of the mathematicians (versus 19 percent CEC) thought that such meetings were unlikely to improve international relations.

Respondents were also asked what specific reasons prompted them to take the trip and were given sixteen options and asked to mark five. The most widely given reasons were:

- 74 percent: to better understand the average Soviet citizen;
- 57 percent: to become better acquainted with Russian culture;
- 54 percent: to be an ambassador of friendship;
- 47 percent: to obtain factual information about aspects of Soviet society;
- 40 percent: to equip myself with firsthand information to disprove falsehoods current in the United States about the Soviet Union [only 10 percent of the mathematicians chose this option]
- 39 percent: to acquire firsthand information I can disseminate among friends;
- 35 percent: to enrich my personality by visiting a new country;
- 27 percent: to confirm my belief that Soviet and especially Russian people are good, no matter what kind of government they have;
- 27 percent: to counteract misinformation Soviet citizens have about the United States, and explain the truth about the United States;
- 21 percent: to put factual foundation under the ideas I already have about the Soviet Union;
- 13 percent: to see the country my ancestors came from;
- 12 percent: to improve knowledge of Russian language [23 percent of the mathematicians chose this].

Most of these responses were congruent with the declared mission of the CEC.

Among the mathematicians the most popular choice (49 percent) was "to enrich my personality, etc." and the second most popular (45 percent) "To become acquainted with Russian culture." These were clearly more apolitical reasons.

Given my interest in the relationship between attitudes toward American society and the views of the Soviet Union, the respondents were also asked to choose among different characterizations of both American and Soviet society. The most popular option (74 percent) concerning the United States (and indicative of a social-critical disposition) was that it was "a pluralistic society with high standards of living but with many serious unresolved social problems and defects." Far below was the number of those, 14 percent, who believed that it was "democratic and pluralistic striving to extend social justice." The unqualified positive assessment—"a land of freedom and unlimited opportunity"—was held by only 6 percent. Likewise, the most unqualified condemnation—"an irresponsible and wasteful society, obsessed by consumption and controlled by a power elite"—was also chosen by only 5 percent.

The mathematicians were somewhat less critical of American society, as shown in their response to the statement that emphasized the "serious and unresolved social problems and defects" of the United States: 67 percent chose it versus 74 percent of the CEC respondents.

In evaluating the seemingly judicious view (the first option, cited above) held by almost three-quarters of the respondents of American society, we do not know which part of the statement carried more emotional weight: the acknowledgment of positive aspects (pluralistic, high standards of living) or the negative (serious social problems and defects).

Another question sought to gauge the views about convergence between American and Soviet society (widely held at the time) offering these alternatives:

- 44 percent (as against 26 percent of the mathematicians): "the United States and the USSR are becoming similar in their use of technology and growing bureaucratization";
- 33 percent: "becoming similar insofar as the values and aspirations of their average citizens are concerned";
- 9 percent: "becoming more alike with regard to the standard of living";
- 6 percent: "becoming similar in most areas of life."

Here again, almost three-quarters subscribed to what is essentially a belief in convergence, and the mathematicians' responses were largely similar.

Another group of questions probed the conceptions of the Soviet Union: 44 percent chose "a society that modernized itself at great cost and at the expense of personal and political freedom" (versus 51 percent of the mathematicians);

- 30 percent: "made great progress in modernizing itself under very difficult conditions";
- 18 percent: "a totalitarian society that remains in many ways underdeveloped and intolerant of . . . dissent and diversity";
- 7 percent: "a peace-loving country . . . which created a truly popular system of government."

Again it may be asked which component of the most popular answer carried more weight: the accomplishments of modernization or its costs.

It was my assumption that those who held the most negative conceptions of American society would be more susceptible to more favorable perceptions of the Soviet Union. This assumption was not completely supported by the responses. The most negative view of American society held by the small number (5 percent) of respondents (i.e., "an irresponsible and wasteful society, obsessed with consumption and controlled by a power elite") proved compatible with assessments of the Soviet Union: ranging from the most favorable ("a peace loving country which made more social and economic progress in a short time than any other country and which created a truly popular government") held by the smallest number to "a society that made great progress in modernizing itself under very difficult conditions." A handful ascribed to the more critical view: "a society that modernized itself at great human cost and at the expense of personal and political freedoms." Only the most unambiguously critical assessment "a totalitarian society . . . etc." was shunned.

The most widely held view of American society that incorporated both positive and negative aspects ("pluralistic, high standards of living" and "serious and unresolved social problems and defects") was compatible with the entire available range of assessment of the Soviet Union, including the most unfavorable.

The most unambiguously favorable views of America ("a land of freedom and unlimited opportunity") did not invariably coincide with the most negative view of the Soviet Union, but sometimes allowed for the less judgmental and most widely chosen one, that is, "a society that modernized itself at great human cost, etc." Still, more typically the highly favorable views of America went along with the more critical views of the Soviet Union.

While most of these perceptions of the two societies were not starry-eyed or unrealistic, the options offered in the questionnaire might have restricted the expression of the most strongly felt or salient attitudes. There was also a list of various features of Soviet society, positive and negative ("assets or weaknesses"), of which I solicited approval or disapproval. For the most part, the responses were predictable and unremarkable. For instance: 87 percent approved or strongly approved of free medical services and similar percentages of universal literacy. As to "political participation of the broad masses" (which, of course, did not exist), 55 percent had no comment, probably because they were bewildered by the suggestion that it existed or were not sure how to respond given a measure of favorable disposition; on the other hand, 39 percent approved, which meant that they mistakenly believed that it existed. Eighty-five percent disapproved of "the persistence of anti-Semitism"; 93 percent supported the raising of the standard of living; 77 percent disapproved of the one-party system; 57 percent of the privileges of the party-elite, although 25 percent professed to be "indifferent," and 12 percent had no opinion. Both of the latter responses suggest that the issue was not salient or well known.

There were some interesting divisions of opinion about the state of control over the means of production: 42 percent did not favor it as against 33 percent who did; 19 percent professed to be indifferent. But almost two-thirds disapproved of "the absence of private enterprise" (that is a condition identical to "state control over the means of production"); only 15 percent approved; a quarter were indifferent or offered no opinion. There were no noteworthy differences in the responses of the two groups to this group of questions.

Since the majority of the CEC respondents failed to return the second questionnaire it was not possible to make meaningful comparisons between attitudes before and after the trip. Still, there were self-assessments about the impact of the trip on various opinions, and beliefs. I asked, "in which of the following areas did the trip change your feelings, opinion or attitude?" Eleven such areas were listed, including Soviet living standards, domestic and foreign policy, Soviet social problems, people's attitudes toward the government, and others. Respondents could choose between "great, considerable, some or none" as to the degree of change in their attitudes. There was an open-ended follow-up question asking to explain "what the change consisted of" to shed some light on the quality of the change. A far greater portion of the CEC people reported "great change" in regard to some attitude than did the mathematicians. For example, while 18 percent of the CEC respondents reported "great change" regarding their views about Soviet people, only 2 percent of the mathematicians did so; likewise 12 percent versus 2 percent regarding Soviet domestic policies; 21 percent versus 6 percent regarding living standards; 21 percent versus 8 percent regarding physical aspects of Soviet cities, and so forth. Overall the responses in the "great change" column totaled 122 points for the CEC members as against 45 points for the mathematicians.

All reports of changing attitudes would have been more meaningful and informative if we had known exactly what they had replaced or modified. Thus, for example, only 22 percent of the CEC people registered "great" or "considerable" change in their view of Soviet social problems; the rest (78 percent) presumably learned little or nothing, or nothing new. This could also mean that their previous views (whatever they were) had been confirmed during the visit. Presumably the subjects least affected by the visit were those about which they could learn the least (e.g., social problems) or the countryside (they did not see) or anti-Semitism.

EXPECTATIONS AND EXPERIENCES

A close reading of the post-visit responses, and especially those to the open-ended questions, makes clear that despite the Soviet goal of controlling the exchanges, many Americans found opportunities for informal contacts and conversations with Soviet citizens, usually on the street and in other public places. The mathematicians, too, reported many informal and apparently candid exchanges of opinion and information with the natives.

Clearly, many Soviet citizens in major urban areas (as well as in resorts such as Sochi on the Black Sea) were not deterred from seeking unauthorized contact with Americans. But there were exceptions. A mathematician reported, "I met several Russians who had relatives in the U.S.A. but they were afraid to communicate (by mail) with them." In seeming contradiction to this observation, the same respondent found "Soviet citizens critical of their government."

The responses do not make clear what proportion of the encounters and conversations reported by the CEC contingent occurred with the preselected "ordinary" Soviet citizens as distinct from those outside this category. Likewise, we have no way of knowing how many of the thirty-four invitations to the homes of Soviet citizens reported by the CEC participants were officially planned or authorized and how many were not.

Responses to the open-ended questions reveal a great variety of attitudes and experiences, positive as well as negative, conditioned in a large measure by the expectations of the travelers as they themselves made clear. It is impossible to quantify what portion of the experiences were generally positive or negative; most were mixed.

These responses also remind one of the inherent difficulty of bridging the gap between the multiplicity and uniqueness of personal experiences conveyed in a multitude of ways and words and the social scientific endeavor that seeks to fit such responses into neat, compressed, and clear-cut categories. The most widely reported experience of both groups of visitors was that the Soviet people they met were friendly, warm, helpful, outgoing, and avidly interested in American ways of life and especially the standards of living and were impressed by the freedom to travel.

The other most widely shared and deplored experience was that of bureaucratic inefficiency shaping the practical arrangements for the trip (CEC) as well as the life of the natives observed; as one visitor noted, the Soviet people spend much of their life "waiting in line for everything."

It was another widespread perception of the visitors that Soviet people were healthy and beneficiaries of a superior health care system provided by their government. These observations were made in the same period when statistics began to show the decline in public health that continued unabated through the remaining decades of the Soviet Union (and into the postcommunist era as well). It is doubtful that more than a handful (if any) visitors had reason to visit Soviet hospitals or were provided with truthful statistics of public health.

The wide range of expectations and the "revelations" resulting from testing them against experience are reflected in the comments that follow. A student CEC participant wrote: "I expected Soviets to have a downtrodden, brow-beaten attitude . . . [but] They are extremely proud. . . . One of the [Soviet] students said, 'So what if we don't have color TV and washing machines—we will be on the moon first, without them.'" A theater agent was "disappointed in the performing arts—expected a high degree of excellence. Found . . . inferior and backward acting technique." She also found the "Soviet character less vivacious, less demonstrative than expected. . . . Though people were warm and friendly . . . [they] rarely laughed . . . or showed uninhibited emotion." By contrast, other visitors commented on the expressive, emotional nature of the people they met.

A mathematician from Chicago "found the cities much better than expected and the countryside somewhat worse. . . . The Russians were much more openly critical of bureaucrats, past mistakes, civil liberties restrictions, etc. than I expected." The part played by expectations and their meeting realities is further shown in the comments of a chemist from Princeton, New Jersey, who found "the people warm and eager to be friendly though tempered by fear . . . living standards much lower than expected . . . anti-Semitism intense and terrible . . . Soviet cities backward . . . [and] class distinctions" noticeable. Class distinctions were also observed by a mathematician from Philadelphia who was "shocked by the meanness of a Soviet mathematician toward the serving waitress. Such attitude is unthinkable either in Paris or the USA."

There were considerable differences of opinion among those who found cities poorly planned and buildings neglected and those who found the (same) cities clean and well planned. A librarian from Detroit wrote: "Soviet living standards are much more behind the U.S. than I thought. . . . [but] The physical aspects of Soviet cities were better than I expected . . . cleaner than the major U.S. cities. . . ."

There were also those who found the country "incredibly more poverty stricken than I had thought . . ." whereas others found the improvements in the living standards impressive, especially compared to prerevolutionary conditions, although they were not in a position to ascertain what the latter were like. A "homemaker" from Grand Rapids, Michigan, thought that Soviet "life is even more Spartan than I had imagined; although they claim anti-Semitism doesn't exist . . . it does; likewise with class distinction; I did not realize that drinking was such a problem, especially with young people."

Expectations also played a crucial part in assessing the overall impact of the trip, as in the response to the question seeking explanations for any attitude change that might have occurred: "Soviet life seems to be freer than I had imagined [a self-employed sales representative from Great Neck, New York, wrote]. . . . People were even warmer and friendlier than I had thought they would be. . . . [They] looked neat, well groomed and nicely dressed. . . ." On the other hand, he confessed to greatly underestimating "the extent of anti-Semitism. . . ."

Several of the CEC participants were aware of the restraints on these exchanges. A high school teacher wrote, "Visitors to the USSR are bound by Intourist [the official tourist agency] regulations over every aspect of the tourist's necessities—accommodations, food, etc. Visitors are also circumscribed . . . to travel outside of designated areas. . . . Everything is controlled by the government." Another high school teacher wrote, "These contacts [at organized events such as seminars, lectures] were much less fruitful for they were 'planned' and were more formal and official, less frank and less an exchange of ideas." On the other hand, he found (on other occasions) Soviet people's attitude toward their government "much more critical than expected," whereas the physical aspects of Soviet cities were "less drab than expected." A retired businessman from Elmira, New York, thought that "personal contact with Russians at organized events was very limited and non-productive." Even in private, informal talks "discussions were limited by language barriers, in most cases, and therefore confined to generalities and expressions of friendship. . . ." Notwithstanding these difficulties, his "impressions represented a change for the better, largely because our press and official propaganda apparently deliberately misrepresents almost all aspects of Soviet life."

Yet another high school teacher observed, "The [Soviet] people at the lectures were up on the platform handing out the official line. . . . No one was allowed to express a difference of opinion in public." A college senior wrote of those met at the organized events, "Very well indoctrinated by the Party— always evaded questions, said what they were expected to say. . . ." In more spontaneous encounters, another respondent wrote: "immediate agreement was found" that "Stalin and Khrushchev were bad" as was the suppression of the Hungarian Revolution of 1956 while "the Beatles were good." A professor of mathematics "was surprised at the political apathy and/or essential agreement with the government." He was also "surprised to find petty dishonesty when cab drivers and chauffeurs . . . asked for . . . payment in dollars. . . ."

A "planning analyst" from Washington, D.C., found that a meeting of minds [with Soviet people] was only achieved on matters such as "peace and friendship and [other] bland generalities." He was also among those who found far more anti-Semitism and deeper class and status cleavages than expected. His concluding comment was that the trip was an "interesting, fascinating experience but [the Soviet Union] a strikingly depressing place to live for a person interested in ideas or politics."

Positive impressions dominated the observations of a research chemist from Los Angeles: "People are happy. They have more money and a higher standard of living than I had been led to believe. They . . . seem in complete accord with the government . . . its program and policies." He also found them "very relaxed. . . . [They] laughed and enjoyed themselves easier than Americans. . . . Everything seemed very clean and neat in the cities. . . ." A secretary from Nebraska came to the conclusion "that a system which has managed to provide freedom from want and from fear of illness may actually provide [create?] a different kind of people . . . who have the capacity to make a better world." These feelings were not shared by a mathematics professor from Cleveland, Ohio, who during his visit "had the persistent feeling that anything could go irreparably wrong anytime . . . and [that] people seem[ed] poorer than in Mexico . . . counting the value of freedom and the value of time (waiting time)." His "single most memorable experience" was the refusal to be served in a restaurant that was not full because "I was a foreigner." A "merchant" from Detroit listed his most memorable experience as the witnessing of "two policemen beating up a teenager because he was singing at the railroad station." Other memorable experiences reported included "being photographed by the secret police" and getting things stolen from the dormitory and hotel rooms where visitors stayed.

Not all mathematicians were better informed or more sober in their judgments and conclusions. One (who did not disclose either his residence or place of birth) believed that Soviet standards of living were "about the same as the

American." Of the Soviet people, he wrote, "They are rugged, healthy, pioneering, outgoing and friendly, talented, generous and proud. I consider them very much like us." He also believed that they were healthier than the French ("but otherwise very European") and more "independent than in Mexico." Another mathematician offered this interpretation of the attitude and behavior of Soviet people: "A patient people—willing to live under decreased freedom of movement and low [living] standard so future generations can benefit."

A professor of mathematics from Cincinnati, Ohio, also had offered a sanguine assessment of Soviet people and society: "They are happy, confident and proud and with good reason. Public transportation is excellent, goods are adequate and plentiful, and housing, though cramped, is cheap. . . . This is obviously a country on the move."

A mathematician from Ossining, New York, wrote: "people I met seem very honest and forthright similar to what you might expect from a Midwestern rural community." A mathematician from Rhode Island took an upbeat, yet curiously mixed position summing up his impressions: "Beautiful country, extremely nice, polite and friendly people, their attitude seems relaxed; class structure is not apparent. . . . Their morals seem to be very strict. The standard of living . . . is much lower than I would expect. The inefficiency of the bureaucratic system is amazing."

Sometimes the open-ended responses comments contradicted the others. Thus, the same mathematician who chose the most negative characterization of the Soviet Union (i.e., "a totalitarian society that remains in many ways underdeveloped and intolerant of any political, philosophical or intellectual dissent and diversity") also wrote that "the people surprised me; I often thought if I didn't know where I was I would never have guessed that I was in Russia. The people seemed happy and enjoying life. . . . There didn't seem to be any people following or watching others—I guess I expected to be in some sort of police state."

Among the notable misperceptions of American society on the part of Soviet citizens reported by the visitors was disbelief that blacks could own cars and that most Americans own private automobiles. Many also reported profound and genuine incomprehension of a pluralistic, open society where the government did not control everything and having a passport was a commonplace experience.

TAKEN-FOR-GRANTED DURABILITY

None of these visitors had the slightest idea, premonition, or experience leading them to question the durability of the Soviet system and the Soviet empire (not that the experts on such matters did so at that time). Whether they perceived the Soviet system as repressive or progressive, its people impoverished or well provided for, none could foresee that a quarter-century later the system would unravel and abruptly collapse. No conversations or experiences were reported that called into question or cast the slightest doubt on the overall stability and persistence of the Soviet system.

More surprisingly, no reference was made by the visitors to any discussion they might have had with Soviet people about the 1956 revelations of Khrushchev; likewise little was said about the Soviet dissidents of the period, Solzhenitsyn included. None of the visitors was in a position to detect the profound alienation of a critical mass of Soviet citizens that, in conjunction with the eroding political will and self-confidence of the rulers, would bring down the system in the early 1990s.

In the final analysis, American attitudes—popular or official—played little part in the changes percolating within Soviet society during the 1960s, 1970s, and 1980s. The exposure of Soviet citizens to American visitors, however limited in scope, might have made a small contribution to altering warped and stifled views of the world outside the Soviet Union, and especially of its alleged arch-enemy, the United States; these encounters helped to make a small number of Soviet citizens more aware of options and possibilities, fraying the mental-ideological straitjacket the regime imposed on its people.

Chapter Seventeen

Alexander Yakovlev

Alexander Yakovlev's name is largely unknown to the American public, although he was a major political figure during perestroika, a key advisor to Gorbachev, and a high-ranking official in the Soviet political hierarchy for most of his adult life.

Born in 1923, Yakovlev came from a poor peasant family; his father had four years of education and was the first chairman of the local collective farm. His mother was an illiterate, "downtrodden peasant woman and a religious believer to the end of her days." Yakovlev became a Party member in 1943. He worked in the Central Committee of the Party between 1953 and 1973 in positions connected with ideology and propaganda and became head of the Party's propaganda department in 1969. He was ambassador to Canada from 1973 to 1983; in 1983 he was appointed director of the Institute of International Economy and Relations. Under Gorbachev he was restored in 1985 to his position as head of the Party's propaganda department, and in 1986 he became secretary of the Central Committee in charge of ideological matters. In 1987 he was appointed to the Politburo.

Prior to *A Century of Violence in Russia* (2002), Yakovlev had published another important book in English, *The Fate of Marxism in Russia* (1993), a pathbreaking study that examines the link between Marxism and the political practices and institutions of the Soviet Union and other "actually existing" communist systems.

A Century of Violence in Soviet Russia provides a remarkable range and amount of information despite its compactness, enumerating and illuminating the major phases, trends, and events associated with the repressive policies of the Soviet system. Like the earlier, more theoretical work, it amounts to an exploration and summation of what went wrong with what used to be called, charitably, "the Soviet experiment." But unlike the other volume, *A Century of Violence* focuses on specific institutional and moral failures and the human costs the system exacted; it identifies the groups and strata of the population that suffered most. As such, it may be compared to *The Black Book of Communism*,[1] which attempted to document and examine the crimes not only of the Soviet Union but of all other existing or extinct communist states. There are, however, important differences. None of the contributors to *The Black Book* were ever communist officials, let alone high-ranking ones, and, due to its scope, *The Black Book* could not be as detailed and thorough as the work here introduced.

Readers accustomed to dispassionate, scholarly analyses of political phenomena and traumatic historical events should be warned: this is not a detached, bland discussion wrapped in neutral social scientific terminology—it is an emotionally charged expression of deeply felt pain and moral indignation that accumulated during a lifetime of witnessing the suffering, misery, and mendaciousness inflicted by the Soviet system. Doubtless Yakovlev's personal pain was intensified, even in retrospect, by the fact that he himself devoted much of his life to that system.

There are many critiques of communist systems by authors of different backgrounds and nationalities; what makes this volume unusual is the biography and stature of its author. It is hard to think of any other communist official of comparable rank and distinction who so explicitly, sweepingly, and powerfully repudiated the system he was a part of, who was as much an insider and a product of the system as Alexander Yakovlev. Only Milovan Djilas occupies a comparable position: he was similarly highly placed (in the Yugoslav communist ruling elite) and his indictment of Soviet-style communism is notable for its depth and scope.[2] Trotsky, too, renounced the Soviet regime in its Stalinist incarnation, but he remained a Marxist and even a Leninist, and his critiques of the Soviet system are less far-reaching than Yakovlev's. Unlike other insider critics of communist systems, Yakovlev did not defect, nor was he exiled. He still lives in Russia, devoting much of his life since the collapse of the Soviet system to the fate of its victims in his capacity as head of the Commission on the Rehabilitation of Victims of Political Repression.

While for most readers Yakovlev's insider position and perspective will immeasurably add to the authenticity of this book, there may be some for whom the intensity of his disillusionment and moral passion may cast doubt on the credibility of his message. They are likely to be the same people for whom the demise of the Soviet Union has had the unhappy result of rendering the United States the only superpower. They are even more likely to be disturbed by Yakovlev's unqualified rejection of Marxism and not just the Soviet system. In their eyes it is a grave transgression to link Marxist theory to the policies and practices of a communist system such as the Soviet Union used to be. Yakovlev has no doubt of such a linkage, as he also made clear in his earlier book.

Yakovlev's critiques of the Soviet system will not be easy to discredit. He is neither a pampered Western intellectual in search of a cause nor a defector who can be accused of having been bought off by Western lucre. It will be interesting to see the response of those who find it hard to stomach his conviction that Marxism, too, bears significant responsibility for the human toll exacted by communist systems.

Yakovlev ranks as a major historical figure on several grounds. In the first place, he made crucial contributions to the political changes associated with Gorbachev, to the liberalization of the Soviet system that hastened its end. He was also a key contributor to the intellectual and spiritual ferment that led to perestroika and glasnost, promoting the quiet and gradual evolution that preceded Gorbachev's reforms and providing their intellectual foundations. Known as "the father of glasnost," he belonged to the small group of Party intellectuals who (as another close associate of Gorbachev, Anatoly Chernyaev, puts it) "were in many ways the ambassadors to Gorbachev of a larger liberal intelligentsia, one whose humanist, 'Westernizing' philosophical and practical orientation had been developing for over two decades. . . . [They were] collectively described as 'Children of the 20th Congress,' reformist thinkers who kept alive the unfulfilled hopes of Khrushchev's 'thaw' for broader liberalization of Soviet society and integration with the international community."[3] Yakovlev was also among those who tried to keep Gorbachev on a steady course of reform and to bolster his liberal-democratic policies against the resistance of the nomenklatura and his own fluctuating political impulses.

Yakovlev has been unique among former Soviet officials and ideologues in confronting the relationship between Marxism and the debilitating flaws of the Soviet system. *The Fate of Marxism in Russia* is the major expression of that effort in English, but the reader will find references to the same theme in this volume.

Among his other contributions, Yakovlev has devoted a great deal of his time since the early 1990s to documenting and rehabilitating the victims of Soviet communism and has remained a voice of critical conscience in the postcommunist period. In the course of these activities he has acquired many detractors at both ends of the political spectrum. In recent years he has been among the most outspoken critics of the many serious deformations of

Russian public life and politics associated with old-style communism, right-wing nationalism, and anti-Semitism. He understands keenly the deep roots of the historical pathologies that the Soviet system represented and that made the transition to a political democracy and civil society difficult:

> The land of Rus accepted Christianity from Constantinople in A.D. 988. Characteristics of Byzantine rule of that era—baseness, cowardliness, venality, treachery, overcentralization, apotheosis of the ruler's personality—dominate in Russia's social and political life to this day. In the twelfth century the various fragmented Russian principalities . . . were conquered by the Mongols. Asian traditions and customs, with their disregard for the individual and for human rights and their cult of might, violence, despotic power, and lawlessness became part of the Russian people's way of life.
>
> The tragedy of Russia lay first and foremost in this: that for a thousand years it was ruled by men and not by laws. . . . They ruled ineptly, bloodily. The people existed for the government, not the government for the people. Russia avoided classical slavery. But it has not yet emerged from feudalism; it is still enslaved by an official imperial ideology, the essence of which is that the state is everything and the individual nothing.

These circumstances presumably also help account for what Yakovlev does not hesitate to call the "slave psychology" of the Russian people, which remains a major obstacle to the genuine liberalization of the society and its economic reconstruction. Thus Yakovlev connects both the pre-Soviet and Soviet past and the postcommunist present, and his reflections on recent developments are pessimistic.

A Century of Violence is an impassioned, bitter, and emotional indictment of the Soviet system from its earliest days and a methodical and detailed inventory of its misdeeds. Yakovlev has no illusions about the "purity" of the early Soviet goals and policies allegedly promoted by Lenin or, for that matter, about the personality of Lenin, whom he regards as having been as evil and unscrupulous as Stalin. ("Stalin did not think up anything that was not there under Lenin: executions, hostage taking, concentration camps, and all the rest.") This is a major departure from the conventional wisdom that has long prevailed among Western academic specialists, who detect significant discontinuities between the policies and personalities of these two figures.

A survey, in effect, of the worst repressions of Soviet history from Lenin to perestroika, *A Century of Violence* contains a wealth of information, including case histories of victimization, based on both Yakovlev's personal experience and his privileged access to archival sources. Yakovlev systematically probes the policies and individuals behind these repressions, whose victims included children and adolescents, Mensheviks, Social Revolutionaries, Anarchists, and other socialists (early allies of the Bolsheviks), the peasants, the intelligentsia, the clergy, the nationalities and Jews, former prisoners of war (in World War II), and civilians taken to Germany as forced laborers. Yakovlev holds the Soviet system responsible for the deaths of at least sixty million Soviet citizens. He is particularly strong in his coverage of the repression of the intelligentsia, touching on many famous groups and individuals, including those silenced, exiled, or imprisoned in the 1920s; the "Trotskyist terrorist" writers in Leningrad in 1937; Pasternak, Daniel, Sinyavsky, Brodsky, and, later, Solzhenitsyn.

Another strength of the volume is its treatment of the ethnic-national policies and repressions directed at the Ukrainians, Volga Germans, Kalmyks, Crimean Tatars, Ingush, and others and its detailed discussion—particularly relevant today—of the mistreatment of the Chechens.

While many of the major events and policies discussed in this volume are known, at least in their general outlines, many others are likely to be unfamiliar, even to specialists. As early as 1918, for instance, there was labor unrest in Motovilikha, a village in Perm province, where "the workers demanded a stop to special food privileges for Soviet government and Party workers, an end to summary executions, guarantees of freedom of speech and assembly." Yakovlev also brings to light Lenin's predilection for hostage taking as a means of consolidating the system; the mistreatment of close to half a million Soviet prisoners of war returned after the Soviet-Finnish war; the communications between Romain Rolland (the pro-Soviet French writer) and Stalin about the punishment of children and adolescents; Meyerhold's complaint to Molotov about his treatment in prison; the numerous intrigues and denunciations among various writers and artists; the persecution of theater companies and moviemakers in the 1930s; the fate of the Korean minority; the huge number of Soviet workers severely punished simply for being late for work; the alleged organizations of Jewish bourgeois nationalists in the Stalin Works in Moscow and at the Kuznetsk metallurgical complex; the preparations to deport Jews at the time of the "doctors' plot" before Stalin's death; and the suppression of the 1962 food riots in Novocherkassk. Yakovlev also demolishes the myth, widespread in the West, of Yuri Andropov's liberal credentials. It may also surprise some readers that Yakovlev regards the early twentieth century as the brightest, most promising era of Russian history.

Yakovlev's revelations and graphic descriptions of the many misdeeds of the system are only one noteworthy aspect of this book. Another is what we learn about the transformation of his own beliefs and attitudes, how and why he became profoundly critical of the system he helped legitimize and keep in power for decades.

The case of Yakovlev illuminates the process of political disillusionment in our times. It raises the intriguing question of what it takes to reject a political system and its legitimizing ideas for a man raised in, fully committed to, and well rewarded by it, a high-ranking member of the political elite who spent much of his life in the rarefied heights of the nomenklatura. Even more significant and unusual is that this sweeping, unconditional rejection of the system comes from a man with a long and deep involvement with official doctrine, with ideology, and with the task of convincing the population of the virtues and legitimacy of the system. In an interview in 1994 he linked his disaffection precisely to his involvement with ideology: "The main thing that changed my worldview was the fact that my ideology was my business. . . . I took the work seriously. And gradually, step by step, more and more often, it nauseated me. Then I went back again to the primary sources. . . . When you get older faith alone is not enough, you want to look more deeply. And as soon as you begin to analyze what you believe it begins to crack."[4]

Three sets of experiences played a major role in the undermining of Yakovlev's beliefs and commitment to the system. The first was acquired during World War II, in which he served and sustained serious injuries, the second was Khrushchev's historic revelations during the Twentieth Party Congress in 1956, and the third was his demotion in 1972 as the result of an article he wrote criticizing Russian nationalism and anti-Semitism.

His doubts and disillusionment during World War II were stimulated by the inhumane treatment of former Soviet POWs: "A serviceman taken prisoner was regarded as having committed a premeditated crime. . . . Soldiers and commanding officers who had broken out of encirclement were treated as potential traitors and spies. . . . When, at the beginning of 1942, a group of us young officers arrived at the Volkhov front . . . we saw this practice take place under frontline conditions." Soviet soldiers were supposed to fight to the death regardless of the circumstances. There was also apprehension on the part of the authorities that exposure to life outside the Soviet Union, even for prisoners of war or slave laborers, might have implanted attitudes that would erode unquestioning loyalty to the system. Sometimes former Red Army officers who had been liberated from prison camps or had broken out of encirclement were assigned to "assault battalions," which "were employed in situations where it was almost impossible to stay alive." It is hardly surprising that such experiences gradually undermined Yakovlev's political faith; what is more surprising is that they did not have a similar impact on many others and did not impair their capacity to work. for the regime.

Another particularly disturbing experience was Yakovlev's witnessing the return of Soviet POWs from Germany:

> I remember the Vspolye train station in Yaroslavl a year after the war, the rumor that a train would be passing through with some of our soldiers . . . from German prisoner of war camps. I was still on crutches, but I went with the others . . . to watch. Railway cars, small windows with iron bars; thin, pale, bewildered faces at the windows. And on the platform, women weeping and wailing . . . running back and forth between the cars looking for their husbands, brothers, sweethearts. . . .
>
> The people on the platform . . . couldn't understand why these boys from the Nazi camps were being transported like criminals to the Urals and Siberia. I remember the tortured faces, the total incomprehension, theirs and mine.

The second major blow to Yakovlev's loyalties and beliefs (as to those of many others of his generation) was Khrushchev's famous speech at the Twentieth Party Congress in February 1956. Yakovlev was present and what he heard, he says, "plunged me into the deepest dejection, if not despair. Everything seemed unreal, even that I was sitting there in the Kremlin hearing words that were destroying everything I had lived by, shattering the past, rending the soul. Everything crumbled, never to be made whole again." Nevertheless, Yakovlev remained a highly placed functionary for decades to come, leading what must have been a difficult inner life:

> I had been honest in my previous faith, and I was equally honest in rejecting it. I came to detest Stalin, . . . who had deceived me so cruelly and trampled on my romantic dreams. From then on I devoted myself to searching out a way to put an end to this inhuman system. . . . All this took the form of hope, not action. . . .
>
> I lived a double life of agonizing dissimulation. I conformed, I pretended, trying all the while not to lose my bearings and disgrace myself. No longer interested in working for the Central Committee, I looked for an out and found one. . . . I sensed a need to reeducate myself, to reread everything I'd read before, go back to original sources—Marx, Engels, Lenin, the German philosophers, the French socialists, the British economists, all the fountainheads of my outlook on the world.

Even before the Twentieth Congress, Khrushchev made public statements disclosing the rampant mismanagement of the economy; these Yakovlev "jotted down" and found distressing. To wit:

> We've been squandering the accumulated capital of the people's trust in the Party. We can't go on endlessly exploiting the people's trust. . . .
>
> We've become like priests and preachers: we promise a kingdom in heaven, but in the here and now there are no potatoes. Only our long suffering Russian people would put up with something like that. . . . We are not priests, we are Communists, and we must give them this happiness here on earth.
>
> When I was a worker, there was no socialism, but there were potatoes, and now we have built socialism and there are no potatoes.

The third set of experiences that helped change his worldview was set in motion in 1968 in Prague, where he was sent to oversee Soviet journalists covering the Soviet invasion. At the time he was deputy head of the propaganda department of the CPSU Central Committee, and this was a vital assignment. Officially the dispatch of troops was described as friendly assistance, but Yakovlev was shocked by what he found. "I saw gallows with effigies of Soviet soldiers hanging there. . . . People were shouting 'Fascists, Fascists.'" Yakovlev has summed up the experience as "an important school for me. . . . It had a great sobering effect."5

As to the article that led to his demotion as head of the Party's propaganda department (and to his exile to Canada as ambassador), he recalls, "No sooner had I written an article in 1972 on the dangers of chauvinism, nationalism, and anti-Semitism in the USSR — hung out the dirty laundry, as it were — than I was removed from all Party work. Moreover, I remain labeled to this day as a 'Russophobe' and a leader of 'kike-masons' and supplied with . . . different surnames Epshtein, Yankelevich, Yakobson." In other words, Yakovlev continues to pay a price for defying both the elements in the old Soviet hierarchy and the anti-Semitic groups and attitudes that have resurfaced over the past decade.

In Yakovlev's summation, the most serious damage (and the hardest to repair) has been to what Trotsky called the "human raw material." Political reform, institutional change, free elections, and new laws are welcome and essential, but they will not create a stable, democratic, and decent society unless the basic attitudes and values of the people change, or those of a critical number of people change. Yakovlev writes, "The Bolshevik regime is guilty not only of the deaths of millions of people and the tragic consequences for their families, not only of creating an atmosphere of total fear and lies, but of a crime against conscience, of producing its notorious 'new historic community of people' distorted by malice, doublethink, suspiciousness, and pretense. Lenin and Stalin and their henchmen . . . destroyed the nation's gene pool . . . undermining the potential for the flowering of science and culture."

This is indispensable reading for anybody who wants to grasp the nature of the Soviet system, the full range of its crimes against its people, the sources of its collapse, and the grave problems it left behind.

NOTES

1. Stephane Courtois et al., *The Black Book of Communism: Crimes, Terror, Repression* (Cambridge, Mass.: Harvard University Press, 1999).

2. Most notable are Djilas's *The New Class* (New York: Praeger, 1957) and his *Conversations with Stalin* (New York: Harcourt, Brace & World, 1962).

3. Anatoly S. Chernyaev, *My Six Years with Gorbachev* (University Park: Pennsylvania State University Press, 2000), xvii, xv–xvi.

4. Quoted in Robert V. Daniels, "Overthrowing Utopianism" [review of Yakovlev's *The Fate of Marxism in Russia*], *New Leader*, 14–18 February 1994, 17.

5. Jonathan Steele, *Eternal Russia: Yeltsin, Gorbachev and the Mirage of Democracy* (Cambridge, Mass.: Harvard University Press, 1994), 175. In a conversation I had with Yakovlev in 1998 in Washington, D.C., he confirmed that his visit to Prague had made "a terrible impression" on him; he asked Soviet tank drivers why they were there, and they had no idea.

Chapter Eighteen

Violence of Higher Purpose

Communist systems existed in areas of diverse historical and cultural traditions inhabited by different ethnic groups. As time went by, these systems became more differentiated in their policies, including the degree of repression they engaged in. These systems ranged in size and population from Albania to China, in longevity from the Soviet Union (seventy-four years) to Sandinista Nicaragua (ten years), in economic development and level of urbanization from Czechoslovakia and East Germany to Ethiopia and Angola. Many of these systems could also be described—at least in their origins—as "revolutionary."[1] Forrest Colburn wrote:

> What is strikingly similar about the twenty-two cases of contemporary revolutions . . . is not their structural origins, but the common values and shared behavior of their leaders. . . . [S]uccessful revolutionaries, once in control . . . proved to have had remarkably similar ideas about how to remake their societies. . . . The shared intellectual culture of contemporary revolutions centered on a commitment to "socialism."[2]

Communist political violence ebbed and flowed, surged and diminished over time. There are identifiable high points (as, for example, the 1930s in the Soviet Union and the 1960s in China) and long periods of routine, less life-threatening policies of repression. But the common ideological foundations of communist systems shaped their policies of repression, which centered on the crucial—theoretical as well as practical—distinction between supporters and opponents. Igal Halfin noted, "Far from dispensing with the division of human souls into good and evil, Communism endowed this tradition with the status of a thoroughly scientific observation. The Communist conceptual architectonics was full of black-and-white oppositions: proletariat versus bourgeoisie, revolution versus counterrevolution, progress versus reaction. . . ."[3]

Another widely shared philosophical premise was that "the leaders of the Communist Party, unfettered by a 'bourgeois' legal code or a capricious judicial system, were fully entitled to punish enemies of the state. They were empowered to do so because of their privileged relationship to historical laws."[4]

The common heritage of the Marxist-Leninist worldview also enabled the rulers and planners of repression to think in abstract, impersonal categories and overlook the specific, empirical consequences of their policies for particular groups and individuals. Simon Leys observed (in the Chinese context): "[T]he Communists always believed that mankind mattered more than man. In the eyes of the party leaders individual lives were merely a raw material in abundant supply—cheap, disposable and easily replaceable. Therefore . . . they came to consider that the exercise of terror was synonymous with the exercise of power. . . ."[5]

The political police forces (or "state security" organs) communist states developed to perform these tasks were larger, more powerful, and more highly differentiated than regular police forces charged with ordinary crime control and prevention. They had similar organizational structures because the first communist state, the Soviet Union, was the model for such forces and provided assistance in establishing them. Police and military officers from various communist states attended Soviet training schools; Soviet advisors assisted their East European counterparts in the preparation of the post–World War II show trials. The East German state security arm (the Stasi) came to play a prominent role in third-world communist systems. As a former high-ranking Vietnamese communist functionary wrote, "the state of our security forces owes a lot to the East German Stasi and the Soviet KGB. These two organizations trained our cadres in various specialized subjects and exchanged experience about methods of detection and investigation. . . . [T]he Cong [the Vietnamese political police] became just as overmanned as the armed forces."[6]

All communist penal systems made a sharp distinction between political and nonpolitical crimes and criminals. In every one of them the latter were treated better and were often given, informally, power over the political prisoners. The authorities considered political criminals a much greater threat than ordinary criminals, who were not accused of calling into question the system or of trying to undermine it. Sometimes those classified as political criminals were also accused of common, nonpolitical crimes, including, in the Soviet case, "hooliganism." The purpose of such accusations was either to obscure the political origins of the persecution of particular individuals (especially if they were known in the West) or to complete their moral discreditation.

In at least four communist states—the Soviet Union, Cuba, China, and Romania—those accused of political crimes were sometimes simultaneously classified as suffering from some type of mental illness and were detained in special psychiatric institutions. The most widely practiced and best known was the Soviet detention of outspoken dissidents in psychiatric hospitals,[7] but in China, too, according to recent reports, there is "a secretive system of psychiatric hospitals around the country that are affiliated with local public security bureaus [the Chinese political police]. . . ." In one instance, a Chinese dissident was held for seven years in such a hospital for unfurling a protest banner in Tiananmen Square in 1992.[8] These spurious attributions of mental illness were probably made for two reasons. One was to make the system appear more humane and less punitive; the other, more sinister and totalitarian in its implications, was the belief that questioning and criticizing the system *itself* amounted to a kind of mental disease.

It is among the remarkable paradoxes of history that communist systems claimed the lives of vast numbers of their citizens in spite of the ideologically derived expectation that they would be far less repressive than both their historical predecessors and other contemporary noncommunist societies. This expectation rested on the belief that communist governments would enjoy unparalleled popular support and legitimacy, that they would be veritable embodiments of consensus and harmony and therefore would have little need to resort to force in dealing with their citizens. As Engels wrote (and as Lenin quoted approvingly):

> Society, thus far based upon class antagonism, had need of the state . . . for the purpose of forcibly keeping the exploited classes in the condition of oppression. . . . [But] when at last it [the state] becomes the real representative of the whole of society, it renders itself unnecessary. As soon as there is no longer any social class to be held in subjection . . . nothing more remains to be repressed, and a special force, the state is no longer necessary. The first act by virtue of which the state really constitutes itself the representative of the whole of society—the taking possession of the means of production in the name of society this is at the same time, its last independent act as a state. State interference in social relations becomes, in one domain after another, superfluous and then withers away of itself. . . .[9]

This presumption of unfolding social harmony was at the heart of the optimistic assessments of the future of the state as an agency of coercion; the same presumption also served as the theoretical basis for establishing a one-party system that would be adequate to represent all interests in a society that had banished major divisions and conflicts. In more recent times, even in communist Ethiopia, which rapidly embraced overt terror, "the Revolution began with a famous slogan and song: Without blood, without blood. . . ."[10]

Admittedly, the use of force was not expected to disappear at once but gradually—hence the expression, "the withering away of the state." This anticipation was predicated on the elimination of social contradictions, "antagonisms" associated with the conflict-ridden, exploitative class societies of the past; in the new socialist system there was going to be little conflict requiring massive state regulation and little discontent to be repressed (and this applied not only to political conflicts but also to antisocial or criminal behavior, which was expected to disappear since its root causes, exploitation and inequality, were to be eliminated).

The remaining opponents of the new society were expected to be a mere handful—a notion rooted in Marx's mistaken idea that a fundamental polarization of capitalist societies was destined to take place, leading to a huge increase in the size of the exploited masses and a decline in the number of the exploiters. After the revolution the few former exploiters that remained were to be annihilated as a class (though in practice, many of them were annihilated as individuals as well) and deprived of the means to cause trouble for the new government. In other words, the new system was supposed to rest on such overwhelming popular support that it would require little coercion to maintain itself. Lenin wrote:

> What class must the proletariat suppress? Naturally only [!] the exploiting class, i.e., the bourgeoisie. The toilers need a state only to suppress the resistance of the exploiters. . . . [Whereas] the exploiting classes need political rule in order to maintain exploitation . . . [t]he exploited classes need political rule in order completely to abolish all exploitation, i.e., in the interests of the vast majority of the people, and against the insignificant minority consisting of the modern slaveowners—the landlords and capitalists.

Lenin (before the October Revolution) was also exceedingly and unrealistically optimistic about the prospects for the elimination of bureaucracy (the mainstay of coercion and organized political violence in this century): "since the majority of the people *itself* suppresses its oppressors a 'special force' for suppression is *no longer necessary*." He also wrote that the

> suppression of the minority of exploiters by the majority of wage slaves *of yesterday* is comparatively so easy, simple and natural a task that it will entail far less bloodshed than the suppression of the risings of slaves, serfs or wage slaves and it will cost mankind far less. . . . The exploiters are naturally unable

to suppress the people without a highly complex machine for performing this task: but the *people* can suppress the exploiters even with a very simple "machine," almost without a machine, without a special apparatus. . . .[11]

These were extraordinarily groundless beliefs and anticipations, and Lenin himself rapidly abandoned them after his seizure of power. Thus, for example, in 1922 he demanded the arrest and execution of a "very large number" of residents of the small town of Shuya because they had opposed the confiscation of consecrated articles from local churches. Lenin wrote, "Now it is the time to teach these people such a lesson that for decades to come they will not dare to even think of such opposition."[12]

Indeed, it quickly became apparent that none of the predictions cited above were correct: conditions in the Soviet Union (and in the other communist states to emerge later) were far from conducive to the shrinking of bureaucracy and the restrained use of coercion by the party-state. On the contrary, communist states created coercive agencies of unprecedented size and complexity, agencies that came to be charged not merely with tracking down and punishing those suspected of political unreliability (manifest, potential, or imaginary), but also with overseeing vast construction projects utilizing the labor of those arrested.

The major reason for these developments was that the popular support that had been anticipated quickly evaporated—or, arguably, never existed; the programs and policies of the Soviet Communist Party (and those of most other communist states) did not elicit the wholehearted support of the majority. In fact, these policies—for example the collectivization of agriculture—stimulated the growth of opposition. At every step of the way people had to be pushed, prodded, and coerced along the path of rapid, state-controlled industrialization and political regimentation.

Secondly, communist governments placed a high premium on total conformity, which could not be achieved by persuasion but only by intimidation. The political culture of the party was permeated by intolerance and dogmatism; means were unflinchingly subordinated to ends that could not be questioned.

By the early 1930s the resistance to collectivization and the purges (in the USSR) called for a new justification of intensified repression already institutionalized, on a smaller scale, under Lenin. The new theory of political conflict promulgated by Stalin claimed that it was the very successes of socialism that called forth the vicious resistance of the enemy (sometimes called the cornered enemy). This resistance called for stern measures, even if it was only the resistance of a determined and vicious minority. Stalin said:

> We must smash and throw out the rotten theory that with each forward movement we make, the class struggle will die down more and more, that in proportion to our successes the class enemy will become more and more domesticated.
>
> This is not only a rotten theory but a dangerous theory, for it lulls our people to sleep, leads them into a trap and makes it possible for the class enemy to rally for the struggle against Soviet power.
>
> On the contrary, the more we move forward, the more success we have, then the more wrathful become the remnants of the beaten exploiter classes.... [T]he more mischief they do the Soviet state, the more they grasp the most desperate means of struggle as the last resort of the doomed.[13]

This became the official justification of the waves of terror unleashed during the 1930s.

The isolation of the Soviet Union contributed to its besieged mentality: it was plausible to claim, as Soviet leaders repeatedly did, that internal enemies were conspiring with those abroad. Alleged conspiracies were integral parts of the widely publicized show trials and essential for justifying the mass terror. Conspiracy themes were also incorporated into routine accusations against the anonymous victims of the terror. "Who recruited you?" was a standard question in countless interrogations. The "organs of the state security" (Cheka, NKVD, GPU, MVD, KGB, etc.) were in effect counterconspiracies seeking to uncover and smash those of the enemy. In all this, there was an element of psychological projection: "totalitarian regimes see other regimes [and one may add, groups and individuals as well] as being as ruthless, duplicitous as themselves, and they act accordingly...."[14]

It is important to note that although the repression inflicted by communist states had not been anticipated in their theoretical blueprints, these policies nonetheless had deep and arguably idealistic roots: they were by-products of the urgent desire to reshape societies (and human beings) and to remove all obstacles from, and opposition to, this endeavor. As Solzhenitsyn wrote:

> To do evil a human being must first of all believe that what he is doing is good. ... The imagination and the spiritual strength of Shakespeare's evildoers stopped short at a dozen corpses. Because they had no *ideology*.
>
> Ideology—that is what gives evildoing its long-sought justification and gives the evildoer the necessary steadfastness and determination. That is the social theory which helps to make his acts seem good instead of bad in his own and other's eyes....
>
> That is how the agents of the Inquisition fortified their wills: by invoking Christianity; the conquerors of foreign lands by extolling the grandeur of their Motherland; the colonizers by civilization, the Nazis, by race; and the Jacobins (early and late) by equality, brotherhood and the happiness of future generations.[15]

More recently, Alexander Yakovlev, former member of the highest Soviet political elite (in charge of ideology and propaganda under Gorbachev), came to the conclusion that the roots of Soviet political violence could be discerned in the Marxist-Leninist ideological legacy and inspiration: "Fundamentally, the responsibility for the genocide . . . that took place in Russia and the entire Soviet Union rests on the ideology of Bolshevism."[16] He did not believe that the mass killings could be ascribed to a siege mentality, the backwardness of Russia, or Stalin's personality. He wrote:

> [B]elief in the inevitability of the coming Communist world served to justify the numerous and senseless victims of the class struggle. . . .
>
> The idea that one should not fear creating victims in the course of serving the cause of progress, that the revolutionary spirit of the proletarian masses must be preserved at any cost is very characteristic of Marx. . . .
>
> Moral criteria are simply not appropriate under the conditions of a revolutionary coup d'etat; they are "revoked" by the brutality and directness of class warfare. . . . This special "class" morality . . . leads to indulgence of any actions. . . . Its justification comes from the special vision of the historical path of development, its final goals for the full renaissance of humanity.

He repeatedly stressed the idealistic underpinnings of communist political violence:

> Dostoevsky's Grand Inquisitor speaks of love for humanity. But complete contempt for an actual individual flows from this love. . . .
>
> . . . [A]ll of this was committed under the guise of concern about humankind, but with complete disregard for the specific individual. Terror is the way of remaking human material in the name of the future. . . .
>
> Marx finally shed the discussion about humanity and love. . . . He no longer spoke of moral justice. . . . All this grew into the conviction that everything that corresponded to the interests of the revolution and communism was moral. That is the morality with which hostages were executed . . . concentration camps were built, and entire peoples forcibly relocated. . . .
>
> Can everything be justified in the name of progress? And is it really progress? What gives one group of people the right to sentence to death civil society, or popular custom centuries in the making?[17]

Yakovlev's reflections reaffirm the distinctive feature of communist political violence: its initial idealistic origin and intent—that is to say, it was *violence with a higher purpose*. By contrast, much historic violence, including recent outbreaks of ethnic hostility, have little or no idealistic justification. The Nazis, the Turks, the Hutus, the Serbs, and others (engaged respectively in slaughtering Jews, Armenians, Tutsis, and Albanians) had no interest in "remaking human material in the name of the future"; they just wished to get rid of those belonging to groups considered different, threatening, competing, or inferior, although sometimes even these types of violence were colored by the conviction that a better world would be created after the inferior or poisonous group was removed. Most intergroup (ethnic) violence is based on a visceral, taken-for-granted group hostility aggravated by competition for important and scarce resources, usually land. In Rwanda, Bosnia, Kosovo, the Sudan, Cyprus, Sri Lanka, and Israel (and Palestine), groups have sought greater control over their lives while other groups have sought to prevent them from achieving this goal. Schemes for improving human nature, or a desire for major social transformation and utopian social arrangements, had played a negligible part in these conflicts and massacres.

Communist political violence flowed from a utopian vision of the future, from the great goals pursued, and from the intolerance the service of these ideals inspired, as well as from an intense attachment to power. The means had to be subordinated to historically unparalleled ends that required extraordinary measures. In a nutshell, this is the part played by ideology or belief in the repression communist states introduced.

The future orientation of the revolutionaries and their successors helped to resolve or reduce the tension between ends and means: the Bolsheviks did not "consider the chance of attaining certain goals to be lessened by the . . . protracted and large-scale use of means which [were] . . . at extreme variance to them. . . ."[18] The accomplishments unfolding in the future were going to outweigh and cleanse the questionable means employed in their pursuit—this was the unshakeable conviction of generations of communist leaders and revolutionaries in the Soviet Union and other communist states. The committed revolutionary steeled himself in the face of the pain and suffering his policies caused. Lenin said that "there are no . . . serious battles without field hospitals near the battlefields. It is altogether unforgivable to permit oneself to be frightened or unnerved by field hospital scenes. If you are afraid of the wolves, don't go into the forest."[19] This was an attitude Edward Ochab, a Polish functionary, shared: "I became . . . a professional revolutionary. I read Lenin's *What Is To Be Done* . . . where Lenin maintains that the socialist revolution needs 'professional revolutionary' cadres . . . who would be prepared to spend months crawling along sewers and would be in charge . . . of organizing the masses. That was when I said to myself that's me."[20]

Self-discipline, mastery of personal feelings, and commitment to the cause made it possible to transcend reservations or revulsion about the means used. Again, as Leites put it, "The Bolshevik must eschew free-floating empathy. . . . Bolshevism shares the feeling expressed by a character in Dostoevsky's *A Raw Youth*: 'It doesn't matter if one has to pass through filth to get there as long as the goal is magnificent. It will all be washed off, it will all be smoothed away afterward.'"[21]

Leites also wrote that "Bolshevik doctrine rejects the virtue of empathy with and pity for all human beings. . . . The awareness of distress of others would reduce one's capacity to perform those acts which would ultimately abolish it."[22] This might be called the surgeon's view of pain; he must remain indifferent to the bodily sensations of the patient in order to heal him. Thus, in the political struggle, "instead of feeling guilty about the sufferings which one imposes on others . . . one attempts to feel self-righteous about directly and actively imposing suffering on others—for the sake of the future abolition of suffering."[23]

Hence the political violence of communist systems was instrumental rather than expressive or passionate, not the kind that would satisfy some personal instinct or impulse, although occasionally and illicitly it might have done so.[24]

The use of violent means was also made easier by perceiving them as both defensive and revolutionary. Trotsky wrote, "The man who repudiates terrorism in principle—i.e., repudiates measures of suppression and intimidation toward determined and armed counter-revolution, must reject all idea of political supremacy of the working class and its revolutionary dictatorship. The man who repudiates the dictatorship of the proletariat repudiates the Socialist revolution. . . ."

Earlier, Trotsky pointed out that the dictatorship of the proletariat is a necessity because no agreement is possible with the bourgeoisie: "only force can be the deciding factor."[25]

Leites grasped with great clarity the mentality required by impersonal, deliberate, ideologically motivated mass murder, the willingness to "dirty one's hands." Still, there remained, in all probability, a lingering awareness of the dissonance between ends and means.[26] This awareness helps to explain the secretiveness surrounding much of the political violence in most communist systems, and probably the Nazi secretiveness as well.

The uninhibited use of political violence and coercion also followed from the paternalism of professional revolutionaries (subsequently transformed into functionaries) who believed that they were acting on behalf of, and in the interest of, the masses, while in fact they were sharply separated from them. The deep class cleavages in Russia (and in other similarly or even more backward communist countries) bolstered this elitism.

Even Stalin's extraordinary power-hunger and vindictiveness toward his real or imagined enemies is in part explained by his conviction that he was a chosen instrument of history, the executor of great and lofty goals bequeathed by both Marxist-Leninist theory and Russian history. Similar beliefs doubtless also motivated Mao, Castro, Kim Il Sung, Ho Chi Minh, and other communist leaders. Such convictions did not inspire restraint or attention to proper procedure.

Despite the controversies that have surrounded it since the late 1960s, it is the theory of totalitarianism that best explains the principal characteristics of communist political violence and coercion. The latter were inseparable from the unconstrained exercise of power, from the urge to dissolve distinctions between the public and private realms (by completely subordinating the latter to the former), and from the attempted politicization of every aspect of life. Because political meaning was attached to virtually everything the citizens did, political crime and deviance became defined very broadly, leading to the mistreatment of vast numbers of people, most of whom had not the slightest interest in politics and were not inclined to question let alone endanger the power of the party-state.

Communist leaders were (at least in the beginning) inspired by ideas promising secular redemption; they possessed enormous concentrated power unchecked by any institutional arrangement, countervailing social force, or tradition.[27] At the same time, in all probability the personalities of the supreme leaders also played a part in the forms political violence took. Stalin, Mao,[28] Castro, Mengistu (of Ethiopia),[29] and Mathias Rakosi (of Hungary) were exceptionally ruthless, deceitful, and vindictive individuals who attached little value to individual human lives. They each had the proven capacity to turn on or betray their closest collaborators, friends (if any), or comrades-in-arms if they were suspected of the slightest disagreement or diminished loyalty.

No communist system was free of repression, but the severity of repression fluctuated over time (North Korea may be an exception, since its repressive policies seem to have changed little over the years). The routine reliance on political violence and coercion was at once a defining characteristic of communist systems and a telling indicator of the failure of their policies and their lack of (or limited) legitimacy. Communist systems' habitual reliance on repressive policies may also be seen as the institutionalization of their leaders' intolerance.

The decline and fall of communist states coincided with declining repression, growing corruption, and the underlying weakening of the political will of their ruling elites.[30] Those still in power—in China, Cuba, North Korea, and Vietnam—did not hesitate to use force to crush and stifle dissent or opposition and have remained highly repressive. Nonrepressive, tolerant communist systems "with a human face" have never came into existence. Hungary in the late Kadar years did move in such a direction but it eventually fell apart.

In the final analysis, the repressive character of communist states can be explained by a combination of universal and historically specific factors. The first includes the longstanding and entrenched human potential and disposition to dehumanize, demonize, and mistreat others (those defined as outsiders, strangers, and enemies) without compunction and for a wide variety of reasons; most commonly such hatreds and scapegoating are associated with competition and conflict for scarce resources (not only material). Social, ethnic, and religious differences between groups further aggravate such dispositions.

Preconditions for the type of massive violence and coercion must also include the availability of certain minimal technological and administrative means for carrying out large-scale repression, lethal or nonlethal. Victims must be transported (on trains, trucks, or boats) to particular locations (for incarceration or execution); firearms are required for the rapid and efficient killing of large numbers (absent gas chambers); barbed wire is an essential ingredient for the creation of concentration camps and for rapidly confining large numbers of people.

The second set of factors consists of more specific historical, and ideological elements. Most communist states had no democratic, liberal, or individualistic political culture or traditions; reflexive submission to authority was more readily forthcoming in these societies. Most of these countries were also economically underdeveloped, inegalitarian, and scarcity-ridden.

Arguably, ideology—that is to say, certain structured and militant beliefs— was most important in channeling frustrations and resentments into politically defined and legitimated violence and aggression and such beliefs also led to the mistreatment of designated groups in the purported service of bringing about a radical break with past deprivations and injustices—although these beliefs were held only by small elite groups.

Communist systems were relentlessly ends-oriented. These ends provided the assurance and legitimation needed to coerce, or outright eliminate, all those who stood in the way of the great experiment in human liberation, the creation of a better world. In each of these societies small but determined minorities (mostly politicized intellectuals or quasi-intellectuals) found new meaning in the attempt to radically transform societies and human beings; politics became, at least initially, a quasireligious quest that stimulated ruthlessness and intolerance. As Hilton Kramer, among others, has pointed out: "Socialism had indeed supplanted religion as the source of 'political idealism,' and from that fateful shift there have flowed many of the horrors of the modern age."[31] This idealism or utopianism did not endure, but the practices and institutions created in its pursuit remained in place decades after revolutionary fervor had gradually given way to the love of power and privilege among the ruling elites.

The decline and fall of communist systems shows that the love of power and privilege bereft of ideological and moral certainties is insufficient for keeping such systems going, especially when they are also incapable of meeting the less than utopian needs of their people. As Forrest Colburn has written, "Politically intoxicated . . . revolutionaries have shoved their poor societies into an unsustainable recasting of state and economy that has left the majority of people disoriented, politically cynical, and materially more impoverished. . . . The brutal confrontation of dreams with intractable political and . . . economic realities . . . explains the dispiriting outcomes of contemporary revolutions."[32]

In the final analysis the inhumanities here discussed were, for the most part, unintended byproducts of the desire to radically and rapidly change the human condition through the inherently limited and crude means at the disposal of human beings.

NOTES

1. The nonrevolutionary communist regimes were those established in Bulgaria, Czechoslovakia, East Germany, Hungary, Poland, and Romania as a result of the arrival and prolonged stay of Soviet troops during and after World War II in these countries.

2. Forrest D. Colburn, *The Vogue of Revolution in Poor Countries* (Princeton, N.J.: Princeton University Press, 1994), 13–14. Milovan Djilas also believed that in communist states "everything, including the economy [was] subordinate to ideological power" (see his *Fall of the New Class: A History of Communism's Self-Destruction* [New York: Knopf, 1998], 312).

3. Igal Halfin, *Terror in My Soul: Communist Autobiographies on Trial* (Cambridge, Mass.: Harvard University Press, 2003), 14.

4. David Chandler, *Voices from S-21: Terror and History in Pol Pot's Secret Prison* (Berkley, Calif.: 1999), 150.

5. Simon Leys, "After the Massacres," *New York Review of Books*, October 12, 1989, 17.

6. Bui Tin, *Following Ho Chi Minh* (Honolulu: University of Hawaii Press, 1995), 115.

7. Peter Reddaway, *Psychiatric Terror: How Soviet Psychiatry Is Used to Suppress Dissent* (New York: Basic Books, 1977); Petro G. Grigorienko was subjected to this treatment as recalled in his *Memoirs* (New York, 1982); see also Alexander Yakovlev, *Century of Violence in Soviet Russia* (New Haven, Conn.: Yale University Press, 2002), 147–48.

8. Erik Eckholm, "A China Dissident's Ordeal: Back to the Mental Hospital," *New York Times*, November 30, 1999. The use of psychiatric wards in China for detaining political prisoners is also described by Liu Binyan in *A Higher Kind of Loyalty* (New York: Pantheon, 1990), 225–27. Concerning similar policies in Cuba, see Charles J. Brown and Armando M. Lago, *The Politics of Psychiatry in Revolutionary Cuba* (New Brunswick, N.J., 1991). In Romania dissidents were sent to psychiatric institutions for periods ranging from a few months to several years. (See Dennis Deletant, *Ceausescu and the Securitate: Coercion and Dissent in Romania, 1965–1989* [New Armonk, N.Y.: M.E. Sharpe, 1995], 93–101.)

9. Quoted in Lenin, *State and Revolution* (Moscow: Foreign Languages Publishing House, n.d.), 25–27.

10. Davit Wolde Giorgis, *Red Tears* (Trenton, N.J., 1989), 21.

11. Lenin, *State and Revolution*, 39, 68, 144–45.

12. Quoted in Mikhail Heller, *Cogs in the Wheel: The Formation of Soviet Man* (New York: Knopf, 1988), 36. Lenin's inclination to political violence is also documented in Richard Pipes, ed., *The Unknown Lenin* (New Haven, Conn.: Yale University Press, 1996).

13. Quoted in Robert V. Daniels, *A Documentary History of Communism* (New York: Random House, 1960), 57. Stalin made the statement in 1937 in a speech to the Central Committee of the Party.

14. Ted Galen Carpenter, "Democracy and War," *The Independent Review* (Winter 1998): 436. Edward Shils also noted that "The phantasy of conspiracy requires the reality of counterconspiracy so that in the end the world becomes an arena in which two conspiracies operate, the wicked conspiracies of the enemies and the legitimate and morally necessary conspiracy of Bolshevism" (*The Torment of Secrecy* [Carbondale: Southern Illinois University Press, 1974], 30).

15. Alexander Solzhenitsyn, *The Gulag Archipelago*, vol. 1 (New York: Harper & Row, 1973), 173–74.

16. Yakovlev, *Century of Violence*, 15.

17. Alexander Yakovlev, *The Fate of Marxism in Russia* (New Haven, Conn.: Yale University Press, 1993), 7, 11,17, 29, 38, 39, 56–57.

18. Nathan Leites, *A Study of Bolshevism* (Glencoe, Ill.: Free Press, 1953), 105.

19. Leites, *A Study of Bolshevism*, 105.

20. Quoted in Teresa Toranska, *"Them": Stalin's Polish Puppets* (New York: Harper & Row, 1987), 88.

21. Quoted in Leites, *A Study in Bolshevism*, 208, 106.

22. Leites, *A Study in Bolshevism*, 348.

23. Leites, *A Study in Bolshevism*, 352.

24. Presumably such impulsive, sadistic enjoyment of violence motivated the Japanese soldiers in Nanking as well as the participants in pogroms, lynchings, and in other spontaneous outbursts of ethnic violence.

25. Leon Trotsky, *Terrorism and Communism: A Reply to Karl Kautsky* (Ann Arbor: University of Michigan Press, 1960), 20, 23.

26. Heinrich Himmler, for one, quite candidly addressed the problem of ends and means with respect to the final solution of "the Jewish question" in a speech to SS of-

ficers in which he acknowledged that it was unpleasant to contemplate the mounds of corpses and required strong character, as he saw it. See Joachim C. Fest, *The Face of the Third Reich* (New York: Patheon, 1970).

27. Zbigniew Brzezinski, "Patterns of Autocracy," in *The Transformation of Russian Society*, ed. Cyril Black (Cambridge, Mass.: Harvard University Press, 1960).

28. On these aspects of Mao's personality, see Li Zhisui, *The Private Life of Chairman Mao* (New York: Random House, 1994).

29. "Mengistu once confided to me that he enjoyed chairing meetings in this hall . . . because he was able to sit right above the basement where all former aristocrats whom he despised were imprisoned" (Giorgis, *Red Tears*, 126). This was by no means the only reflection of Mengistu's unappealing personality. For other examples of his megalomania and ruthlessness see Giorgis, *Red Tears*, 18–21, 33–34, 332, 352.

30. This is the central argument of Paul Hollander, *Political Will and Personal Belief* (New Haven, Conn.: Yale University Press, 1999).

31. Quoted in Patrick A. Swan, ed., *Alger Hiss, Whittaker Chambers and the Schism in the American Soul* (Wilmington, Del.: ISI Books, 2003), 314.

32. Colburn, *The Vogue of Revolution*, 77.

Chapter Nineteen

The North Korean Gulag

North Korea is the only surviving communist regime that has managed to preserve intact the worst, most oppressive characteristics of such systems. These include isolation, a grotesque personality cult of the leaders (father and now son), breathtaking mendaciousness, an exceptional degree of militarization, and the catastrophic economic policies that have led to famine and the death of an estimated 2 million people. It has also kept the Gulag system going.

The Aquariums of Pyongyang: Ten Years in a North Korean Gulag by Kang Chol-hwan and Pierre Rigoulot is, to the best of my knowledge, the first and only account in English by a survivor of the North Korean Gulag and by extension the North Korean police state. The author was forced into a camp with his family in 1977, at age nine, and was released ten years later. (He escaped from the country through China in 1992.) This is an extraordinarily informative, indeed revelatory, volume; it is also well written and moving.

It is especially interesting to learn something about this country from one of its natives at a time when the United States is trying to sort out its relationship with North Korea and searching for a way to deprive it of nuclear weapons. Yet, as far as I can tell, this first-rate book has not been reviewed in any major publication.

Thus our ignorance of North Korea persists. Occasional high-level delegations visit the country, but they are carefully prevented from learning anything other than what the officials wish them to learn. The book makes it clear that North Koreans are intimidated to a degree that most Americans cannot conceive of. It also helped me to understand—though not entirely—how President Carter came to the conclusion in 1994 that the North Korean people "revered" their leader—then Kim Il Sung—and that Pyongyang was "full of pep" with shops reminding him of Wal-Mart! While Western admirers of North Korea are not as numerous as those of Stalin's Russia or Mao's China used to be, there are a handful, such as Bruce Cumings, a professor at the University of Chicago, who has for some time taken it upon himself to be an apologist of this murderous regime.

The author of this book was born in North Korea to a prosperous, pro-communist North Korean family that had lived in Japan until the division of the North and South. They made the unfortunate decision to return to participate in the socialist transformation. (Many such families, wooed by the regime, returned from Japan and were initially well-treated and provided with privileged living conditions.) The author's grandfather handed over his "immense fortune" to the authorities, but eventually got in trouble with the regime and disappeared in 1977—he simply did not come home one day. They learned later that he was "picked up work and taken away to a hard-labor camp without even the chance to pack a bag."

A few weeks later the rest of the family was taken from their comfortable apartment in Pyongyang to Yodok, one of the many camps in the remote areas of the country. The camp was divided into "villages," each for a "specific category of detainees"—Mr. Kang's family was interned in the village for those repatriated from Japan—who were forbidden any contact with prisoners from other villages.

The detainees "had missing teeth, their hair was caked . . . and overgrown, and they were filthy . . . more striking than their physical appearance was the aura of weakness that oozed from their every pore . . . and a pervasive sense of desperation." During the orientation session, the new arrivals were told by an official that "you people don't deserve to live, but the Party and our Great Leader have given you a chance to redeem yourself. . . . We will discuss all this further at our next meeting for criticism and self-criticism."

In the camp hunger was endemic, working conditions harsh, and "during our years of detention, rags were often the only clothing we had. . . . After a few months . . . the appearance of our rags bothered us no more. . . . The only thing that mattered was keeping warm." Special punishments were meted out, including the "sweatbox" for offenses such as "stealing three ears of corn, responding to a guard's command with insufficient zeal, missing a role call." Prisoners could be put in it for weeks or months, and most of them did not survive.

In the sweatbox, a prisoner is forced to crouch on his knees in "a kind of shack . . . devoid of any openings . . . shrouded in total darkness . . . given so little to eat that he will devour anything that comes within arms' reach . . . most often a wayward cockroach or centipede. . . . The secret of survival was to eat every insect. . . . Hardly anyone exited the sweatbox on his own two feet. If the prisoner had to relieve himself he raised his left hand; if he was sick . . . his right. No other gestures were allowed."

The author's work assignments included burials, which conferred two advantages: a little extra food and, more importantly, access to the clothing of the dead. Malnutrition was such that rats were regularly eaten: "If I were to improve my nutritional intake and realize my dream of becoming the family's provider of meat, the better option was rat [compared to the risk of stealing rabbits]. One of my coworkers—a camp veteran—was the first to introduce me to the dish. . . . Despite my revulsion, I could not resist . . . because the rat was truly delicious. Though the rodents were everywhere, trapping them was difficult." After figuring out how to reuse the traps he increased his catch and was able "to supplement the family's small food ration."

Public executions were another regular feature of camp life. Attendance was obligatory. While executions were usually by firing squad, on one occasion, two members of an elite military unit were hung for trying to escape from the country. "Once both men were finally dead, the two or three thousand prisoners in attendance were instructed to pick up a stone and hurl it at the corpses while yelling: 'Down with the traitors of the people!'"

After his release, Mr. Kang saw that life as a "free" citizen of North Korea was appalling. Corruption was widespread, a direct response to the endemic scarcities and deprivations. His escape from the country was a long and complicated undertaking. China initially impressed him as a wonderfully free and prosperous country, given his experiences in North Korea—though getting from China to South Korea was almost as difficult as escaping from the North.

This book, like all others that deal with similar experiences in comparable settings, compelled me to ponder how such monstrous systems come about and persist and what precisely motivates the human beings in control of them at the highest level. Theories of totalitarianism help to answer these questions—but far from completely. Regrettably, the general conclusion is that exceptionally repressive political systems have a unique capacity to unlock and put to their use the worst aspects of human nature.

North Korea remains the classic embodiment of totalitarianism, perhaps the only one left in the world today. It has withstood isolation, famine, the collapse of Soviet communism, and liberalization in the rest of the communist world. It would be a monumental mistake if Western concessions born out of fear of its nuclear weapons were to prolong the existence of this repugnant and inhumane regime.

Chapter Twenty

Admiring North Korea

Anyone who knows the history of the colossal and surrealistic misperceptions of communist regimes on the part of many Western intellectuals will find this volume [Bruce Cumings's *North Korea: Another Country*] at once familiar and distinctive. It is appearing against the background of the reasonable expectation that something might have been learned from the long history of such misperceptions and their resourceful encouragement by the officials of such regimes. Most of these states no longer exist, and from their ashes emerged further evidence confirming their mendacity and disproving the propaganda they steadfastly disseminated for both domestic and foreign consumption.

Bruce Cumings, a professor at the University of Chicago, strangely enough, has chosen North Korea—the only surviving communist state to preserve intact the worst, most oppressive characteristics of such systems—as the recipient of his affections and the object of his efforts at political rehabilitation. These sentiments are inspired in part by his respect for the Korean people, culture, and tradition and by his failure to distinguish sufficiently such traditions from the realities of the murderous regime in the North. Evidently, Cumings belongs to the long line of Western academic intellectuals who are fully persuaded that the United States bears responsibility for much that is wrong with the world, including the existence of political systems and movements that are its most dedicated adversaries. Not only does he believe that the United States is largely responsible for the (in his opinion, defensive) brutality and pugnacity of North Korea, he is equally eager to acquaint the reader with the alleged achievements of this regime. These include "compassionate child care" and superior health and education benefits (the kind all communist regimes routinely have claimed among their accomplishments). He approvingly quotes a writer who averred that prior to the recent economic disasters, typical North Koreans lived "an incredibly simple and hardworking life but also [had] a secure and happy existence, and the comradeship between these highly collectivized people [was] moving to behold."

The author is eager to dispel any impression of North Korean aggression against the South (which culminated in its 1950 invasion); he even uses the disingenuous argument that the conflict was a civil war and that the 38th parallel is "not an international boundary." He dwells on the sufferings the United States inflicted during that war, and thus creates a framework for his apologetic reinterpretation of the paranoid garrison state North Korea has become. His emphasis on the inhumanities of U.S. air warfare is reminiscent of the argument that the U.S. bombing of Cambodia somehow prompted the massacres of Pol Pot. Thus a very familiar theme pervades the narrative: "Beleaguered" North Korea (like other communist systems, whose conduct was not entirely praiseworthy) did some bad things, but it was due to feeling and being threatened and victimized by the United States.

In a disclaimer early on, we are assured that the author has no sympathy for the North; there are indeed critical statements scattered throughout the book, including the admission that the regime does not promote human freedom (but this admission is hastily qualified with "not from any liberal's standpoint"). Cumings has no love for the grotesque personality cult of the leaders, but he cannot resist remarking about "U.S. support for dictators who make Kim Jong Il look enlightened"; nor does he endorse the garrison state (he notes that conscripts have to serve ten years). But he laments the bad press North Korea gets. He has little doubt that the misconceptions about this much maligned political system are rooted in the ignorance of Americans (blended with racism) and nurtured by the sensationalistic mass media and unscrupulous politicians.

The reader's doubts about the depth and genuineness of Cumings's criticisms of the regime are further stimulated by the fact that he was considered sympathetic or dependable enough by the North Korean authorities to be allowed (or invited?) to make a television documentary. Such doubts deepen when one reads his many contemptuous references to the defectors from the North and their "tales" (which reminded me of Noam Chomsky's dismissive references to the "tales" of Cambodian refugees about the atrocities they witnessed).

In a triumph of selective perception, he manages to interpret the most damning indictment of the North Korean Gulag available—*The Aquariums of Pyongyang*, by Kang Chol-Hwan and Pierre Rigoulot—as providing support for his views of the system. As he sees it, the book is "interesting and believable" because it is not the "ghastly tale of totalitarian repression that its original publishers . . . meant it to be." But it is precisely and resoundingly just that, as any reader without a soft spot for North Korean tyranny would readily discover. Cumings writes that "conditions were primitive and beatings were frequent [in the camp described in that book] but the inmates also were able to improvise much of their upkeep on their own . . . small animals could surreptitiously be caught and cooked." He delicately refrains from mentioning that these small animals were mostly rats, and a regular part of the narrator's diet. That book makes abundantly clear that hunger and malnutrition were endemic; inmates stealing food or trying to escape were executed. Cumings also fails to mention these public executions the inmates were obliged to attend, stressing instead that families were commendably kept together and that "death from starvation was rare." In any event, reaching for moral equivalence, he suggests that these deprivations ought to be put in proper perspective by our "longstanding, never-ending gulag full of black men in our prisons"—which should disqualify us from "pointing a finger."

As one reads on, it becomes an increasingly compelling question how it is possible for a professor of history at a great institution of learning—the University of Chicago—to have any sympathy for such a regime. One explanation may be that, like other similarly disposed visitors to communist countries, Cumings was favorably impressed by the remnants of a traditional social order reflected in the conduct and interaction of ordinary people, their respectful manner, and sense of community. On his conducted tours he rejoiced in the prevailing orderliness and cleanliness—the little old ladies sweeping the streets (presumably without any official encouragement!)—and contrasted these appealing conditions with their absence in South Korea and other noncommunist third-world countries. Among the revealing and novel information he provides is that "every citizen who travels, checks into a hotel, or dines at a public restaurant is required to carry a sanitation pass, verifying that he or she has been to a public bathhouse within the past week."

Cumings is aware of the flaws of North Korea, but they have no perceptible emotional impact on him. He generally withholds moral judgment, owing to his zeal to rehabilitate the regime and to his reflexive indulgence in moral equivalence (the United States and South Korea are no better).

Sections of the book offer some useful information about the cultural-historical background and recent economic difficulties of North Korea and about the personal lives and character of its two leaders (dead and living). It is, however, of far greater interest as a document illustrating the stunning persistence of the political attitudes of academic intellectuals durably estranged from their own society and predisposed to find virtue in others opposed to it, and in the surviving idealized social arrangements of the past.

Chapter Twenty-one

The Fiftieth Anniversary of the Hungarian Revolution

My recollections of the Hungarian Revolution of 1956 and the subsequent illicit nocturnal border crossing into Austria provide indelible illustrations of the connections between the personal and the political. While the immediate consequences of the Revolution were, for the most part, tragic, I was among its beneficiaries. Fifty years later I remain convinced that leaving Hungary was a wise decision and one that, at one stroke, quite dramatically changed my life. Rarely does a walk of a few hours in the countryside have such far-reaching consequences. It was a gamble, as I could have been arrested before reaching the border or at the border. Life in the West, in unfamiliar surroundings without family and friends, could have turned out to be grim. I left with nothing but the clothes on my back, including a crumbling, American-made leather jacket I have preserved to this day. The jacket hangs in a closet and I wear it on November 19 to impress my friends who will join me in a small celebration of my border-crossing anniversary.

Leaving Hungary did not assure unalloyed contentment and the elimination of all problems of life. But by doing so the political realm ceased to dominate and deform the personal one. I gained access to higher education, a professional life, and a modicum of intellectual creativity. More important—and perhaps the hardest to convey to those who had no opportunity to make such comparisons—I exchanged life in a repressed and regimented society for one in a free world, which I do not put into quotation marks.

The border crossing was the culmination of longings that I used to believe would never be consummated. Conditions for getting out were not auspicious between 1948, when the communist regime was established, and 1956. The Iron Curtain (of which the Berlin Wall was the best-known and most conspicuous part) was not a figure of speech.

Political and personal elements were intertwined in my motivation to leave Hungary. There was, to begin with, a growing distaste for the intrusive and mendacious political system that even a high school student was bound to experience firsthand (for instance, we were required in school to sign petitions demanding the strictest punishment for the defendants in the Hungarian Purge Trials). There was no way to ignore or avoid the singularly repetitive, numbing, and self-righteous political propaganda that engulfed all of us, in and outside school.

I also recall, among the reasons for my questioning the system, the spectacle of party functionaries and government officials riding around in large, luxurious, chauffeur-driven American (!) cars while most people suffered a wide range of shortages and the official propaganda claimed that an egalitarian society was being built. Even in my mid-teens I could discern the yawning gulf between official pronouncements and practices, proclaimed ideals and social realities. That is to say, I rejected the regime in the first place because of its addiction to fraudulent propaganda.

I also believe that the vast majority of Hungarians (and people in other communist countries) came to reject the system above all because of their experience of the insistent, routine misrepresentations of reality they could check against their daily experiences. To be sure, objective realities—the declining standard of living, the loss of free expression, the abuses of power, restrictions of religious practices, and so on—also mattered a great deal. But these grievances were more strongly felt since the authorities endlessly claimed that we lived in growing harmony and abundance in the most enlightened and just social system and under the benevolent guidance of wise and beloved leaders.

The second set of experiences relevant to my departure were more personal. One night in June 1951 a police truck arrived at the apartment building where we lived to collect our family, which had officially been classified as "politically unreliable" or "class enemies." We were taken under police guard to a freight train terminal where similarly designated people were assembled for shipment to villages in Eastern Hungary defined as "forced dwelling places" that we were not permitted to leave. Upon arrival at the railway station of the designated village, we were met by a small crowd assembled by the local party organizers who shouted denunciations at the newly arrived enemies of the socialist state.

Our political classification resulted from my maternal grandfather's prewar social status: he used to be a well-to-do, self-made businessman. His properties had been confiscated by the communist authorities years before the exile. He lived with my parents and myself, hence we were considered one family, all members of which were hopelessly contaminated by his capitalist past.

About 50,000 people similarly classified were exiled from Budapest in 1951 and dumped into villages to live under crowded and primitive conditions. This measure was officially explained as a stage in the class struggle and one that also alleviated the housing shortage in the capital.

The exile closely followed my matriculation from high school and it meant that I could not attend university, to which I had been admitted. After two years in the village I was conscripted into the army, but having been a politically unreliable element, I was placed into a so-called construction battalion. Instead of getting military training, we performed manual labor at various construction sites. I worked at the construction of military barracks, the Hungarian Nuclear Research Institute, and a state farm. Following discharge from the military I sought employment as a laborer in construction, since such a job entitled one to temporary permission to live in Budapest.

Between October 23, 1956, and the massive Soviet offensive that began on November 4, I gave little thought to getting out of the country. I was on the streets most of the time, observing events and participating in demonstrations, distracted from plotting my escape. A chance meeting with a truck driver in mid-November led to my joining a group of strangers driven by another driver to a small town by the Austrian border. There were about fifteen of us, including children and a baby. At night the truck deposited us near the border and we were shown by the locals the way to Austria. We began our walk through the open fields. After about an hour we saw in the moonlight two figures standing by a ditch who turned out to be Hungarian border guards. We approached. Silence ensued. At last one of the guards remarked, "Why are you going in such a big group?" This sounded like a friendly question and was followed by the guards pointing us in the right direction.

After arriving in Vienna, I was among three hundred Hungarian students the British universities undertook to help to continue or commence their studies. I arrived in England on November 30, and in January began my studies at the London School of Economics. (I knew some English and quickly picked up more.)

I chose to study sociology because it seemed interesting. I had never heard of such a field before. After graduating in the summer of 1959, I came to America for graduate studies that led to a Ph.D. from Princeton in 1963. A nontenured teaching job at Harvard and more than three decades at the University of Massachusetts at Amherst followed. In 2000 I retired from teaching, but not from writing. I have produced twelve books over the years. My personal life in America had little to do with matters political. But the past found expression in my books, many of which, in one way or another, have some connection with the experience of having lived in a communist society.

I spent the first twenty-four years of my life in Hungary, close to three in England, and forty-seven years in the United States. I remain fluent in Hungarian and pass for one when I visit, which I do every year since the collapse of the communist system. I still have relatives and friends in Hungary, and I like Hungarian food. I don't have a love-hate relationship with Hungary or Hungarians. I used to think of myself as a so-called rootless cosmopolitan—a term of disapproval Andrei Zhdanov, the Soviet cultural commissar under Stalin, coined. This is no longer quite true. With the passage of time, I sank roots in western Massachusetts. I have found New England very much to my liking, being an outdoorsman and nature lover. I don't even mind the occasional bears visiting our backyard. After the excitements of growing up in Hungary, surviving both Nazism and communism, and witnessing the Revolution, I appreciate a settled and secure academic life. I have an American wife, a daughter, a stepdaughter, a dog and a cat, and two kayaks. I have published books critical of anti-Americanism, but that does not mean that I am uncritical of everything in this society, far from it.

I learned that political conditions inevitably, and often painfully, shape personal lives. In the course of my reluctant participation in the building of Soviet-style socialism in Hungary, I met many peasants and workers, supposed beneficiaries of the system, who were its most embittered victims and adversaries. It became clear to me that repressive political systems, even if they proclaim impressive idealistic aspirations, will cease to be idealized (as they often are from a distance) once the human costs of their practices are experienced or understood. Warren Beatty would not have directed *Reds* if he had known how far apart the ideals and realities of Soviet communism were from one another. Nor would he have produced the movie if he had known real people who had lived under such a system, or if he had given thought to the question of why the ideals he admired lent themselves so readily to distortion and misapplication.

My life in the West deepened the conviction that personal freedom has a reality and meaning that can be truly appreciated only by those who have lived under circumstances defined by its absence.

Chapter Twenty-two

Crossing the Moral Threshold: The Rejection of Communist Systems in Eastern Europe

There is no shortage of explanations—political, economic, or cultural—of why communist systems were unpopular in Eastern Europe and why uprisings erupted as they had in 1953 (East Germany), 1956 (Hungary and Poland), and 1968 (Czechoslovakia). Of these uprisings, the Hungarian was the most significant, its demands the most far-reaching, its popular support the most widespread, and its human toll the greatest.

There were numerous well-founded grievances against communist regimes in Eastern Europe: the standard of living declined due to rapid, forced industrialization, the collectivization of agriculture, mismanagement, and decline of work ethic; nationalistic sentiments were deeply offended by the slavish imitation of everything Soviet; the populations were terrorized by the political police modeled on the KGB; grotesque, compulsory cults of Stalin and his local emissaries flourished; cultural life was homogenized and politicized; political indoctrination became part of formal education and daily life; religious institutions were crushed and religious practices discouraged; meaningless but time-consuming political participation was demanded and extracted from the population, such as voting in one-party elections and attending demonstrations and endless meetings; the freedom of movement was severely curtailed (the Iron Curtain was not a figure of speech); last, but not least, political propaganda was as ubiquitous, pervasive, and irksome as commercial advertising in capitalist countries (but far more monolithic), and unlike advertising its propositions and commands could not be questioned or ridiculed.

Not all these grievances were equally strongly felt at different points in time and in the different countries of Eastern Europe, but there was a continuity and convergence among them that led to the uprisings noted above and the final extinction of communist rule in Eastern Europe at the end of the

1980s. Needless to say, the latter could not have been accomplished without unmistakable indications that the Soviet Union was no longer prepared to impose its will and control over this area and shore up the local governments by military force.

There is an important component of the discontent all these developments and policies generated that did not receive adequate attention, namely, their subjective perception and evaluation by ordinary people and the *moral* indignation and outrage they created. This essay seeks to better understand these more subjective undercurrents of the widespread political disaffection that pervaded these countries and especially the part played by what I will call the moral threshold of their citizens. Much of the discontent, I suggest, had more to do with matters subjective and social-psychological than with objective socialpolitical conditions and deprivations. This is not to diminish the importance of the objective conditions that too were plentiful and consequential.

People can tolerate a wide range of deprivations if they are legitimated or justified in some fashion, or made meaningful. This can be accomplished by custom, communal solidarity, religious belief, law, or charismatic leaders. In traditional societies most people were impoverished but widespread poverty was considered normal and hence not conducive to much, if any, indignation; likewise, time-honored social inequalities were readily accepted as inescapable and justifiable. This was in part the case because alternative social arrangements were unknown and unthinkable, and in part because the deprivations of life here and now were widely believed to be temporary, to be alleviated in some kind of otherworldly existence—in short, because people were sustained by supernatural religious beliefs that helped to diminish the importance of the material (and other) difficulties of life here and now.

The restrictive, repressive aspects of traditional societies were likewise readily accepted because they were longstanding and part of deeply rooted and often religiously sanctioned social arrangements. Traditional societies were successful (up to a point) in controlling and stabilizing personal expectations; stable expectations in turn stabilized social and political institutions and practices.

By contrast, communist systems, (indeed all revolutionary societies) rapidly and abruptly raised a wide range of expectations. As Raymond Aron wrote half a century ago, "A revolution seems capable of changing everything. . . . [It] provides a welcome break with the everyday course of events and encourages the belief that all things are possible."[1]

In addition to these elusive promises and expectations, communist systems were quite specific in their (unfulfilled) promises. They included vast material improvements, freedom from various social restraints (such as traditional societies maintained), a sense of personal liberation that was to be combined with new, sustaining communal ties (a new, improved, and enlightened sense of community), rational, scientific ways of organizing and perfecting society, ample opportunity for participation in public life and political decision-making, the eventual attainment of social equality (to be preceded by modest, temporary inequalities based on indisputable merit), and, most crucially (and implausibly), the elimination of the conflict between personal and public interest, or between the individual and society. Last but not least, these systems also promised to create a new, greatly improved human being, "the new socialist man"—a secular version of the saintly heroes and protagonists of organized religion. The attributes of this new socialist man were most readily and meticulously revealed and elaborated in the figure of the so-called positive hero—an integral part of the socialist-realist literature produced in these countries. Vasily Grossman, the Soviet writer, observed,

> Writers dreamed up out of whole cloth people and their feelings and thoughts. . . . The literature which called itself "realistic" was just as formalized and imaginary as the bucolic romances of the 18th century. The collective farmers, workers and rural women of Soviet literature seemed . . . to be close kin to those beautifully built villages and those curly headed shepherdesses who played on pipes and danced in the meadows among pure-white lambs. . . .
>
> In novels and poems . . . Soviet people were being depicted like people in medieval art, who had represented the Church's ideal, the idea of divinity. . . .

Socialist-realist literature was another ambitious attempt to obliterate the dividing line between actual, perceptible realities and the way things were supposed to be according to the official, ideological blueprints and desires. Arguably it was the most far-reaching, grotesque, and elaborate denial of the realities inhabitants of these communist states were exposed to.

The promises made by these systems were not limited to their early, idealistic, revolutionary stages; they persisted well after the revolutionary objectives were abandoned. The propagandists and ideologues insisted that these promises were fulfilled, that a historically unprecedented, just, and gratifying social system was being built. These claims were put forward and repeated by the enormous, comprehensive agit-prop apparatus that encompassed the mass media, door-to-door verbal "agitation," and the entire system of education. At places of work, special seminars were organized with compulsory attendance requirements that would elaborate and regurgitate the same messages. Slogans were particularly offensive in their brazen defiance of reality. For example, in Hungary the slogan "Tied a gyar, magadnak dolgozol!" that is, "the plant is yours, you are working for yourself!" was plastered all over factory buildings. These were the same places of work where at the end of the shift workers were searched as they exited (to make sure they did not steal), where their earnings were determined by distant authorities, where they had no say in their working conditions and no autonomous unions to represent and protect their interests.[2] To be confronted day after day with such reality-defying slogans in every walk of life was a slap in the face, a daily humiliation. Understating the case, one of the fighters in the 1956 Revolution wrote, "the workers did not feel that they owned the factory, the land, the fruits of their labor."[3]

Given the comprehensiveness and relentlessness of the propaganda campaigns, the public in communist states was well acquainted with *both* the official claims of rectitude and accomplishment *and* their lack of fulfillment (through daily personal experience). This led to the sentiments and attitudes here discussed.

A specific kind of outrage was generated by the routine misrepresentations of reality that culminated in the crossing of the moral threshold. The latter refers to internalized moral norms and sensibilities that define in a compelling way what kinds of behavior, policies, or events are morally acceptable or unacceptable, what can or cannot be tolerated. Communist systems created a specific and intense moral outrage by institutionalizing and perpetuating these discrepancies between theory and practice, ideal and actual, promises and the realities they created. This became their particular weakness, at any rate in the long run. Gyorgy Litvan, a Hungarian historian (former supporter, later opponent of the system) wrote, "it was the moral cynicism, or moralizing cynicism, that became the Achilles-heel of Stalinism. The latter was only effective as long as the edifice of faith was intact, but its nakedness was revealed as soon as the edifice began to shake and fall apart. *It was obligatory to moralize* because of the redemptive claims but it was precisely the moralizing that made the system vulnerable."[4]

The mendaciousness of the rulers was widely recognized; people came to resent being lied to and compelled to lie in turn, pressured as they were to participate in hollow displays of loyalty to the system they despised. During their totalitarian phases, these systems were not content with passive acceptance on the part of the population; they were determined to squeeze out displays of approval, a semblance of supporting, enthusiastic participation in the political-public life the authorities created and permitted. Such compulsory participation took several forms: on the official holidays (and some other special political occasions), virtually the entire working population had to take part in huge mass rallies; people were routinely obligated to vote in elections which provided no choice, only the opportunity to endorse the official candidates; workers had to attend at their place of work the political seminars; students at every level in the system of education had to imbibe the official messages in the framework of courses in humanities and social sciences as well as in newly created courses on Marxism-Leninism. Special boarding party schools were also created for those already in elite positions and others groomed for such positions.[5]

While no political system lives up completely to its own ideals or idealized self-conception, communist systems excelled in creating an unprecedented gulf between their policies, promises, and claims, on the one hand, and their performance, on the other. The ceaseless exposure to reality-defying propaganda stimulated a reflexive comparison of the daily reality experienced by the citizens with its official representation and misrepresentation. The political jokes of the period remain a highly informative repository of the popular awareness and responses to these manifold discrepancies and misrepresentations.

Alexander Wat, the Polish author, memorably summed up this phenomenon: "The loss of freedom, tyranny, abuse, hunger would all have been easier to bear if not for the compulsion to call them freedom, justice and the good of the people."[6] Two Hungarian writers, Tamas Aczel and Tibor Meray, made the same point: "most intolerable was the simulation of virtue, the endless proclamation of good intentions: everything was taking place on behalf of 'the people,' in the name of the workers' power. . . ."[7]

It should be noted here that for the deeply committed, idealistic supporters of the system (including those belonging to the political elite), the journey to disillusionment, to the crossing of the moral threshold, was much more prolonged, painful, and halting than for ordinary people. This was a result of their longstanding commitment to the system and the techniques they developed to avert or delay a drastic moral awakening. It was possible to avoid or postpone the crossing of the moral threshold (or face up to the abyss between theory and practice) by refusing to generalize from particular experiences as long as the internalized beliefs of a distinctly religious character were in place. This mindset is revealed by incantations such as those of George Lukacs, who averred that "the worst socialism is better than the best capitalism." His former disciple, Agnes Heller, an early supporter of the regime (later émigré) observed that Lukacs was led to communism by "a search for redemption. He wished to be the new St. Augustine of a universalistic movement such as Christianity used to be. The communist St. Augustine. He longed for a movement that would transform the world. . . . If there was anything he took from his Jewish background it was messianism."[8]

For these believers, the experience of the specific flaws and shortcomings of the system could be neutralized by their faith and commitment and by the attendant capacity to defer to the future the benefits the system was going to deliver; in the absence of such faith, personal experience was devastating. The most widely used technique or defense mechanism was what Arthur

Koestler called "the doctrine of unshaken foundations," [9] the conviction that, notwithstanding apparent problems and deficiencies, the system was headed in the right direction, its positive aspects outweighed the questionable ones — or, more simply, that the ends justified the means. A Hungarian writer, Istvan Eorsi, who moved from sincere devotion to equally sincere opposition to the regime, also used this defense mechanism and a similar terminology: "On the rare occasion when we were stung by the pricks of doubt, we instantly applied the balm of magic incantations to the wound. They included 'essentially' and 'in the final analysis.' Certain aspects of the confession of the 'traitors' [in the show trials] perhaps were not entirely true, but in its 'essentials' and 'in the final analysis' the charges were well founded."[10]

Likewise, Agnes Heller clung to the sentiment that under difficult conditions "the essentials are OK."[11]

Another defense mechanism was described by Miklos Gimes, a dedicated Hungarian communist functionary who became a revolutionary in 1956 and paid with his life for his changed convictions:

> Gradually we came to believe ... that there are two kinds of truth, that the truth of the Party ... could possibly be different and more important than objective, factual truth, that truth and momentary political expediency are identical. ... If there is a truth higher than factual truth ... then lies can be "true" since lies can be useful in the short run; a fabricated political trial can also be "true" since it may yield political benefits. Suddenly we are transported to the outlook which infected not only those who devised the show trials ... which poisoned our public life ... paralyzed our critical thinking and finally prevented us from perceiving basic facts of life.[12]

Wolfgang Leonhard, a communist functionary in East Germany after World War II, had a traumatic and tangible encounter with the abyss between theory and practice when he found out that there was a hierarchy of food services at the party headquarters entailing several classes of meals for different groups of staff members depending on their position.[13] Andras Hegedus, former prime minister of Hungary, also recalls the special, high-quality meals he was served in his office; he was uneasy about them but allowed himself to be persuaded (at the time) that they were justifiable given his devotion and the value of his services to the party.

As an adolescent supporter of the communist regime in Hungary (around the same time Leonhard met his moral threshold, after World War II), I made my own troubling discoveries of what struck me as a serious conflict between theory and practice. These doubts arose from my daily contemplation of the luxurious American automobiles members of the nomenklatura used. On my way to school every day, I walked by a streamlined Hudson parked by the sidewalk with the chauffeur waiting for his passenger (a minister) and I wondered why a much smaller Skoda, VW, or Opel would not be sufficient? What did it mean that under conditions of scarcity when private automobiles were mostly unheard of, these functionaries were provided with large, luxurious vehicles? I was well aware of the egalitarian rhetoric and proclaimed policies of the regime and under the impression they were being implemented. I also believed that discrepancies between luxury and deprivation (as exemplified by the different modes of transportation for high-ranking officials and the "masses") were only prevalent in capitalist systems. The bad impression created by these luxury vehicles was deepened by the curtains on the windows hiding the faces of the occupants in the back, symbolizing their inaccessibility, or perhaps an embarrassed preference for anonymity.

This kind of moral revulsion was an unintended consequence of the extraordinary claims of the official propaganda (and its distant connections with the utopian aspects of the official ideology) designed to make these systems not merely acceptable but convince the citizen of their unprecedented comparative-historical superiority.

It may be asked, how do we know that there was a popular awareness of these manifold moral transgressions, and how was it manifested? Which forms of the discrepancy between theory and practice were the most unacceptable or outright intolerable?

The most obvious evidence of these perceptions and feelings comes from the rapid unraveling, indeed collapse, of these systems at the end of the 1980s and early 1990s. Once it became clear (under Gorbachev) that Soviet troops would no longer guarantee the survival of the governments in Eastern Europe, these systems rapidly fell apart with surprisingly little effort on the part of the rulers to hang on to power, as if they themselves realized their own unpopularity and illegitimacy. Inside the Soviet Union the long-simmering crisis of legitimacy (that began with Khrushchev's 1956 speech at the Twentieth Party Congress) intensified during the years of *glasnost* (which brought to surface much of what had been hidden), culminating in a corresponding loss of political will to cling to power on the part of the Soviet ruling elites.[14]

While it is difficult in retrospect to assess or classify different moral thresholds in various groups or strata of the population, it is possible to speculate about some of its determinants. It is likely that those who held strongly internalized traditional and especially religious values, as well as those who believed in some kind of secular, humanistic values were more deeply offended than others. Not surprisingly, those who suffered at the hands of these regimes also looked for and easily found larger moral causes for their own rejection of these systems.

At last an effort should be made to comprehend the likely motives and mentality of those who devised the counterproductive propaganda campaigns that directly contributed to the discreditation and moral rejection of these systems. The propaganda directed at the populations in communist systems was remarkably heavy-handed, humorless, self-righteous, and repetitive. Little effort was made at anything resembling a more sophisticated effort at persuasion; the population was inundated with unqualified assertions and claims reflecting a totally polarized and oversimplified view of the world and human beings.

Whether or not or to what degree the power-holders themselves believed the propaganda they disseminated or presided over is debatable. They certainly believed in its overall necessity, as something that made a contribution to the survival of the system and to keeping their power. Many citizens of the communist states were convinced that their rulers themselves did not believe their own propaganda, that it was all put forward and disseminated in a totally cynical fashion. If so, this provided further reasons for rejecting the system. As the literary incarnation of a Czech political refugee put it, "what is so debilitating, so *spiritually* debilitating, is that no one believes in the Party line, least of all those who are charged with enforcing it. At least in the past, at the time of the Inquisition . . . or in the early days of the Russian Revolution, those who imposed an ideology believed in it, but in Czechoslovakia, since 1968, no one believes in Marxism or Leninism, and so what they impose upon us is what they themselves know to be a lie.[15]

The key to understanding the nature of communist propaganda that was used in communist systems (as distinct from the propaganda of the communist parties in the West or communist state propaganda directed at the West, or other parts of the world) is that it was inspired by a totalitarian mentality and was integrated with the possession of power. Just as the attitude to power was uncompromising, so was the attitude toward the battle of ideas. No quarter was given and no concessions were made in presenting the case for the official worldview and policies. As Gyorgy Litvan put it, those in power feared that "if only one brick is pulled out, the whole edifice would collapse."[16] This also applied to propaganda.

The qualities of the propaganda were further determined by the monopoly on power of those dispensing it. The communist systems kept up the propaganda barrage in the manner here described since their power rested far more decisively on coercion and intimidation than on persuasion. The possession of power obviously reduces the need for propaganda; the survival of these regimes did not depend on persuading their citizens about the righteousness of their objectives and policies; obedience was exacted by coercive measures, or their threat. Nonetheless, it is likely that the rulers would have preferred to govern on the basis of a genuine popular acceptance of their policies.

Another major stimulant of communist propaganda was the mirage of the new socialist or communist man these systems sought to create. Appropriate models of behavior had to be created, promoted, and disseminated in various ways and settings and this too became a task of propaganda.

Finally, it is also likely that another major source of communist propaganda (as a compensatory device) was the unacknowledged awareness of the leaders of their own questionable legitimacy and lack of genuine or wide popular support.

Communist systems in Eastern Europe, and Hungary in particular, lost their legitimacy not merely because they created repressive police states which imposed a wide range of material, social, and cultural deprivations on their people but also because they violated, basic, elementary moral precepts that had been internalized by the populations of these countries. They created intense moral revulsion because the people rightly felt that these systems engaged in prolonged and determined attempts to drastically redefine their personal experiences of the new social environment—that is to say, to deceive them without the least hesitation. If so, one of the many lessons of the anniversary we are here remembering and honoring may well be that ordinary human beings are capable of moral judgment and these judgments can have profound political and historical consequences.

NOTES

1. Raymond Aron, *The Opium of Intellectuals* (London: Secker and Warburg, 1957), 42–43.

2. Miklos Haraszti, *Worker in a Workers' State* (New York: Universe Books, 1978) is a revealing study of how industrial workers experienced and responded to these realities.

3. *Angyal Istan Sajatkezu Vallomasa* [The Firsthand Confession of Istvan Antal] (Budapest, n.d.), 37. The author was executed for his participation in the armed struggle during the 1956 Revolution. (I translated this and all subsequent quotes from Hungarian sources.)

4. Gyorgy Litvan, *Oktoberek Uzenete: Valogatott torteneti irasok* [The Message of Octobers: Selected Historical Writings] (Budapest, 1996), 335.

5. An illuminating discussion of these schools and their program of indoctrination can be found in Andras Hegedus, *A Tortenelem es Hatalom Igezeteben* [In the Thrall of History and Power] (Budapest, 1988).

6. Aleksander Wat, *My Century* (Berkeley, Calif.: University of California Press, 1990), 173.

7. Thomas Aczel and Tibor Meray, *Tisztito Vihar* [Cleansing Storm] (Munich, 1978), 276. Published in English under the title *The Revolt of the Mind*.

8. Agnes Heller, *Biciklizo Majom* [Monkey on the Bicycle] (Budapest, 1999), 136, 87.

9. Arthur Koestler, "Soviet Myth and Reality," in *The Yogi and the Commissar* (New York: MacMillan, 1961), 123.

10. Istan Eorsi, *Versdokumentumok, Magyarazatokkal, 1949–1956* [Poetic Documents with Commentary] (Budapest, 2001), 8.

11. Heller, *Biciklizo Majom*, 81.

12. Sandor Revesz, *Egyetlen Elet: Gimes Miklos Tortenete* [A Single Life: The Story of Miklos Gimes] (Budapest, 1999), 291.

13. He described this in his *Child of the Revolution* (Chicago: 1958).

14. See Paul Hollander, *Political Will and Personal Belief: The Decline and Fall of Soviet Communism* (New Haven, Conn.: Yale University Press, 1999).

15. Piers Paul Read, *A Season in the West* (New York, 1988), 27.

16. Litvan, *Oktoberek Uzenete*, 336.

Chapter Twenty-three

Ambivalent in Amsterdam

There have been three major ideological-political movements in the twentieth and early twenty-first centuries that most explicitly and purposefully exploited and harnessed the capacity for hatred to the pursuit of political objectives: communism, Nazism, and now radical Islam.

Supporters and leaders of all three movements believed that they could create blissful social systems if only they could eradicate the groups and individuals malevolently obstructing the accomplishment of the great goals. The thirst for destroying these enemies was dependably fueled by a consuming hatred. All three were arrayed against the West, that is to say, against secular, liberal, democratic, and pluralistic societies.

But Nazism and communism were largely secular, or secular-religious—their adherents did not seek fulfillment and glory in the combination of self-destruction with the destruction of their enemies in the expectation of generous otherworldly rewards. These three belief systems also differed in the degree of irrationality their leaders and supporters displayed, reflecting the varying degrees of religious, or quasi-religious, fervor motivating them. "Irrationality" here (as in general) refers to implausible, empirically unfounded beliefs and expectations—for example, those of the suicide bombers who are convinced that their murderous deeds will secure them admission to paradise.

Islamic radicals are also distinguished from Nazis and communists by the prominence and intensity of their hatred, freely and joyously expressed, and the ready embrace of self-destruction rooted in the beliefs in otherworldly rewards. A major question of the present-day political agenda of the whole world, and especially Western nations, is how serious a threat such fanaticism represents and how to cope with it.

In light of these questions and concerns, Ian Buruma's new book is of great interest. Buruma had earlier addressed (with Avishai Margalit) in *Occidentalism* (2004) the more elusive sources of the current Islamic hatred of the West and the rejection of Western values and institutions. In this volume the point of departure is the 2004 murder of Theo van Gogh, an outspoken Dutch critic of Islamic beliefs and attitudes. Why did a young man, who was neither poor nor oppressed, who had received a decent education, who had never had trouble making friends, who enjoyed smoking dope and drinking beer—why would such a man turn into a holy warrior whose only wish was to kill and, perhaps more mysteriously, to die? There is no clear answer forthcoming, but there are numerous plausible, if somewhat contradictory, suggestions offered.

Murder in Amsterdam is the product of a journalistic fact-finding visit consisting of sketches of the major protagonists in the recent violent dramas and interviews with people expressing very different points of views about these events and their background. The chapters are somewhat disjointed, as if hastily put together—albeit by a very knowledgeable native of Holland who had access to the major players and had given much thought to these matters.

Buruma is judicious and discerning, but his efforts to avoid simplification often interfere with determining what his own views are. Sometimes it takes an effort to establish whether or not the views described are his or those of his interlocutors. And when presenting the latter, it is often unclear whether he agrees or disagrees with them. He writes about Ayaan Hirsi Ali, the famous female critic of Islam of Somali origin and former member of the Dutch Parliament, who was forced to live underground because of death threats and who is currently in exile in the United States: "To some she is a heroine, standing up against the forces of darkness, battling for free speech and enlightened values.... Others ... loathe her." Does the "some" include or exclude the writer? Does he question that she stood up against the forces of darkness defending free speech at great risk to her life? Is she mistaken in her belief that many problems "that plague the Islamic world ... can be explained at least in part ... [by] ... a warped view of sexuality," that is to say, the attitude toward women? Is she overly zealous "in her battle for secularism" as he suggests? And is not such zealousness commendable when it combines, as it did, with great courage and integrity? Is she wrong suggesting that the liberation of Muslims in the West "is sabotaged by the Western cultural relativists ... who say, 'It's part of their culture, so you mustn't take it away....'" Here Buruma gently guides the reader to the conclusion that these are unwise positions. He also writes that she "was no Voltaire. For Voltaire had flung his insults at the Catholic Church, one of the two most powerful institutions of eighteenth-century France, while Ayaan risked offending only a minority that was already feeling vulnerable in the heart of Europe." A peculiar judgment, since Voltaire was hardly in imminent danger of assassination and forced to live in hiding, whereas she was hounded by an exceptionally brutal, violent, and hate-filled "minority"—as if that minority status minimized or trivialized the risks she had taken or neutralized the deadly fanaticism of her enemies. In the postscript, Buruma shows more sympathy, apparently more on account of the tragic circumstances of her life than her beliefs. His "country seems smaller without her," he concludes.

Another example of authorial ambivalence is the discussion of the views of Afshin Ellian, a scholar born in Tehran who writes newspaper columns in Holland "harshly critical of political Islam." Ellian believes, in Buruma's telling,

> that citizenship of a democratic society means living by the laws of the country. A liberal democracy cannot survive when part of the population believes that divine laws trump those made by man. The fruits of European Enlightenment must be defended. . . . European intellectuals, in their self-hating nihilism and utopian anti-Americanism, have lost the stomach to fight for Enlightenment values. . . . No religion or minority should be immune to censure or ridicule.

Buruma does not say what he thinks about these sensible and defensible propositions but observes later that "the tone of his [Ellian's] columns is sometimes strident, even shrill." He also appears to distance himself from the opinion of former leftist Paul Scheffer, who thinks that "allowing large communities of alienated Muslims to grow in our midst was a recipe for social and political disaster."

At one point Buruma argues that democracy would only be threatened "if all true Muslims were political revolutionaries." It is hard to see why a smaller, determined group of violent revolutionaries (who enjoy the passive support of more substantial, if undetermined, portions of their community) should be dismissed as nonthreatening.

It is a telling illustration of the attitudes found in the Islamic communities in Holland that van Gogh's killer and his friends demanded that they be provided with apartments by the municipal authorities built in such a way that the "women should be able to go in and out of the kitchen unseen." Buruma quotes an old woman in a declining working-class neighborhood, one of the few Dutch people who chose to stay: "The trouble really began when masses of Moroccan and Turkish families were dumped in our neighborhood. They had no idea how to behave in our society. Garbage bags would be tossed into the street from the second floor. Goats would be slaughtered on the balcony. The worst . . . [is] that we don't speak the same language. You know, when your ceiling leaks and you can't tell the neighbors upstairs to turn off their tap." Again, it's not clear if Buruma thinks these are vicious ethnocentric stereotypes or reasonable enough complaints.

This is not to say that the author never makes his views clear. Toward the end of the book he demolishes a conventional wisdom, writing, "It is unlikely . . . that those who want God's kingdom on earth are going to be satisfied with a better deal for the Palestinians or a U.S. withdrawal from Iraq." Thus on the one hand he recognizes that "violence in the name of faith" is hard to tame or eradicate, but on the other he seems to blame Dutch society for the alienation of the Islamic community, sometimes the Western world as a whole: "Perhaps Western civilization, with the Amsterdam red-light district as its fetid symbol, does have something to answer for."

As to the responsibility of Dutch society, it is not clear if it is the "smugness" and racism that are blamed, or their opposite: the politically correct eagerness to cater to the immigrants' customs and sense of identity and the attendant abandonment of any serious attempt to integrate them.

Thus Buruma oscillates between explaining the instances of violence (and the attitudes giving rise to them) by the character of Dutch society, Islamic beliefs, and broader historical trends and phenomena. He writes (discussing the mindset of van Gogh's killer) that "the death wish in the name of a high cause, a god, or a great leader is something that has appealed to confused and resentful young men through the ages and is certainly not unique to Islam." But the current confluence of violence against the "infidels" with self-destruction has few equals outside the ranks of those imbued with Islamic beliefs. Neither Nazism nor Marxism generated suicidal violence; likewise, the radical leftist terrorist groups in the 1960s and 1970s in the United States and Europe displayed no suicidal impulses, presumably because they had no religiously inspired conviction that a blissful afterlife awaits them as a reward for their murderous good works.

Overlooking these and other differences also contributes to questionable parallels between a traditional Dutch-Protestant self-righteousness and the Islamic variety: "Mohammed [the killer of van Gogh], in a very Dutch delusion of grandeur, expanded his youthful enthusiasm for neighborhood politics to encompass the fate of mankind." Buruma also writes, "In the muddled mind of Mohammed Bouyeri . . . ran a deep current of European anti-liberalism combined with self-righteous moralism and Islamist revolutionary fervor." The attribution of European antiliberalism in this instance is gratuitous and redundant; Bouyeri's behavior was amply accounted for by the other attributes noted.

There is also an implausible and strained attribution of resemblance between costumed Dutch soccer fans celebrating a soccer game and supposedly corresponding attitudes of Muslims: "It [the celebration] was a return to an invented country, no more real than a modern Dutch Muslim's fantasy of the pure world of the Prophet."

Far more persuasive is the parallel between the part played by ideas in the major campaigns of political violence in recent history: "Revolutionary Islam is linked to the Koran . . . just as Stalinism and Maoism were linked to *Das Kapital*, but to explain the horrors of China's man-made famines or the Soviet gulag solely by invoking the writings of Karl Marx would be to miss the main point. Messianic violence can attach itself to any creed." True enough, but once the notion of "messianic" is introduced we have a circularity in the argument, since "messianic" is a key component of the "creeds" in question. It would be safer to say that violent impulses attach themselves to, and find legitimation in, messianic creeds that legitimate the former, and this applies to both Marxism and Islam.

This informative volume would have been more enlightening if its author could have settled in his own mind the respective contributions Dutch society and Islamic beliefs have made to the violence he sought to understand.

Chapter Twenty-four

Travel in the Peloponnesos

Even at a time when it is the conventional wisdom that the world is getting smaller, that modernity crushes cultural diversity and globalization overwhelms local distinctions, travel can still provide some welcome refutation of such claims. Surely, airports all over the world are virtually identical in design and ambience, as are superhighways, parking garages, hydroelectric dams, telephones, TV sets, microwave ovens, and many other products of modern technology. Although we depend on these devices, few of us understand how they work, what laws of physics they obey, and the scientific discoveries they embody. Perhaps here lies one source of aversion to modernity: it makes us humiliatingly dependent on machines and instruments that we cannot comprehend; it also makes us further dependent on the specialized few who can make them work or fix them when they fail to do so.

This, however, is not the whole story. Technology does not completely erase traditional ways of life even when widely relied upon, and it is not equally widely relied upon everywhere notwithstanding its availability and affordability. Even thoroughly modernized Western Europe abounds in spots and corners pleasantly different from North America (and other parts of Europe) to gladden the heart of the traveler looking for remnants of the past and settings different from those he is familiar with. To be sure pristine, technologically untouched areas are impossible to find in Europe—but, in any event, one would not want to spend one's holiday in such places given the physical discomforts. There are limits to the pursuit of authenticity and heartwarming traditional ways of life, even for the romantic critics of modernity. On the other hand, there is an appealing element of adventure and modest risk associated with travel in the less-modernized parts of the world.

It is an endlessly interesting question why so many among the educated and affluent (not that the two invariably go together) are so taken with the past and its physical remnants; why the nostalgia for the imaginary (or real?) times bygone? Interest in the old is not merely a response to the burdens and stresses of modernity, of living in crowded, polluted technological civilization. Already in the middle of the eighteenth and early nineteenth centuries, European writers, artists, and aristocrats traveled to places (foremost among them Italy and Greece) where they sought to discover and rediscover lost virtues, pleasures, and sensibilities. Both the Enlightenment intellectuals and the Romantics somewhat later avidly pursued the past, the remains of traditional societies where they sought instruction and relief from the difficulties of their own as yet barely modern world. James Boswell, Chateaubriand, Byron, Flaubert, Goethe, Heine, Shelley, and Wordsworth were among such travelers.

Werther, an outstanding literary personification of this sensibility, and doubtless reflecting the feelings of his creator Goethe, mused in a small German village of his times: "Nothing can fill me with such true, serene emotion as any features of ancient, primitive life like this. . . . How thankful I am that my heart can feel the simple, harmless joys of the man who brings to the table a head of cabbage he has grown himself. . . ."[1] Romantic nature worship sometimes merged with religious sentiments; Thomas Gray, the poet, was prompted by the Swiss Alps to observe (in 1739): "Not a precipice, not a torrent, not a cliff but is pregnant with religion and poetry. There are certain scenes that would awe an atheist into belief, without the help of other argument."[2]

These writers and artists, small in number, were the vanguard of a movement, pioneers of what was to come in our times: the popular "journeys of self-discovery" undertaken by large numbers of prosperous, educated, middle- and upper-class people (North American, European, Japanese), especially the young among them. These journeys have in part been prompted by the belief that a certain amount of travel is an obligatory part of one's education. In more recent times the "junior year abroad" programs of many American colleges institutionalized this belief. There are, however, other broader and murkier motives blending with the more straightforward and rational pursuit of some knowledge of the world and the cultures of different societies that travel may yield.

Travel unconnected to utilitarian pursuits (business, colonial exploration, conquest) can be linked to the rise and spread of individualism, to taking oneself seriously, and to the belief in one's uniqueness, or in the imperative to discover it. As Paul Fussell put it, travel is also an "escape . . . from the traveler's domestic identity."[3] The desire for such escape is related to the rejection of a conception of one's identity predominantly rooted in one's social roles; such a conception came to be seen as far too narrow and confining and failing to do justice to the richness, complexity, and uniqueness of one's individuality. Individualism is a by-product of modernity, or incipient modernity, of a heightened intolerance of conditions felt to be constricting, suppressing the wondrous complexity and hidden potentials of the self.

The urge to discover one's "true self" by means of travel is based on the idea that new surroundings would allow, or compel, one to see things differently, to take a new look at oneself, and stimulate the discovery of new aspects of one's personality, leading to, what in these days is called "personal growth." In the new, unfamiliar settings, fewer things would be taken for granted, one's eyes would open to new realities, possibilities, and insights; the traveler would benefit from exposure to the different customs and ways of life and types of people, from the novel and hopefully transforming experiences; no longer will he be captive to stale, ingrained habits and tastes—hence the notion that travel broadens.

A major attraction of travel has been its association with novelty and change, with the suspension of routines and the promise of coming upon new, more fulfilling ways of life. But there is a paradox here, since the traditional societies most of the travelers here discussed seek are, or appear to be, stable and unchanging, which is precisely one of their appeals. How can these two desires, for novelty and tradition, be reconciled? They can insofar as various features of traditional society are the novelty, a welcome departure from the turmoil, busyness, and restlessness of the Western societies most of these travelers come from.

The principal, if not often clearly articulated, appeal of traditional societies lies in the moral and existential certainties they offer; people who belong to them have no great trouble deciding what to do with their lives and do not find it difficult to make moral choices and judgments; nor do they have identity problems—they know all too well who they are, what their limitations are, and they do not entertain grandiose fantasies and desires about reinventing themselves. Of course, by the same token those living in these traditional societies also have fewer choices in matters of importance, but this may be overlooked by those who in our times feel overwhelmed by an excess of choice, or options.

There may be another, more prosaic, explanation. In the past, as in recent times, many journeys were undertaken in part to escape the harsh northern climate: to the Mediterranean, the Caribbean—wherever a milder climate could be found. Certainly the reverse has never been the case: southerners have not been flocking to northern destinations. Of course it has not been only a matter of different climates but also different incomes: populations in the less than balmy climates of northern Europe and North America have enjoyed higher living standards and could more readily afford to travel than those in southern Europe let alone in much of the rest of the world.

The travelers here alluded to tend to assume that many countries other than their own are more exotic, colorful, vibrant, and stimulating. The main character of a romantic novel (and a stand-in for its author, the early nineteenth-century French writer and traveler Francois-Rene de Chateaubriand) thus rhapsodized, "Ancient and lovely Italy offered me its innumerable masterworks. With what reverent and poetic awe I wandered among those vast edifices consecrated to religion by the arts! . . . What a succession of arches and vaults! How beautiful the strains of music heard around the domes, like the rolling of the ocean waves, like the murmuring winds of the forests, or like the voice of God in His temple!"

The character in Chateaubriand's novel also put his finger on another motive for travel, even more pertinent in our times than it was two centuries ago when it was written: "Europeans constantly in turmoil are forced to build their own solitudes. The more tumultuous and noisy our heart, the more calm and silence attracts us."[4] This is exactly what we expect and hope to find in places "off the beaten path," less touched or untouched by material progress. In these fulfilling destinations these travelers hope to come upon the descendants, if not the actual incarnations, of the noble savage and what is left of unspoiled nature. For Americans and urbanized Europeans, even present-day farmers, peasants, or fishermen will qualify as noble savages. A recent visitor to Greece typified these sensibilities as he wistfully recalled, "We stopped for an early breakfast at the Krifos Kipos taverna in the tiny fishing village Agios Nikolaos and watched the caiques come in, hung with kerosene lanterns and laden with the morning's catch of fish." Unhappily, he was also compelled to note that the serenity was punctured by the cries of traveling salesmen advertising their wares with loudspeakers mounted on their trucks.[5]

A sense of security is also associated with traditional societies. In none of the small towns where I stayed on recent trip to Greece (Tolo, Githeo, Kardamili, Methoni on the coast; Stremitsa and Dimistsana in the mountains) did we see any policemen. There was, coincidentally or not, a sense of security and tranquility. Realistically or not, we felt safe.

All this leads to the question of what exactly it takes to pronounce a village or small town "unspoiled." The major requirements certainly include small size, lack of crowds, minimal presence of modern technology, and reminders of the past, mostly in the form of old buildings. No village or town will qualify as "unspoiled" if it is full of cars and tour buses or if it boasts huge parking spaces. TV antennas, too, encroach on the idea of the unspoiled even when sprouting from old houses. Small size does not automatically protect from crowds. This was clearly the case in Rocamadour, France, which I visited a few years ago—a splendid, small medieval town in a rocky hillside full of great Gothic churches and chapels but also one inundated with crowds of tourists filling its small streets, lined with gift shops and restaurants. My wife and I were part of these crowds and therein lies the paradox and insoluble problem of pursuing "unspoiled" places. Given the large number of travelers intent on discovering and visiting them, they cannot remain unspoiled. The same applies to the beauties of nature trampled underfoot by the all of us nature lovers. It is somewhat easier to ration access to the beauties of nature (as the U.S. National Park Service has done in recent years) than to inhabited villages and towns. Cars can be excluded as they are from many small towns in Europe, but that is not the whole solution. Masses of pedestrians feasting on junk food disgorged on the edge of these towns by enormous tour buses or emerging from their own cars encroach on our expectations just as much as traffic jams on the old town square or main street. Rural areas and small towns can also be spoilt, indeed ruined, not just by mass tourism but by industry and commerce. On our recent trip to Greece we were shocked to discover a huge thermal power plant belching fumes in the center of the Peloponnesos in the midst of an otherwise attractive mountainous landscape and not far from the well-preserved remnants of the Byzantine city of Mystra. I do not know when it was built and if there were alternatives to such an obviously polluting plant in that location. There is, though, little doubt that area residents who thereby got their electricity would not willingly unplug their televisions or refrigerators in order to enjoy unpolluted air and unspoiled scenery.

My interest in visiting the Peloponnesos, while not explicitly influenced by the impulses and attitudes sketched above, was certainly colored by them. I have always been interested in remote, scenic, mountainous areas surrounded by or incorporating bodies of water. A large part of the attractions of the Peloponnesos was the scenery: dramatic mountains and gorges, a deeply indented coast, and low population density. Almost the entire southern, eastern, and western coast is dotted with small coastal towns and harbors, complete with Venetian forts. From guidebooks I learned about the old monasteries tucked into a deep gorge, irresistible even for those possessed of a secular mentality.

I was also drawn to the Peloponnesos because of the Mani Peninsula in the south, famous for its desolate landscape, abandoned fortress villages, and fierce early residents—"a proud and courageous people," according to the Michelin Guide, supposedly descended from the Spartans, "exclusive and bellicose" and filled with "a spirit of adventure." Those few remaining "still live in their steep villages dotted with olive trees on the mountain slopes preserving the cult of honor and hospitality," the guide further assured us. In the old days their lives revolved around bloody family feuds and successful attempts to repel invaders from other parts of Greece or from abroad, including the Turks. They were supposedly feared by other Greeks. Most of these original residents have vanished over time.

The Peloponnesos also abounds in famous ruins (such as Epidaurus, Mycenae, and Olympia), which I find of lesser interest since in many instances there is more left to the imagination than to the eye on these sites, at least for those of us archeologically challenged.

My first stop (reached by a two and a half hour drive from Athens's airport) was the small coastal resort town of Tolo. It is near the much better known and more picturesque town of Naflion, which used to be the first capital of independent Greece after the Turkish occupiers were defeated in 1822. (Athens became the capital in 1834.) I am among those who did not realize (or forgot) that Greece has only been an independent nation-state since the early nineteenth century, following the long and unwelcome presence of the Turks; that is to say, it was part of the Ottoman Empire. Other powers, such as Venice, controlled areas on the coast, as did the French in conjunction with the Crusaders; Britain possessed some islands in the Ionian Sea. I suspect that most people also fail to realize how small the population of Greece is (ten million), considering its historical and cultural importance. Of course Greece also produced emigrants ranging in the millions over time.

The only ruins I visited (on the way to the Mani peninsula), and very impressive ones at that, was Mystra (or Mistras), a former Byzantine city founded in the thirteenth century in the foothills of the Taygetos mountains, "occupying an exceptional site," as the Green Guide puts it. It is in the area where Sparta used to be (and there is now a modern city of that name). Mystra is a widely dispersed collection of partially ruined and restored palaces, monasteries, and fortresses at various elevations surrounded by tall, picturesque cypresses and connected by a network of trails and roads. It too was occupied by the Turks, and the churches were converted into mosques. There are excellent views of the Taygetos mountains and the surrounding countryside.

The next major stop was Kardamili, a small coastal town on the Messenian Gulf ("simple holiday resort and fishing village," according to the Green Guide) north of the Mani peninsula and flanked by the Taygetos mountains on the east and north of the Mani Peninsula. We chose it because it abuts the Viros Gorge and numerous hiking trails.

Further coastal explorations followed as we drove north on the pleasant highway circling the Messenian Gulf, stopping briefly in Koroni, a very attractive small port with citadel built by Venetians and Turks, and stopping for a few days in Methoni, further west. Here the major attraction was the huge Venetian fort and nearby Pylos (yet another attractive and lively coastal town) and its nature reserve. In Methoni we were the only guests in a pleasant hotel. From Methoni we took two day trips to Pylos and the nearby nature reserve, where we climbed a modest mountain topped by a partially ruined but still impressive fort overlooking the sea and the large horseshoe-shaped bay, part of the nature reserve. Subsequently we drove north along the shore until turning east and into the mountains to stay in the small towns of Stremitsa and Dimitsana, both located at elevations over 3,000 feet.

Aside from our interest in the monasteries, we went to the area because of the Lousios Gorge, which promised good hiking and in which the monasteries were located. The first and most spectacular monastery we visited (Moni Agios Prodromu) was partly accessible by car. After descending on a switchback road into the gorge, we continued on foot. Less than one hour's walk took us to the monastery located under an overhang of the cliff, part of it built into the mountain. Nearby was a small garden, a spring and some outbuildings. We were the only visitors. We had a glimpse of the living quarters of the monks (a handful only, it seemed), the ossuary where the skulls of earlier residents of the monastery reposed on shelves (hundreds of them), and a small room (quite dark) that had spectacular wall paintings. The wall painting of what appeared to be a saint was in excellent condition, with vivid colors.

It is not easy to put into words what made the visit to this monastery so memorable. For one thing it was something rather unusual; people living in North America or Western Europe rarely have the chance to come upon ancient monasteries hidden in a deep gorge. At the bottom of the gorge was a sizeable and clean stream, much of it white water. The monastery was surrounded by lush vegetation and smaller streams. All was quiet. The few monks went about their business, whatever it was. They were quite friendly, offering water and olives (candy in another monastery). They had electricity and could reach civilization easily if they wanted to. We have no idea how often they would and for what purpose. What did they do with themselves? How much of their time was spent with prayer and other devotions or with cultivating their gardens? How strong is their belief in eternity? These are matters we were in no position to learn about. These monks certainly made a choice by removing themselves from where most people live and from human company (other than fellow monks) and from women, except for visiting tourists or pilgrims. I am sure that in Greece, as in much of Europe and North America, the number of such people is dwindling. Still, there were young men among the monks in this and the other two monasteries I saw.

The serenity, seclusion, and the blending of the site with the natural beauty of the site were among the identifiable reasons for being impressed. Regardless of one's religious beliefs (or, in this case their absence), the monastic life and its reclusiveness hinted at an engagement with the spiritual realm, at a sustained determination to grapple with the pursuit of meaning in life (and death). This idea may, of course, be romantic projection; monks may become monks for all sorts of reasons that do not necessarily include great religious fervor, spirituality, or the desire to do good works. It is also quite possible that the daily, rigidly regulated and routinized rituals of devotion could divert attention from reflection and from deeper, less-structured spiritual quests. Nor did I have proof that these monks engaged in any charitable, humane, or helping activity. And yet they inspired respect and exuded more than a whiff of authenticity.

It must be readily acknowledged that one learns little of importance about people with whom one does not share a common language and way of life, which is usually the case when we travel. In Greece many of the natives spoke some English, but our exchanges were largely brief, functional transactions. Even so, some impressions emerge and linger, superficial as they were by necessity. Driving habits, for example, give some clues to the national character, or aspects thereof, as they vary in a patterned way from country to country. Greece is clearly among the countries—along with France Italy, Spain, and others in Europe—where people drive aggressively, and dangerously, and in obvious disregard of posted speed limits; they also readily honk at other drivers to express displeasure. On the other hand, they are surprisingly tolerant when confronted with double or otherwise illegally parked drivers blocking their way in the narrow streets of small towns and villages, when traffic is at a standstill for one reason or another.

Greek drivers think nothing of passing, or trying to pass, on curvy two-lane mountain roads that carry a fair amount of traffic. Why are these people (mostly men) so impatient, aggressive, and competitive in these situations? One explanation may be that unlike in the United States and parts of Western Europe, the widespread use of cars in Greece is more recent and one may surmise that owning a car is more a matter of pride and self-assertion. But there is also a certain general impatience and less self-discipline more readily found in all Mediterranean countries. In Britain, Holland, Scandinavia, and, above all, in the United States and Canada, people drive in more disciplined, less assertive ways. Greek, French, and Italian driving habits are comparable to those of many American male teenagers. Self-assertion is certainly part of the explanation. The many small shrines on roadsides erected in memory of the victims of such driving habits testify to their consequences.

The other explanation of Greek driving habits, like those of the Italians, is that they don't care much about rules. I recall that on another trip, flying from Athens to an island, some passengers, apparently friends of the pilot, walked casually in and out of the cockpit and quite a few smoked unselfconsciously in nonsmoking areas without earning a reprimand from the flight attendants. On the recent trip I also read in the Greek English-language newspaper about chronic squatting on public lands including nature reserves, about which the government has done little. Nor are environmental regulations enforced, evidently. The paper wrote (in an editorial), "In recent decades, Greece has experienced an environmental disaster at all levels. The postwar model of development led to repeated abuse of the environment. The most fundamental principles regarding the protection of natural resources were violated.... All these years strict laws were not able to prevent the destructive activities of organized interests, mainly due to widespread corruption and lack of proper monitoring mechanisms" (*Kathimerini*, September 24, 2003, 2).

On the other hand, the indifference toward the environment does not seem to extend to the toleration of billboards along the highways, except in the vicinity of Athens. The impressive nature reserve north of the coastal town of Pylos (mentioned earlier) also seemed well protected and clean; it included large lagoons, bird sanctuaries, and the spectacular bay with emerald water. The apparent cleanliness of the sea was another delightful and unexpected finding, and not only in this sanctuary. The fish population sampled while snorkeling was modest both in size and variety compared to the Caribbean, but these waters were by no means a saline desert.

There is a paradoxical relationship between tradition, modernity, and concern with the natural environment. Modernity as manifested in population growth and pressure, in urbanization and industrialization, is clearly bad for the environment. On the other hand, only prolonged modernity creates the kind of mentality that is self-consciously protective of the environment. Only educated, urban people generations removed from rural roots or origins revere nature and the environment. The romanticization of nature in Europe coincided with accelerating industrialization and urbanization. The more traditional a society, the less widespread the self-conscious admiration of nature and the less concern with the environment, partly because people depend very directly on the physical environment for their livelihood—from agriculture, animal husbandry, and forestry to hunting and fishing. Being traditional also means an unquestioning acceptance of these time-honored activities required by survival; nature is taken for granted and exploited without a second thought. But such exploitation remains circumscribed and moderated by primitive technology and lower population densities.

A degree of friendliness toward strangers is also characteristic of more traditional societies found in parts of Greece. I often found people going out of their way to be friendly and helpful, and not because we rented their rooms or ate in their restaurants. This was the case in particular when we needed information or directions in small towns; on such and other occasions people tried to round up a proficient English speaker if their own English was limited or nonexistent. Off the major highways we did not encounter aggressiveness, impatience, and unfriendliness, nor any hostility on account of being American, even though one reads and hears much about Greek anti-Americanism. Such good-natured behavior might have been due to various circumstances. We were tourists in small towns at the end of the tourist season, and people who make their living from tourists are not noted for their hostility or surliness toward them, although there are exceptions: in parts of the Caribbean and in any country where nationalistic pride is wounded by notions of servicing well-heeled strangers. A few years ago some Hungarian intellectuals complained that Hungary was becoming "a nation of waiters." This never seems to have occurred to the Swiss, who have been capable of combining high levels of collective self-esteem with a flourishing tourist industry for well over a century.

It is a test of the satisfactions a particular journey yields whether or not one would consider returning to the places visited. But this rarely happens. The accessible world abounds in attractive and interesting places. An American traveler can go to Britain, France, Italy, Spain, or Switzerland (among others) every year for decades without exhausting points of interest, natural or manmade. As we seek out new places with similar appeals, we are also motivated by a domesticated exploratory impulse. This impulse is not fully rational and by no means universal. Enormous numbers of people are perfectly content not to travel at all, or go to the same places year after year, confining their travel to a particular resort or a second home. The exploratory impulse of the kind here noted rests on a pure if vague curiosity, some kind of unarticulated hope and expectation as to what may be accomplished by visiting different parts of the world.

In the end one must recognize that travel—like so many other human activities—often reflects contradictory desires and beliefs. We want both novelty and a change of pace, but we also wish to immerse ourselves in the stable, time-honored ways of life assumed to persist in some corners of the world; we look for relaxation, for new comforts and luxuries, more interesting food and drinks, but travel, even the most modern and convenient, is almost inescapably tiring and disruptive; we are interested in invigorating new human contacts, but short trips circumscribed by language barriers cannot yield them; we long for the simplicity that eludes us at home, yet we also know that we are hopelessly dependent on the conveniences of modern technology. On our journeys of "self-discovery" we are not likely to discover much about ourselves we do not already know. None of this is to suggest we should give up traveling or that it is not a learning experience. However, one of the things we learn is that no magic breakthrough in personal liberation, enrichment, or self-discovery is accomplished by restlessly moving around, and that the pursuit of authenticity and meaningful life is no less elusive in the new as in the familiar settings.

NOTES

1. Johann Wolfgang Goethe, *The Sorrows of Young Werther* (New York, 1962), 43. (First published in 1774.)
2. Paul Fussel, ed., *The Norton Book of Travel* (New York, 1987), 275.
3. Fussel, *Norton Book of Travel*, 13.
4. Francois-Rene de Chateaubriand, *Atala and Rene* (New York, 1961), 11, 98. (First published 1800.)
5. Nicolas Krauss, "Where the Gods Are Neighbors," *New York Times Travel Section*, June 18, 2000, 9.

IV

THE SURVIVAL AND REPLENISHMENT OF THE ADVERSARY CULTURE

Chapter Twenty-five

The Resilience of the Adversary Culture

The terrorist attacks of September 11, 2001, provide a new vantage point for examining the evolution and current condition of the American adversary culture. This term, coined by Lionel Trilling in his 1965 book *Beyond Culture*, refers to a discernible and durable reservoir of discontent, a disposition of those Americans who habitually find the United States—or at least its government—at fault in virtually every conflict in which it is engaged and its social institutions irredeemably corrupt. It is a culture whose boundaries, both demographic and intellectual, defy precise definition; nonetheless, the concept has been indispensable for identifying a chronic domestic estrangement and the specific beliefs associated with it.

As to the social-demographic boundaries, most of those within the adversary culture may loosely be described as intellectuals, or quasi-intellectuals, and their followers; they are found in the greatest concentrations on major college campuses and in the surrounding communities. Living near a campus generally inclines one to overestimate the adversary culture's importance and influence, whereas distance from such a setting tempts one to write it off as inconsequential. A visit to a campus by someone not inured to its atmosphere illustrates the psychic distance between the two. About five years ago, *New York Times* columnist Maureen Dowd asked former President George H. W. Bush what he had learned at a Hofstra University conference about his presidency; Bush answered: "I learned that there are some real wacko professors scattered out around the country."[1]

As to the political-intellectual boundaries of this culture, it is left of center; its animating views are unswervingly anticapitalist, Marxist, quasi-Marxist; feminists, radical environmentalists, anarchists, and pacifists also qualify. With the collapse of Soviet communism, the composition and major preoccupations of this culture have somewhat changed. Radical environmentalism; antiglobalization and multiculturalism have come into the forefront. Environmentalism fits the adversary culture because of its antimodernist bias. Antiglobalization combines environmentalism and anticapitalism on a global scale to replace what used to be anticapitalism on national scales.

The adversary culture has also adopted postmodernism and deconstructionism. These relativistic positions and postures have been combined, curiously enough, with hearty, unqualified denunciations of American society and Western culture. As in the past, these condemnations rest on nonrelativistic assumptions, on absolute standards used for judging and condemning American society and culture.

Adherents of the adversary culture can be found in numerous settings, organizations, and interest groups. They include postmodernist academics, radical feminists, Afrocentrist blacks, radical environmentalists, animal rights activists, Maoists, Trotskyites, critical legal theorists, militant homosexuals, and lesbians. These groups often have different political agendas but share core convictions and key assumptions: all are reflexively and intensely hostile critics of the United States or American society and, increasingly, of all Western cultural traditions and values as well. It is their core belief that American society is uniquely repellent—unjust, corrupt, destructive, soulless, inhumane, inauthentic, and incapable of satisfying basic, self-evident human needs. The American social system has failed to live up to its original historical promise and, they insist, is inherently and ineradicably sexist, racist, and imperialist.

The adversary culture, by and large, took little notice of the collapse of Soviet communism, the end of the Cold War, and the retreat of state-socialist systems around the world. Its increasing preoccupation with matters domestic reflects the dearth of foreign alternatives to the alleged evils of American society and capitalism. Nevertheless, the supporters of the adversary culture still tend to sympathize with virtually every political entity that opposes the United States. These include the former Soviet Union, China under Mao, Castro's Cuba, Sandinista Nicaragua, supporters of the uprising in Chiapas, Yugoslavia under Milosevic, and the PLO and other anti-Israeli Arab groups and movements. There have been occasional disagreements among these critics regarding U.S. policy toward particular adversaries: a few of them supported the 1991 Gulf War and more of them the intervention in Kosovo. Some recognized that the Taliban's hatred of the United States and all it stands for does not necessarily make it an admirable ally or friend. Barbara Ehrenreich, for example, was disheartened that authentic enemies of the United States abroad were less than enlightened as regards the rights of women: "What is so heart-breaking to me as a feminist is that the strongest response to corporate globalization and U.S. military domination is based on such a violent and misogynist ideology."[2]

In the wake of September 11, some observers somewhat prematurely thought that the adversary culture has undergone substantial change. Hendrik Hertzberg found that only "traditional pacifists . . . and a tiny handful of reflexive Rip Van Winkles" object "to the aims and methods of the antiterrorism campaign. . . . Conservative commentators have had a frustrating time of it rounding up the usual blame-America-first suspects, because so few of those suspects are out there blaming America first."[3] Michael Kelly proclaimed "the renaissance of liberalism" and the marginalization of left-liberal politics in the same period.[4] Even more pointedly, George Packer argued in the *New York Times Magazine*, "September 11 made it safe for liberals to be patriots. Among the things destroyed with the twin towers was the notion held by certain Americans, ever since Vietnam, that to be stirred by national identity, carry a flag and feel grateful toward someone in uniform ought to be a source of embarrassment."[5]

But the adversary culture did not disappear, and its familiar attitudes reemerged. This has been most apparent on the campuses, where anti-U.S. sentiments and attitudes have been conventional wisdom since the later 1960s. Moreover, aspects of the worldview of this culture have been absorbed over time into the mainstream of public opinion through the media and educational institutions.[6] While the adversary culture still overlaps with the Left, a purely political definition does not do it justice. Rather, the attitudes and beliefs in question involve matters not considered central to politics at earlier times: sense of identity, cultural norms, matters of taste. Russell Jacoby's comment about alienation captures what is distinctive about the adversarial disposition: "Alienation once referred to social relations and labor, signifying an objective condition. Later it turned into an irritation or annoyance. 'I am alienated' someone will announce, meaning, 'I am unhappy or uncomfortable.'"[7]

A heightened receptivity to the real or perceived injustices of American society has a long tradition; high expectations and the value placed on nonconformity have deep roots in American social and cultural history. Strong beliefs in the perfectibility of human beings and institutions have for centuries been an essential attribute of the American view of the world, as has an indefatigable optimism regarding the solubility of all social, political, and personal problems. The social critical temper of the adversary culture has always fed on the high expectations that American society has generated and nurtured from its earliest days.

The current adversary culture descends from the 1960s, the last high watermark of social discontent. But while the most obvious and powerful causes were the Vietnam War, civil rights, and women's liberation, the adversary culture may also be seen as a response to the cumulative impact of modernity. Preeminent among the corrosive effects of modernity are the decline of the sense of purpose and community, the weakening of social solidarity and the problems of identity.

The stalwarts of the adversary culture—the likes of Noam Chomsky, Gore Vidal, Susan Sontag, and others—basically blamed the United States for the attack, invoking the "root causes," that is to say, American policies and attitudes. But there were also new dissenters from the conventional adversarial wisdom, such as Christopher Hitchens and Paul Berman.[8] Dissidents on the moderate left included Michael Walzer, who emphatically rejected the oft-repeated proposition that poverty and inequality explain terrorism. He suggested instead a "cultural-religious-political explanation" that emphasized the obsession with an Enemy embraced by people who are "ideologically or theologically degraded."[9] Christopher Hitchens criticized those on the left who were reluctant to acknowledge that "the bombers of Manhattan represent fascism with an Islamic face." He reminded fellow leftists that what Islamic militants "abominate about 'the West' is not what Western liberals don't like."[10] Ellen Willis, a columnist for the *Village Voice* and a journalism professor at NYU, argued that "the lessons of Vietnam" do not apply to Afghanistan and favored committing ground troops in the war.[11] Richard Falk argued that a U.S. military response to 9/11 could be justified and sought to provide a legal-moral framework for "a just response"—although he did feel compelled to observe that "a frenzy in the aftermath of the attacks [is] giving us reason to fear the response almost as much as the initial, traumatizing provocation."[12]

It is hard to know what proportion of those on the left experienced a conflict between newfound patriotic impulses and the adversarial outlook in the aftermath of the September 11 attacks. Most public responses to September 11 from the adversarial left suggest the persistence of sentiments and attitudes traceable to the late 1960s.

THEY HATE US FOR GOOD REASONS

Two major, closely linked arguments have been pursued among those on the adversarial left that converge in assigning ultimate responsibility to the United States for the attacks. The first is that if Arab terrorists harbored profound hatred for this country, this hatred had to be well founded; in other words, the United States must be hateful if it is hated. This proposition has provided a welcome opportunity to enumerate America's historic misdeeds, which supposedly justify such hatreds. The second proposition focuses on the alleged "root causes" of this hatred. The root causes of terrorism and the hatred of the United States (which shade into one another)—members of the adversary culture believe—should be understood rather than condemned. Emphasis on root causes leads to a deterministic, therapeutic view of the terrorists who are seen as "spawned" by compelling social-political and economic conditions beyond their control or full comprehension. They and their beliefs are held to be products of authentic grievances: poverty, inequality, backwardness, and social injustice. Of course this does not explain the motivation of Osama bin Laden, his associates, and the well-educated middle class suicide pilots.[13]

The "root cause" approach also proposes that hostility toward the United States is inspired by American support for corrupt and repressive political systems such as those in Pakistan, Egypt, and Saudi Arabia—as if the Islamic terrorists opposed to these governments were anxious to replace them with political democracies.

The responses of well-known figures of the adversary culture to September 11 illuminate the persistence of their convictions. Their moral indignation and anger focused almost entirely on the actions and policies of the United States and was largely devoid of corresponding sentiments regarding its avowed and murderous enemies. Gore Vidal thus observed that "the USA is the most corrupt political system on earth" and bin Laden was merely "responding to U.S. foreign policy."[14] A particularly curious form of this argument was put forward by a speaker at a Green Party conference: "The World Trade Center Disaster is a globalized version of the Columbine High School Disaster. When you bully people long enough they are going to strike back."[15] According to Professor Thomas Laqueur of Berkeley, California, "on the scale of evil the New York bombings are sadly not so extraordinary and our government has been responsible for many that are probably worse." Frederic Jameson argued that "the Americans created bin Laden. . . . This is therefore a textbook example of dialectical reversal."[16] Susan Sontag was far more enraged by the White House, our "robotic President" and public figures who stood united behind him, than she was by the terrorists: "this was not a 'cowardly' attack on 'civilization' or 'liberty' or 'humanity' or 'the free world' but an attack on the world's self-proclaimed superpower, undertaken as a consequence of specific American alliances and actions. . . . The unanimity of the sanctimonious, reality-concealing rhetoric spouted by American officials and media commentators in recent days seems . . . unworthy of a mature democracy."[17]

Norman Mailer told a Dutch audience, "The WTC was not just an architectural monstrosity but also dreadful for people who didn't work there, for it said to all those people: 'If you can't work up here, boy, you're out of it. . . .' Everything wrong with America led to the point where the country built that tower of Babel, which consequently had to be destroyed."[18]

There was an unmistakable discrepancy between the volume of compassion extended to the wholly unintended civilian victims of U.S. air strikes against the Taliban and the expressions of compassion for the wholly intended victims of the suicide pilots. As on so many similar occasions, moral equivalence was invoked. Noam Chomsky, perhaps the most durable and representative figure of the adversary culture, proposed that the attacks of September 11 were eclipsed by the American bombing of the pharmaceutical factory in the Sudan and numerous other American atrocities.[19] He asserted that "the United States had killed thousands of innocent civilians in Somalia, Sudan and Nicaragua—actions far more 'devastating' than the September 11 attacks—and was now trying to 'destroy the hunger-stricken country' of Afghanistan."[20] Edward Said, similarly prominent, made clear (in the Egyptian daily *Al-Ahram*) that he sees the United States as a genocidal power with a "history of reducing whole peoples, countries and even continents to ruin by nothing short of holocaust."[21] Michael Mandel, a law professor in Toronto, made no bones about his belief that, "The bombing of Afghanistan is the legal and moral equivalent of what was done to the Americans on September 11."[22] Eric Foner of Columbia University could not decide "which is more frightening: the horror that engulfed New York City or the apocalyptic rhetoric emanating daily from the White House."[23] Michael Klare, a professor of "peace studies and world security studies" at Hampshire College (Amherst, Massachusetts), became "despondent" because "the United States was ratcheting up a strong military response to September 11." He professed to be consumed by fear "that U.S. military reprisals would set off a renewed cycle of terrorist attacks and violence."[24] The General Secretary of the American Friends Service Committee said, "[O]ur history teaches us that bloodshed leads only to more bloodshed. . . .We call upon our president and Congress to stop the bombing. . . . Our grief is not a cry for retaliation. Terrorism must be stopped at its root cause."[25] Vivian Gornick (author of *The Romance of American Communism*) agreed: "Force will get us nowhere. It is reparations that are owing, not retribution."[26] Alice Walker "firmly believe[d] that the only punishment that works is love."[27] Richard Gere, the actor, similarly advised, "If you can see the terrorists as a relative who's dangerously sick . . . the medicine is love and compassion."[28] Oliver Stone called the September 11 attacks "a revolt" and equated the Palestinians dancing in the streets at the news of the attacks with those who publicly rejoiced at the news of the French and Russian Revolutions.[29]

Another oft-repeated theme of the adversary culture also reappeared: that America violates its own best values. Thus Russell Means, the American Indian activist who led the 1973 uprising at Wounded Knee, said, "It's what I used to see when I was behind the so-called Iron Curtain touring Eastern Europe. It's what I used to see in Nicaragua and Colombia . . . [namely] the ongoing deprivation of individual liberties and violations of the U.S. Constitution by the Federal Government. . . . The government lost all constitutional responsibility and has become an outlaw."[30]

Terry Eagleton was equally convinced that "They [the Bush administration] will use the crisis as an excuse to trample on our civil liberties,"[31] while the cover of Gore Vidal's new book, *The End of Liberty: Toward a New Totalitarianism*, showed the Statue of Liberty gagged with a U.S. flag. Alexander Cockburn averred that the war in Afghanistan was "about the defense of the American Empire."[32] Two feminists found no difference (moral equivalence again) between the practices of a religious police state and the influence of fashions in American society: "Taliban rule has dictated that women be fully covered whenever they enter the public realm. . . . During the 20th century, American culture has dictated [*sic*] a nearly complete uncovering of the female form. . . . The war on terrorism has certainly raised our awareness of the ways in which women's bodies are controlled by a repressive regime in a far away land, but what about the constraints on women's bodies here at home. . . ? The burka and the bikini represent opposite ends of the political spectrum."[33] Ralph Nader, meanwhile, was led to conclude that "there is an escalation of the corporate takeover of the United States. The ground and soil are ripe for a revolt by the American people."[34]

A fine example of a visceral response to the American flag and what it stands for came from Katha Pollit of *The Nation*, who revealed that "my daughter who goes to Stuyvesant High School only blocks from the World Trade Center, thinks we should fly an American flag out our window. Definitely not, I say: The flag stands for jingoism and vengeance and war."[35] A physics professor at the University of Massachusetts (Amherst) shared these sentiments: "To many ordinary people . . . around the globe the U.S. has done terrible things. . . . If I think about the flag, I have to think about it from the point of view of those people."[36] At Amherst College, war protesters (allegedly students from nearby Hampshire College) burned the flag while chanting "this flag doesn't represent me."[37]

It was not only the celebrities of the adversary culture who found the events of September 11 an appropriate occasion for reaffirming their animosity toward American society. There were demonstrations on nearly 200 campuses and in several major cities as a "nationwide network of more than 150 student antiwar groups . . . [emerged] holding campus vigils, protests, and teach-ins."[38] The correspondence columns of local newspapers in and around college campuses were flooded with letters expressing sentiments similar to those of the better known critics of the United States quoted above.

A professor of journalism at the University of Massachusetts, Amherst, regarded the attacks as the "predictable result of American policies . . . [that] ignored the suffering of Palestinians. . . . How can we fail to see that *our policy has created zealots and suicide bombers*" [my emphasis].[39] He, too, was convinced that the adversaries of the United States are helpless pawns of social and historical forces, whereas the United States and its amoral leaders always have alternatives to choose from and can therefore be held morally culpable.[40] A professor in the sociology department at the same university proposed that we must "find a way to reduce those alienating actions whereby we create our own enemies."[41] At a Haverford College meeting on September 14, an emeritus professor suggested that "the United States was the most violent nation on earth and ended by saying, 'We are complicit.'" At a teach-in at the University of North Carolina, "one lecturer told the students that if he were President he would first apologize to the widows and orphans, the tortured and impoverished and all the other millions of other victims of American imperialism." University of Texas Professor Robert Jensen told his students and peers that the attack "was no more despicable than the massive acts of terrorism . . . that the U.S. government had committed during my lifetime."[42] Barbara Foley, professor of English at Rutgers University, warned her students, "Be aware that whatever its proximate cause, the ultimate cause [of the attacks] is the fascism of u.s. [*sic*] foreign policy over the past many decades."[43]

Members of the Middle East Studies Association, a professional academic group, also reached the conclusion that the United States bore primary responsibility for the terrorist attacks (which, by the way, they refuse to designate as such).[44] At the 2001 annual meeting of the association, one panelist said, "We have not shown that our actions differentiate us from those who attacked us." An elderly professor in the audience declared, "We ought to be reminded of our responsibility for Hiroshima and Nagasaki and understand that we are not so good," receiving a round of applause. The moderator fully endorsed his view.[45]

STYLE AND SUBSTANCE

Many academic members of the adversary culture also have in common an irresistible attraction to obscure theorizing and arcane jargon, preferring esoteric turns of phrase and opaque abstractions to concreteness and specificity. One explanation may be the parochial elitism of numerous academic intellectuals who write mainly for one another and whose inaccessible language and terminology "signifies" their vanguard status. The second explanation may be the more important, however. The discontent that animates many critics of American (and Western) society and has become a major source of their sense of identity and self-esteem is murky and shapeless. Its origins may not be clear even to those consumed by it; diffuse and contradictory grievances, impulses, unfathomable sentiments, and personal resentments are inherently difficult to express in precise and accessible language. Form follows function: lack of clarity in style reflects amorphous motives and beliefs; Russell Jacoby calls them "postcoherent thinkers."[46] A statement of the "Transnational Feminist Practices Against War" illustrates what he has in mind:

> As feminist theorists of transnational and postmodern cultural formations . . . we offer the following response to the events of September 11 and its aftermath: First and foremost, we need to analyze the thoroughly gendered and racialized effects of nationalism and to identify what kinds of inclusions and exclusions are being enacted. . . . We see that instead of a necessary historical material and geopolitical analysis of 9-11, the emerging nationalist discourses consist of highly sentimentalized narratives that . . . re-inscribe compulsory heterosexuality and the rigidly dichotomized gender roles. . . . A number of icons constitute the ideal types in the drama of nationalist domesticity.[47]

It is among the attractions of obscurity that what people cannot fully comprehend is more difficult to criticize and refute. But it is also the case that some people are impressed by what they cannot fully understand, what promises some great, lurking, not fully penetrable revelation. A paragraph from the newly popular volume *Empire*, coauthored by an American literary scholar and an imprisoned Italian terrorist, provides further illustration:

> In the logic of colonialist representations, the construction of a separate colonized other and the segregation of identity and alterity turns out paradoxically to be at once absolute and extremely intimate. The process consists, in fact, of the moments that are dialectically related. In the first moment difference has to be pushed to the extreme. In the colonial imagination the colonized is not simply an other banished outside the realm of civilization; rather it is grasped or produced as Other, as the absolute negation, as the most distant point on the horizon.[48]

Doubtless there are connections and affinities between the attractions of obscurity, profound political misjudgments, and commonsense-defying beliefs. As Orwell observed, only intellectuals are capable of believing certain kinds of nonsense. Could, for example, anybody without the benefits of higher education and not living in an academic setting believe (with Michael Hardt and Antonio Negri, the authors of *Empire*) that the 1992 Los Angeles riots were "the most radical and powerful struggles of the final years of the 20th century"?[49]

THEN AND NOW

The adversarial generation of the 1960s holds on to a conception of America that is both malignant and inauthentic, and to a sense of identity of the fearless fighter for truth and social justice. This is the generation that had the opportunity and pleasure to glorify its youth by linking it to the causes of the 1960s. Perhaps therein lies the key to its durability, and in the critical mass of those who came of age together when a generic, youthful idealism converged with the rise of idealistic social movements and causes of the time.

But age and mortality are taking their toll on the leading figures of the adversary (and counterculture) rooted in the 1960s. Eqbal Ahmad, William Sloan Coffin, David Dellinger, William Kunstler, Norman Mailer, Susan Sontag, I. F. Stone, and Edward Said passed away. Other influential representatives of this culture are pushing their seventies or are older, including the Berrigan brothers, Noam Chomsky, Ramsey Clark, Angela Davis, E. L. Doctorow, Barbara Ehrenreich, Richard Falk, Stanley Fish, Tom Hayden, Frederic Jameson, Jonathan Kozol, Ralph Nader, Victor Navasky, Michael Parenti, Theodore Roszak, Paul Sweezy, and Howard Zinn. Even Bill Ayers, the cheerfully unrepentant Weatherman-bomber, is in his mid-sixties. The beliefs of this aging subculture, however, are being passed on to segments of the younger generations. American society since the end of the Cold War has continued to produce high expectations (that cannot be met) and the corresponding disappointments often turn into social criticism. Some young people are consumed by the same blend of incoherent discontent and diffuse idealism that characterized the protestors of the 1960s. They, too, seem to be in the grip of the conviction that "something is terribly wrong" with this society — a conviction that precedes the identification of the specific wrongs. When subsequently identified, the specific flaws become proof of the prior, underlying belief in pervasive corruption and thoroughgoing moral decay.

This smaller generation of "peace activists" today also resembles earlier ones in that they appear to be not so much opposed to all wars but only those waged by the United States (or Israel). Given their conviction that American society is profoundly unjust, any war its government may wage is bound to be judged immoral. However, should there appear on the horizon some new "national liberation movement" or militant cause that uses a congenial and idealistic rhetoric, the putative devotion to peace would vanish and be replaced by support for the new, liberating, and authentic revolutionary violence (Chiapas? Shining Path? Maoists in Nepal?).

A recent sympathetic portrait of such young people in the *New York Times* educational supplement demonstrates how present attitudes replicate those prevalent in the 1960s. The "typical student activist" of our times portrayed in the article is one of the leaders of "Students for Social Equality." He "is fueled by a nagging anger over the fact that there are haves and have-nots, oppressors and the oppressed." (His father is a general contractor on Long Island, and both parents are Republican.) His favorite words are "love," "unity," "solidarity," and "justice," along with "beautiful"—as in "unity is beautiful." In his conversation with the reporter "he searches for the roots of his unrest." He and others like him (one of them radicalized by the writings of Howard Zinn) radiate "an ardor not seen for several decades." The main character in the article was smitten by an antiglobalism demonstration: "It was amazing how many people were out acting on their beliefs and coming together. It was beautiful." A protest at the military training center at Fort Benning, too, "was a really beautiful protest, really spiritual." Union Square in New York City became a "magical place of unity" at an anti-Afghanistan war demonstration. Among the activists, the reporter observes, "there is a lot of raging against the machine."[50]

Many readers, at least of a certain age, will recall that "raging against the machine" was the main theme of Mario Savio's fiery oration during the Free Speech demonstrations at Berkeley in 1964. Then and now "the machine" stood for impersonality, lack of community and feeling, "profits above people," and the fear of being crushed by forces over which one has no control. Then, as now, for many of the alienated the personal realm and its concerns ultimately dwarf and displace what is truly political. American society will continue to generate a mixture of high expectations, unease, and discontent that is its hallmark and that of modernity.

NOTES

1. Dowd, "Happy in Free Fall," *New York Times*, May 7, 1997.
2. Ehrenreich, *Village Voice*, October 9, 2001, 54.
3. Hertzberg, *New Yorker*, November 5, 2001, 37.
4. Kelly, "A Renaissance of Liberalism," *Atlantic Monthly*, January 2002, 19.
5. Packer, "Recapturing the Flag," *New York Times Magazine*, September 30, 2001, 15.

6. Roger Kimball has called this the "mainstreaming of radicalism." See his *The Long March* (San Francisco: Encounter Books, 2000), 26. See also Gertrude Himmelfarb, *One Nation, Two Cultures* (New York: Knopf, 1999).

7. Jacoby, *The End of Utopia* (New York: Basic Books, 1999), 121.

8. Podhoretz, "Return of the 'Jackal Bins,'" *Commentary*, April 2002, 29.

9. Walzer, "Five Questions About Terrorism," *Dissent* (Winter 2002), 6.

10. Hitchens, "Against Rationalization," *Nation*, October 8, 2001, 8. See also his "Minority Report," *Nation*, October 22, 2001.

11. Letter, *New York Times*, November 1, 2001.

12. Falk, "A Just Response," *Nation*, October 8, 2001, 15.

13. Daniel Pipes refutes the argument that poverty causes terrorism in "God and Mammon: Does Poverty Cause Militant Islam?" *National Interest* (Winter 2001/2002).

14. *New Statesman* (London), October 15, 2001, 18–19; see also "Author Vidal Blames U.S. for Conflict," *Boston Globe*, November 24, 2001.

15. *Progressive Review*, October 29, 2001.

16. Laqueur and Jameson quoted in Tony Judt, "America and the War," *New York Review of Books*, November 15, 2001, 4.

17. Susan Sontag, "The Talk of the Town," *New Yorker*, September 24, 2001, 32.

18. Mailer quoted in *New Republic*, November 26, 2001, 8.

19. Quoted in David Horowitz, *The Ayatollah of American Hate* (Los Angeles: Center for the Study of Popular Culture, 2001), 7.

20. Quoted in *New Republic*, December 10, 2001, 9.

21. Quoted in *Weekly Standard*, October 8, 2001, 35.

22. *Globe and Mail* (Toronto), October 9, 2001.

23. Foner in the *London Review of Books*, October 4, 2001.

24. Klare, *Hampshire Life* (Northampton, Mass.), September 28, 2001, 8, 10.

25. Letter, *New York Times*, October 9, 2001.

26. *New Republic*, October 15, 2001, 10.

27. Walker, *Village Voice*, October 9, 2001, 54.

28. Quoted in *New Republic*, October 29, 2001, 10.

29. "Voices of Reason? Not in Hollywood," *Boston Globe*, October 23, 2001.

30. Associated Press Symposium, "How Have We Been Changed?" *Daily Hampshire Gazette* (Northampton, Mass.), October 13–14, 2001.

31. Quoted in Judt, "America and the War," 4.

32. "The Left and the Just War," *Nation*, November 22, 2001, 10.

33. Joan Jacobs Brumberg and Jacquelyn Jackson in *Boston Globe*, November 23, 2001.

34. Quoted in *The New Republic*, November 19, 2001, 10.

35. Pollit, "Put Out No Flags," *Nation*, October 8, 2001, 7.

36. Quoted in "How Words Spoken Sept. 10 Came Back to Haunt the Speaker," *Wall Street Journal*, October 10, 2001.

37. "Pro-America Rally Upset by Flag Burners," *Daily Hampshire Gazette*, October 19, 2001.

38. Lisa Featherstone, "A Peaceful Justice?" *Nation*, October 22, 2001, 18.

39. Bill Israel, "A Policy of Neglect and Cowardice," *Mass. Daily Collegian* (Amherst, Mass.), September 12, 2001.

40. Such selective determinism has been with us for a long time. See Paul Hollander, "Sociology, Selective Determinism and the Rise of Expectations," *American Sociologist* (November 1973).

41. Jay Demerath, September 15, 2001, departmental e-mail, University of Massachusetts, Amherst.

42. Each incident or statement quoted in "The Best and the Brightest," *Wall Street Journal*, October 2, 2001.

43. Foley, quoted in *New Criterion*, October 2001, 2.

44. The same is true of spokesmen for the major human rights organizations who argue that "terrorism" lacks clear definition. See *Commentary*, January 2002, 28.

45. Quoted in *New Republic*, December 3, 2001, 15, 17.

46. Jacoby, *The End of Utopia*, 141. See also Jay Tolson, "Wittgenstein's Curse," *Wilson Quarterly* (Fall 2001).

47. E-mail posted by Augustin Lao-Montes of the Department of Sociology at the University of Massachusetts, Amherst, October 29, 2001.

48. Quoted in *New Criterion*, October 2001, 20.

49. Quoted in *New Criterion,* October 2001, 20.

50. Abby Ellin, "The Making of a Student Activist: How a Long Island Boy Learned to Start Worrying and Hate the Bombs," *New York Times* (*Educational Supplement*), November 11, 2001, 26–28. See also Andrew Hsiao, "Make Noise Not War: A Peace Movement Grows in New York and Beyond," *Village Voice*, October 9, 2001.

Chapter Twenty-six

The Chomsky Phenomenon

Discussing a volume devoted to critiques of Noam Chomsky's (or anyone else's) ideas should entail a balanced evaluation of the views in question. But such an evaluation is difficult to accomplish when the individual in question is possessed of an unwavering self-righteousness and when the views examined are so extreme, unbalanced, and immoderate that their quality could only be overlooked by one of his most devoted disciples. Needless to say we are not talking here about Chomsky the linguist (his original, if by now distant, claim to fame) but about Chomsky the political commentator, world class social critic, relentless detractor of U.S. foreign policy, scourge of Israel, defender of Holocaust deniers, and dedicated proponent of the belief that the United States has been responsible for most evil in the world, and is ruled by an elite that is the most corrupt, ruthless, and depraved ever known in history. We are also talking about the man who has been propounding these views for almost half a century with a singular zeal, implausible repetitiveness, and unflagging determination

Unknown even to critics of his political ideas who are ready to concede his excellence in linguistics, Chomsky's contributions to that field have also been questionable and increasingly obsolete, two linguists in this volume argue. To wit, "a remarkable feature of Chomsky's linguistic writings is how few of them (the percentage has shrunk to almost zero over time) are professionally refereed works in linguistic journals" write Robert Levin and Paul Postal, both professors of linguistics. Whatever the quality of his intellectual contributions to political discourse or linguistics, his apparent impact and durable popularity as well as the abundant laudatory literature about him already in print justify a comprehensive critical examination of his ideas such as this volume provides, the first of its kind.

Chomsky's political beliefs and pronouncements deserve critical analysis not because of their originality but because of the extraordinary certitude with which they have been held, the unusual manner in which they have been expressed, and their popularity among educated publics. According to Larissa McFarquhar's portrait of him in *The New Yorker* (March 31, 2003), he was "preoccupied with politics even as a child and his views have not changed significantly since he was ten." He has also been alleged to be one of the ten most often cited authors of all times and his recent pamphlet 9-11 was translated into twenty-three languages and published in twenty-six countries.

There have been many critiques of Chomsky but until the appearance of this volume they have been scattered, inaccessible and unsystematic. The volume here reviewed does remedy this state of affairs up to a point. Part I, entitled "Chomsky, The World and the Word," contains two essays on his views on foreign affairs (on Southeast Asia and the Cold War) and one on his critiques of the American mass media, a somewhat dubious grouping. In part II, "Chomsky and the Jews," we learn about his animus toward Israel and of his support of the Holocaust deniers. Part III is entitled "Chomsky and the War on Terror" and its two essays respectively address his attitude toward 9/11 and his anti-Americanism. (Since anti-Americanism informs and permeates all his nonlinguistic utterances, this chapter could have been put anywhere.) The remaining two essays in part IV reassess his contribution to linguistics. The contributing authors (in addition to the editors who wrote the introduction as well as two substantive chapters) are Paul Bogdanor, Werner Cohn, Eli Lehrer, Robert Levine, Stephen Morris, Thomas Nichols, Paul Postal, Ronald Radosh, and John Williamson.

While the volume does address Chomsky's major preoccupations—U.S. foreign policy and its supposed subordination to economic interests (capitalism), the misdeeds of Israel, the corruptions of the American media, as well as his work in linguistics—gaps remain. For instance, a concluding, overview chapter would have been useful to tie together the individual chapters, and the organization of the volume could have been more coherent. A chapter on his inimitable polemical style and its possible connection to his ideas about language would have been interesting. Also missing is a chapter that could have tried to explain the origins of his beliefs and attitudes, something biographical or psycho-historical, as distinct from, and in addition to, expounding and dissecting them. While he is by no means the only Jewish detractor of Israel, his hostility is so intense and extreme that some specific explanation is called for, especially when it is combined with his defense of the Holocaust deniers. The editors note briefly that "His animus toward Israel is so great . . . that it seems to call for a psychological explanation, especially given the fact that his father . . . was a Hebrew teacher; his mother wrote children's stories about the heroism of Jews trying to form a new country in the face of Arab hatred; and Chomsky himself was once a member of a pro-Israel youth group." Unfortunately these matters are not followed up or amplified perhaps because the editors considered it inappropriate to try to connect the personal and the political.

To say the least, Chomsky has been a controversial and polarizing figure ever since he exchanged the role of acclaimed linguist for relentless social critic during the Vietnam War. While he has a huge and devoted following abroad as well as in the United States, he has also been widely criticized for his intemperate and extreme pronouncements even by those on the left who share many of his beliefs. In particular, his respectability suffered damage due to his downplaying of the Cambodian massacres under Pol Pot, confidently and scornfully dismissing the refugee accounts of their magnitude in his 1977 *Nation* article and his book, *After the Cataclysm*, published in 1979. His inexplicable support for the French Holocaust denier Robert Faurisson and his followers gave pause to many. He has also shown an episodic enthusiasm for discredited third-world dictatorships that apparently impressed him with their revolutionary-socialist credentials and rhetoric, such as Vietnam, Cambodia, Mao's China, Cuba, Grenada, and Sandinista Nicaragua. He has argued tirelessly that the United States was determined to destroy or contain such countries because they offered inspiring alternatives, irresistible examples of social change and reform that could have spread all over the world, and even to the United States.

Since 9/11 new waves of global (and domestic) anti-Americanism lifted him once more to greater prominence as he resumed the role of giving expression to the feelings of all those unyieldingly hostile to the United States at home and abroad. In particular, he advanced with great relish and confidence the view that the United States deserved the acts of terror (9/11) given its own, far greater acts of evil over time as the foremost terrorist entity in the world.

Having been the prototypical public intellectual, endlessly disseminating his ideas in books, articles, interviews, public appearances, and the mass media, and one whose sense of identity appears to be have been rooted in relentless, moralizing social-political criticism, Chomsky should be of great interest to the sociologist of knowledge as well as to students of political morality and political psychology. Even among the many committed critics of American society and U.S. foreign policy he stands out by virtue of the uncommonly extreme and strident character of his indictment. Widespread receptivity to his views in the most varied geographic and cultural settings stimulate further scrutiny of the Chomsky phenomenon, although it appears that his most devoted followers in this country are concentrated among the aging former activists of the 1960s, as well as among groups of college students both at home and abroad. He stimulates further curiosity (of a more psychological nature) on account of displaying an exceptional self-assurance that permeates all of his utterances; he rarely fails to suggest, matter-of-factly and casually, that only the most morally depraved or intellectually stunted would disagree with his views.

It is characteristic of Chomsky's style that the most outlandish propositions are delivered as self-evident; they are matters of course, taken for granted verities embedded in a quasi-rationalistic style. He routinely lubricates and lards his arguments with expressions such as: "it is surely not in doubt that"; "assuming that facts matter"; "nobody with even a shred of honesty would disagree"; "if we are not moral hypocrites we would agree that"; "it is an obvious truism that"; "the available facts lead to one clear conclusion"; "observers of evident bias and low credibility" (those with whom he disagrees) while others supporting his beliefs are "widely respected" with "excellent credentials." "Evidence from sources that seem to deserve hearing" invariably support his contentions, while authors he dismisses "might have troubled to inquire into the source of [their] allegations." Views he rejects are never "subject to possible verification" or possess "a shred of credibility." There are also endless references and appeals to the "serious reader," "serious observer," or "serious analyst" who would unfailingly endorse his views as would those of "minimal intelligence" or honesty.

Chomsky's statements, beliefs, and public postures confirm (if more confirmation is needed) that received notions of the nature of intellectuals need substantial revision. As readers of *Society* know, it used to be widely assumed that the key, defining characteristic of intellectuals is a generally (rather than selectively) critical, questioning, and skeptical mindset that is not confined to the critiques of particular, predetermined trends, policies, institutions, or social-political phenomena. Nor is such an attitude compatible with the trusting acceptance of assertions emanating from political entities favored, let alone with support for political systems that institutionalize the suppression of free expression. The "true intellectual" is also supposed to eschew rhetorical excess and should be capable of making well-grounded, sober distinctions between different social-political phenomena and different kinds of human folly and misconduct.

The proverbial critical intellectual is expected to protest and expose social injustice, political repression, and fraudulent political rhetoric wherever encountered; his interest in appearance and reality, theory, and practice is not supposed to be confined to any particular social setting or political entity.

Needless to say the true intellectual is also anxious to discover facts and information relevant to his argument and truth-seeking and not only those which support and confirm his existing beliefs and preferences. He or she should be capable of making a determined attempt to approach the social-political world with an open mind, instead of a doctrinaire, predictable, and predetermined set of ideas that leads to selective perception and misrepresentation.

If indeed the attributes noted above define the "true intellectual," then Chomsky falls short; it would be more reasonable to classify him as a certain kind of "true believer" whose beliefs are, however, largely negative. Chomsky endlessly exposes evil (as he sees it) and seethes with moral indignation but is surprisingly reticent to offer alternative ideas about desirable social-political arrangements except for his occasional endorsements of some third-world dictatorships that earned his sympathy because of their socialist rhetoric and hatred of the United States. He offers next to nothing approximating a transformative social-political blueprint or vision, nothing specific as to what social-political arrangements should replace the endemic corruption and evil dominating American life and institutions as he sees them. In all these respects there is a strong resemblance between Chomsky and Michael Moore, except that Moore does not claim to be an intellectual or an impartial, supremely rational observer of the social-political world.

What then are the major critical findings of the various authors in this volume? The most serious is that Chomsky's political assertions are riddled with misrepresentation, and the evidence for his assertions is questionable. This is not merely a matter of exaggeration and distortion, which too abound in his statements. Two linguists, Paul Postal and Robert Levine, who have known and worked for him, observed that "the two strands of Chomsky's work [the political and the linguistic] manifest exactly the same key properties: a deep disregard and contempt for truth, a monumental disdain for standards of inquiry . . . and a penchant for verbally abusing those who disagree with him." He makes claims and assertions that can be disproved without much difficulty, including his frequent insistence that he did not make the often-embarrassing statements in question. A striking case in point was an article in the *New Yorker* (cited above) in which he was quoted as saying in class (at MIT) that the United States in World War II supported anti-Soviet military units under Nazi control which slowed down the liberation of Nazi death camps by the Soviet forces, resulting in increased number of inmates killed in these camps; hence, the United States contributed to the Nazi killing of innocents. The author of the chapter (John Williamson), having read these statements, asked Chomsky (by e-mail) for some evidence and elaboration of the allegation. Chomsky responded (by e-mail) "first by saying that MacFarquhar [the author of the article] had manufactured all the statements attributed to him on the subject; and then by referring me to an obscure source that he said would support the claim which he said he hadn't made." John Williamson also asked the reporter if indeed Chomsky had made the statement, which she confirmed and also made available videotape of Chomsky's statement unambiguously vindicating her. The source Chomsky referred to as supporting his allegation (he denied making) "proved no such thing" as many quotes from it (cited in the Williamson essay) make clear. Williamson reached the conclusion (after a prolonged e-mail exchange with Chomsky) that "no fact outweighed his opinion; no historical resource, no matter how impeccable, could shake his *idée fixe*."

More generally, several contributors to the volume note Chomsky's questionable use of sources or references which often have no relevance to his assertions: "His admirers often cite the huge number of footnotes . . . as proof of his impeccable scholarship. But the copious references are there to create a kind of pseudo-academic smog: many of them . . . are so vague as to be useless. Quite often his citations . . . only lead the reader back self-referentially to another of Chomsky's own works in which he makes the same unsupported assertion. . . ." He is also criticized for "mutilating quotations that his readers are unable to verify" and for "a strategy for creating a Potemkin village of intellectual authenticity."

Chomsky's support of leftist, third-world dictatorships is another source of criticism. On his guided tour of North Vietnam in 1970 he discerned "a high degree of democratic participation at the village and regional level" that he was in no position to perceive relying as he did on his guides to interpret North Vietnamese political realities. Even worse was his attempt to justify Vietcong terror: "Don't accept the view that we can just condemn the [National Liberation Front] terror, period, because it was so horrible. I think we really have to ask questions of comparative costs . . . if we are going to take a moral position on this—and I think we should—we have to ask both what are the consequences of using and not using terror. If it were true that the consequences of not using terror would be that the peasantry in Vietnam would continue to live in the state of the peasantry of the Philippines, then I think the use of terror would be justified." This was a classical ends-justify-the-means reasoning further undermined by Chomsky's obvious inability to know how the peasants in Vietnam lived under the communist regime and how that compared with peasant life in the Philippines—of which, in all probability, he knew even less.

As quoted in the May 2002 *New Criterion* (by Keith Windschuttle), he once called China under Mao "an important example of a new society in which very interesting and positive things happened . . . in which a good deal of collectivization and communization was really based on mass participation and took place after a level of understanding has been reached in the peasantry. . . ." Again it would be interesting to know what enabled him to reach these conclusions other than the predisposition to sympathize with a putatively socialist system.

While less favorably inclined toward the Soviet Union than the third-world regimes noted above, he bitterly denounced Vaclav Havel for comparing the United States favorably to the former Soviet Union. He wrote: "It is also unnecessary to point out to the half a dozen or so sane people who remain [!] that in comparison to the conditions imposed by US tyranny and violence, East Europe under Russian rule was practically a paradise. . . ." In 1966 he wrote in the *Harvard Educational Review* that not only did the United States support and encourage terror in other countries but "[American] schools are the first training ground for troops that will enforce the muted, unending terror of the status quo in the coming years of a projected American century; for the technicians who will be developing the means for the extension of American power; for the intellectuals who can be counted on . . . to provide the ideological justification for this . . . barbarism. . . ."

He compared Israeli conduct in Lebanon with the massacres of Pol Pot he had earlier tried to minimize. Even more grotesquely he saw moral equivalence between Israel's rescue of its hijacked hostages from Entebbe, Uganda, in 1976 and the Japanese attack on Pearl Harbor, writing that the Israeli action should be compared to "other military exploits, no less dramatic, that did not arouse such awed admiration in the American press," notably the Japanese attack on Pearl Harbor.

Chomsky's political judgment and discernment is further reflected in his recent claims that the American bombardment of the chemical factory in Sudan (which was carried out at night to minimize casualties) was more vicious than the attacks of 9/11: "The terrorist attacks were major atrocities. In scale they may not reach the level of many others, for example, Clinton's bombing of the Sudan . . . destroying half its pharmaceutical supplies and killing unknown numbers of people. . . ."

Then there is his claim of "the silent genocide" the United States was preparing to commit against the people of Afghanistan by preventing food supplies to reach them ("we are in the midst of apparently trying to murder 3 or 4 million people, not Taliban, of course, their victims"—a claim totally groundless notwithstanding his insistence that it was supported by "grim warnings from virtually every knowledgeable source."

The problem with such and other similar assertions is not merely that they are untrue and therefore unethical. Just as insidious is his contribution to the steady corruption of the capacity for moral discernment and judgment by resolutely lumping together phenomena that are in fact morally and factually quite dissimilar. Chomsky has been the most ardent and determined practitioner of the groundless attribution of moral equivalence to different political entities and actors, which, on closer inspection reveals that behind the apparent equivalence looms the unsurpassable evil, represented by the United States and Israel. Not only did he routinely equate the United States with the U.S.S.R. (always making clear that he found the former far more dangerous and immoral than the latter), he also routinely compared the United States (and Israel) to Nazi Germany—a practice that continues.

Chomsky has always dismissed opposition to communist systems and movements as a smokescreen for nefarious American policies and objectives. He wrote that "The ideology of anti-communism has served as a highly effective technique of popular mobilization in support of American policies of intervention and subversion in the postwar period." In other words, it was an opiate of the people rather than a set of ideas justifiably critical of such systems.

There is finally Chomsky's puzzling defense of Faurisson and his fellow Holocaust revisionists/deniers. After all, one can be a determined, no-holds-barred critic of the United States, capitalism, globalism, Israel, or the whole Western world (as many have been) without supporting individuals and groups whose fantastic beliefs are embedded in and conditioned by anti-Semitism. Chomsky has always claimed that he supports Faurisson merely as a gesture in defense of free expression, or intellectual freedom. But even if this were true, he has been exercising his libertarian impulses quite selectively: the world is full of groups and individuals expressing foolish, grotesque, or hate-filled beliefs; yet, Chomsky did not rush to their defense unless he could implicate the United States or Israel (or their allies) in the infringements of free expression. Genuine civil libertarians "while they will give legal aid to Nazis . . . will not associate with Nazis, collaborate with Nazis politically, publish their book with Nazi publishers, or allow their articles to be printed in Nazi journals. On these counts alone, Chomsky is not civil libertarian," as Werner Cohn argues in this volume. Nor would civil libertarians defend Faurisson (as Chomsky had) "as an 'apolitical liberal' whose work was based on 'extensive historical research'" and dispute his anti-Semitism. Chomsky further argued, in defense of Faurisson, that "everyone should have the right of free speech, including fascists and anti-Semites, but that Faurisson was neither of these." It should also be noted that while Chomsky repeatedly asserted that he did not share Faurisson's views, he never actually criticized him.

It is hardly surprising that Chomsky's selective concern with the right to free speech does not include those who criticize him or whose views he finds distasteful. Even in the classroom he cannot tolerate disagreement and was observed "to berate for a long time" a student who disagreed with him and ignored his attempts to speak. "People cried out 'Let him talk!' but to no avail. Another student stood up . . . but Chomsky ignored him. People made loud, disgruntled noises in protest of his treatment but Chomsky ignored those too."

While we do not know what motivates Chomsky, it is possible to offer some suggestions to account for his influence and popularity. Clearly, he appeals to all those who, for whatever reason share his beliefs and especially his emotions but are incapable, or less capable, of articulating them with the same skill and conviction. In all probability the most important appeal of his messages is their pungent, resounding simplicity served up, as it were, with trimmings of intellectual sophistication. As other ideologues, secular or religious, he offers a monochromatic, conspiratorial worldview in which evil is unambiguously identified and denounced, over and over again, an activity that satisfies a deep-seated scapegoating impulse in his audiences shared in some measure by all human beings.

It should not be too difficult for social historians to explain why, at this point in time, it is the United States (and Israel) that have become the most inviting targets of these sentiments for groups dissatisfied with their lives and the world around them and consumed by a variety of grievances which combine the personal and the political.

Chapter Twenty-seven

The Banality of Evil and the Political Culture of Hatred

There was a time when the most stunning and premeditated forms of political violence, exemplified by the Holocaust, were associated with the "banality of evil"—a concept introduced by Hannah Arendt. She popularized the idea that the Holocaust was a form of bureaucratized mass murder carried out by "desk murderers" who had no strong feelings about it, perfectly ordinary human beings, such as Eichmann and his associates, impersonal and interchangeable "cogs" in the gigantic killing machine. Anybody could have performed the task, no political passion or ideological conviction was involved or required. It was implied that this type of violence was emblematic of modernity and mass society, as were their key characteristics: anonymity, standardization, homogenization, impersonality, as well as increasing specialization and reliance on technology. Stanley Milgram's experiments concerned with obedience to authority further bolstered the notion that people are able and willing to inflict pain and suffering on total strangers for no reason other than their willingness to obey authority, as the Nazi executioners did.

In the wake of these theories it has become widely accepted—with a curious mixture of horror and relish—and especially among intellectuals, that all of us are potentially amoral, robotic monsters, but monsters without convictions, distinction, or originality. There was something morbidly fascinating about the contrast between extraordinary moral outrages (such as the Nazis perpetrated) and the pedestrian, mundane character of the perpetrators. The popularity of these ideas was nurtured by the questioning of modernity that brought us technology, mass production, efficiency, bureaucracy, impersonality, and the decline of community. These ideas were especially congenial with the protest movements of the 1960s whose stock in trade were impassioned critiques of impersonality, dehumanization, and faceless bureaucracies.

The "banality of evil" approach also lent itself to a generous extension of the idea of "complicity" and the rejection of American (or any other Western) society. If *anybody* could readily become a mass murderer, or assist in mass murder, and if beliefs and motivation are largely irrelevant to behavior, then no society is immune to genocidal temptations. Moreover the allegedly homogenized mass societies nurturing modern technology (such as the United States) might have a special affinity with devising new, efficient forms of mass murder, even genocide. Not by accident did "genocide" and "genocidal" become favorite epithets of the social critics and political activists of the 1960s (rarely directed at truly genocidal political systems).

It may also be recalled here that the 1960s generation of radicals took great pleasure in comparing the United States to Nazi Germany (they spelled America with a "k") and whenever possible threw at it terms like "fascist," "nazi" and "genocidal"; they also liked to compare American institutions to the gestapo, storm troopers, or Auschwitz.

The Vietnam War further stimulated the inclination to associate mass murder with technology and view the United States as a genocidal state intent on killing simple peasants impersonally with sophisticated technology, preferably from high altitudes rather than in manly, authentic, face-to-face combat. American soldiers in this perspective were "professional killers" and implicitly, their lack of passion was also held against them by many anti-war activists. Repeatedly, critics of the United States contrasted favorably the supposedly poorly armed, deeply committed, simple guerillas, operating in small groups with the mechanized might of the U.S. forces for whom fighting was a "job" to be performed impersonally and efficiently.

The recent waves of political violence committed by Islamic groups and individuals dealt a heavy blow to the theories and ideas Arendt popularized. A greatly neglected factor of political conflict and violence suddenly and dramatically reemerged, namely fanatical hatred and religious-political convictions legitimating the ruthless violence such hatred inspired. Rarely in history has the relationship between belief and behavior been so clear as in the actions of the Islamic suicide pilots and bombers fortified and reassured by conceptions and personifications of evil defined with great clarity and held unhesitatingly. There was nothing banal, impersonal, dispassionate, or detached about their beliefs and behavior. A pure, fierce hatred of evil motivated them as well as deeply felt beliefs in otherwordly rewards. (More down-to-earth motives also played a part as families received substantial material compensation for their "martyred" sons or daughters in addition to a marked improvement of their social standing in the community that applauded suicide bombings.)

In numerous Arab countries and communities a political culture evolved that joyously enshrined hate and violence as a sacred mission directed at the designated objects of hate. In these settings virulent hatred is inculcated from an early age; it is disseminated by the mass media, in schools and places of worship, sanctioned by both religious and political authorities.

It is one thing to kill or harm one's enemies in a matter-of-fact and defensive manner and something quite different to publicly rejoice in and glorify such killings. It is the hallmark of a political culture drenched in self-righteous hate that it encourages individuals to display joyously their bloody hands on television after they committed murder, as was the case last year when two Israeli soldiers were lynched on the West Bank. This political culture also helps to account for the behavior of people who dance in the streets when hearing about the indiscriminate mass murder of their supposed enemies, as was the case in numerous Arab cities after September 11. One can also associate the same political culture with the attitude of parents who express great happiness upon hearing of the "martyrdom" their children incurred in the course of blowing to bits innocent civilians.

Whatever the ingredients or sources of such hatred—material deprivation, lack of education, frustration, resentment, sense of inferiority, the scapegoating impulse—it has become the dominant force fueling political conflict and violence in many parts of the world. The "root causes" are not poverty but relative deprivation or frustrated expectations and the overpowering but comforting belief that others are responsible for one's misfortune. It is also highly relevant here that (as reported in a recent *New York Times* op-ed piece) opinion polls in the West Bank and Gaza found "that better educated Palestinians were more likely than others to approve of violence."

There is certainly nothing banal or inauthentic about the violence of the suicide bombers enthusiastically killing themselves in the pursuit of their ideals. Religious beliefs and a climate of public opinion legitimate and nurture such hatreds, which in other cultures most people would find embarrassing to display in public, let alone act on them.

It is perhaps the authenticity of such violence and the belief that its perpetrators are among the virtuous victims of the West (mainly of the United States and Israel) that impels the hardcore supporters of the adversary culture to take a more charitable view of it and its perpetrators. Even if these warriors have not attracted as much open sympathy as the Vietcong used to, they benefit from the identity of their enemies in the eyes of the radical-left beholders. The latter cannot help being drawn to virtually any group or individual passionately opposed to and willing to take militant action against the United States and Israel since they regard the United States "the great Satan" and the source of all evil and injustice in this world and Israel its ally and lackey.

In the wake of 9/11 these attitudes have taken several forms. One was the search for "root causes," which invariably led to the conclusion that the

United States and Israel are in the final analysis responsible for the violence directed against them. Another expression of the same attitude was the solicitousness shown toward those accused of or suspected of the terrorist violence against the United States and Israel. A great surge of concern about their civil and human rights and welfare swept through left-liberal circles, which would be praiseworthy had such concern been shown also for the corresponding rights and welfare of the victims of the various anti-Western, anti-American, and anti-Israeli terrorists.

At numerous universities administrators have been anxious to protect the sensitivity of Arab students and adherents of Islamic beliefs deeming offensive any expression of American patriotism including the display of the American flag. Campus critics of the U.S. war on terrorism in Afghanistan and elsewhere were assured a far more supportive environment than those supporting it. Symbolic gestures of support and solidarity were also extended by Western "peace activists" who rushed to Arafat's headquarters in Ramallah and to the besieged terrorists in the Church of Nativity in Bethlehem and sometimes interposed themselves between Israeli bulldozers and their targets in the occupied territories. There have also been many attempts to deny that Islamic religious beliefs could have inspired, influenced, or legitimated the murderous political impulses and behavior of the suicide bombers and other terrorists. These attempts are reminiscent of past disputes about the relationship between Marxism and the practices of communist states. The repressive nature of these states could not be directly blamed on Marx and his theories but nonetheless there was a connection, at the very least in the sense of entitlement to ruthlessness on behalf of great ideals to be realized. The paradise awaiting the suicide bomber is a religious notion not invented by the individuals in question who act on this idea. None of the other violent enemies of Western societies in recent times (the Weathermen, the Red Brigade in Italy, the Baader-Meinhof gang in Germany, the IRA in Ireland, the Basque terrorists, etc.) were suicidal. They did not have the kind of religious assurance and encouragement their Islamic counterparts possess at the present time.

The evil of Nazism was not banal, nor is the evil of the suicide bombers. Whatever the social and political circumstances which contribute to their actions, they do not provide moral license or mitigation for their behavior; these are individuals who, according to all indications, choose their actions freely, with utmost deliberation, and under no compulsion other than the prodding of their beliefs and the enthusiastic support of their community.

Chapter Twenty-eight

The Left and the Palestinians

Support for the Palestinian cause—that is to say, Palestinian statehood and the right of return of Palestinians to Israel—has become a major item on the political agenda of the left in Western countries.

In demonstrations against globalism or the war in Iraq, there are pro-Palestinian contingents; on American college campuses pro-Palestinian organizations (often allied with Islamic ones) thrive. Western "solidarity groups" visit the West Bank and Gaza and often interpose themselves between rioting or demonstrating Palestinians and Israeli troops. Sometimes they join the demonstrators. They were also deployed around the headquarters of Yasir Arafat to protect him, while their representatives visited and hugged him. At any given time, hundreds of Western sympathizers are in the Palestinian areas to lend whatever aid and comfort they can. Boycotts and embargos against Israel are proposed and organized; academic intellectuals advocate excluding Israelis from academic organizations and institutions. The International Solidarity Movement (solidarity with the Palestinians) supports the Palestinians' "legitimate armed struggle." Tom Paulin, the well-known English poet and teacher at Oxford University, writes about "the Zionist SS" and reveals that he never believed in Israel's right to exist. He also encourages the shooting of Jewish settlers in occupied territories.

While these groups are in a state of intense moral indignation about Israeli atrocities, their condemnation of Arab-Islamic acts of terror is either nonexistent or muted and perfunctory. Acts of terror against Israeli civilians (what Martin Peretz called "the utter routinization of the savage killing of innocents") attract little moral attention or energy; they are reflexively attributed to the misbehavior of Israel (or the United States) or to the famous root causes which amount to Israeli (or American) culpability.

The key to these skewed perceptions and uneven moral judgments is to be found in a deeply internalized victim-victimizer scenario. Ever since its victory in 1967 in the Six-Day War, Israel and its Jewish population ceased being seen as victims (or potential victims) by many liberal Western intellectuals—and no further events would dislodge this perception. There is a certain parallel here with the comparative perceptions of the United States and the Soviet Union during the Cold War, when the latter retained an underdog status in the eyes of many Western beholders despite its enormous military power and conquests and gradually became the moral equivalent of the United States.

A similar moral equivalence is widespread today in comparisons of unrestrained Palestinian violence against Israel and the often harsh Israeli countermeasures seeking to deflect it. It is overlooked that Israel kills civilians inadvertently in the pursuit of terrorists, while the terrorists deliberately target civilians in ways to maximize Israeli casualties and openly rejoice when these goals are accomplished.

The support for the Palestinians cannot be understood in isolation from grasping why Israel is detested, just as past (or persisting) sympathy for communist systems could only be understood when seen as an integral part and product of the profound hostility to Western, capitalist democracies.

In all probability, the current denigration of Israel is part of a similar, broad rejection of all things Western. Israel in the eyes of radical leftists (and arguably even in those of less than radical leftists) is identified with everything they abhor in the West: capitalism, consumerism, individualism, scientific rationality, and other Western intellectual and philosophical traditions. Especially delegitimating Israel is its close political-military relationship to the United States.

By the same token, idealization of the Palestinians may well be a substitute for the kinds of projections and longings, which in the past found their target in communist systems, movements, and guerillas. With the collapse (or transformation) of most communist systems, there are no admirable alternatives left to the perceived evils and corruption of the West with the problematic exception of Cuba. Hence the new and admittedly smaller generation of political pilgrims goes to Palestine.

Palestinians are embraced not merely because they are adversaries and apparent victims of Israel; they also came to personify and revitalize idealized conceptions of the third world and its inhabitants which flourished in the 1960s and 1970s. They are the new noble savages leading virtuously simple and deprived lives (the latter can in part be ascribed to Israeli policies). The young men and children throwing stones at Israeli tanks have become symbols of what is seen as the heroic struggle of powerless, authentic, nontechnological fighters against the powerful, technologically advanced, impersonal monster encased in tanks and armored personnel carriers—images similar to those of the lean, small Vietcong fighters battling manfully with minimal equipment the impersonal might of the United States. In both cases there was more involved than sympathy for the underdog: the struggle also symbolized a confrontation between the virtues of a preindustrial social order and its authentic actors, and the vices of the dehumanized military-industrial-scientific complex embodied in the United States. As Susan Sontag observed at the time, there was no "existential agony" or alienation among the North Vietnamese.

There is another possible explanation for the increased appeal of the Palestinian cause during the last few years while the intifada and suicide bombings unfolded. It may well be that Palestinian violence is not merely accepted as a justifiable response to Israeli policies, but is actually applauded. Once more there are probable parallels with the appeal of communist movements and insurgencies of the past and their righteous violence. Many Western intellectuals had a longstanding and barely (if at all) suppressed admiration for what they saw as the morally superior, passionate, invigorating, authentic use of violence in a wholesome, liberating cause. Sartre, Franz Fanon, Carlos Fuentes, Regis Debray, C. Wright Mills, Norman Mailer (and many less illustrious figures)—all these sedentary and verbose intellectuals believed in the redeeming uses of authentic violence in overcoming unadventurous ways of life, trapped and paralyzed as they felt between theory and practice and in their comfortable middle-class lifestyle. Political (and sometimes nonpolitical) violence came to be seen as the magic device with which to bridge the gap between theory and practice, rumination and action, good intentions and genuine commitment.

Palestinian guerrillas and especially the fearless suicide bombers embody such authenticity and unwavering commitment. They do put their lives on the line and joyously, serenely destroy themselves (and many more others) for the good of the cause. They symbolize a profusion of self-transcendence unparalleled in recent times. Professor Gayatri Spivak of Columbia University explained (or tried to) why this was the case:

> Suicide bombing—and the planes of 9/11 were living bombs—is a purposive self-annihilation, a confrontation between oneself and oneself, the extreme end of autoeroticism . . . the destruction of others is indistinguishable from the destruction of the self. . . . Suicidal resistance is a message inscribed in the body when no other means will get through. It is both execution and mourning, for

both self and other. For you die with me for the same cause, no matter which side are you on. Because no matter who you are, there are no designated killees [sic] in suicide bombing. . . . There is no dishonor in such shared and innocent death. (Quoted in *The New Republic*, July 29, 2002, 9.)

While left-liberal intellectuals in the West have serious reservations about religious fanaticism (especially when associated with Judeo-Christian beliefs and practices), Islamic religious fanaticism gets the benefit of doubt since it is a product of the third world and the cultural diversity it represents and as such cannot be rejected out of hand. Even when such religious fanaticism and the violence it inspires is hard to take, it is always possible to fall back on the root causes: the suicide bombers are poor, oppressed, and weak; they are desperately trying to call attention to their condition. Little is said about the hefty awards given to their families or about the fact that many of the violent activists and their organizers are neither poor nor uneducated.

The Palestinians, real and imaginary, are neither the first nor the last representatives of righteous rage against the evils alienated Westerners feel surrounded by in their own societies.

Chapter Twenty-nine

The Personal and the Political in Lessing's Fiction

The Sweetest Dream continues Lessing's long-standing preoccupation with the intimate connection, most insistently proclaimed in our times by radical feminists, between the personal and the political. The book may also be seen as a further and most explicit stage in Lessing's journey of distancing herself from her old leftist convictions and from all radical-utopian beliefs. What she seeks to convey here has certainly been proposed before, by philosophers, political scientists, and clear-headed intellectuals: that there is no political or social solution for personal problems, especially for the most difficult and intimate ones. Likewise, sweeping schemes of social engineering founder on their own unintended consequences and the imponderables of human nature. The determined, self-conscious mixing of the personal and the political, more often than not, yields unpleasant results.

This is a novel mainly focused on England during the 1960s, but it spans half a century from World War II until the late 1990s. In a short preface, Lessing expresses the hope that she "managed to recapture the spirit of the Sixties" (she does, most successfully) and conveys justifiable irritation with the (British) Campaign for Nuclear Disarmament ("there has never been a more hysterical, noisy and irrational campaign"), which embodied many of the questionable beliefs and attitudes of the period.

Unlike most books focusing on the 1960s and written on either side of the Atlantic, and especially on ours, *The Sweetest Dream* is not infused with nostalgia for that supposedly golden era of youthful idealism and personal liberation. Quite to the contrary, Lessing embarks on a highly critical, although not totally unsympathetic, examination of the period and the types of people who seemed to set and embody its tone most characteristically. I can only think of Saul Bellow (and especially his *Mr. Sammler's Planet*) as offering a comparably profound critical reflection of that era's problematic aspirations and the human beings emblematic of them, who firmly believed that all good things are compatible, including no-holds-barred "self-realization," warm communal relationships, and the revolutionary transformation of all social institutions and practices. This was "the sweetest dream."

It was a period when large numbers of people were seized by the conviction that what mattered most were good and pure intentions, which by themselves vindicated the actions they inspired. Even more remarkably, these people believed that human love, kindness, and a sense of solidarity could be extended and expanded effortlessly and without discrimination.

In this book these impulses find expression, among other things, in the commendable but somewhat muddled generosity of the major character, Frances (a "neurotic nurturer" as "the kids" see her); she takes into her spacious home various "strays" who belong to "a tribe of youngsters 'disturbed' for one reason or another," confusedly rebellious middle-class youth (including the offspring of her former spouse). These idealistic young people habitually refer to their parents as "shits." Frances the nurturer is a kind and largely apolitical woman who nonetheless absorbed many of the beliefs and impulses prevalent in the subcultures of the 1960s. She is a victim both of these beliefs and of her own decency.

It is her former husband, "comrade Johnny," who is the prime exhibit of the foolishness, irresponsibility, and hypocrisy of which a thoroughly politicized human being is capable. The son of wealthy parents, he was educated at Eton, but as a young man became involved with the British Communist party; he remains through much of his life a full-time functionary. Staunchly pro-Soviet until almost the very end of "the Soviet experiment", later in life Johnny switches to a more broadly based leftist "third-worldism," admiring Castro and assorted African dictators. What does not change is his unwavering alienation from his own country and his contempt of capitalism—if indeed it is capitalism that is the deepest animating impulse behind Johnny's relentless hostility toward his own society and the nonsocialist Western world.

Johnny exemplifies what happens when the political realm invades and absorbs the personal: the withering of the personal. He is never at a loss to spout soothing (or rousing) agit-prop rhetoric, but is singularly "challenged" in the department of ordinary human concerns and feelings. He is serenely unconcerned with the welfare of his children from his failed marriages; he supports them neither financially nor emotionally. He is a windbag and inveterate freeloader, a parasite with a clear conscience getting free meals from his first wife, whom he despises on account of her low level of political consciousness. ("My wife . . . does not understand that the Struggle must come before family obligations.") Why worry about such mundane matters when you are dedicating your life to the liberation of the masses and the future of humanity? Life holds no mysteries for him, and he has a ready answer and the remedy for every question and problem. In this, he reminds me of Homais, the pharmacist in *Madame Bovary*, another irresponsible, cheerfully impersonal windbag, beholden to soothing platitudes extracted from the vulgarized beliefs of the French Enlightenment.

American readers may be surprised by the many similarities between the ethos and representatives of the 1960s in England and in this country. For example, in the English private school described, "pupils came and went, with little regard for time-tables or exams. When teachers suggested a more disciplined approach, they might be reminded of the principles that had established the school, self-development being the main one." Similarly familiar is the physical appearance of the people populating these pages who wear the "current uniforms of non-conformity" and wish to be seen as "Che Guevara clones." In England too, in these circles, the epithet "fascism" was thrown around with abandon: "they all used the word fascist as easily as they said fuck, or shit, not necessarily meaning much more than this was somebody they disapproved of." The mentally ill, these English youngsters believed, "are just like us." The tribal massacres in Africa were dismissed as products of a "different culture," another expression of cultural diversity that should not prompt "judgmental" attitudes. A group of true believers (in the novel) could listen to the revelations of a former inmate of the Gulag "as if the tale did not concern them." They are people (like the American believers in the innocence of the Rosenbergs) "who cannot change once their minds are made up."

These similarities are all the more surprising since the two countries and societies are in fact very different; Britain was neither involved in the Vietnam war, nor did she have to face the historic burden of slavery—two factors frequently invoked to explain the social-political movements of the 1960s in the United States and the alienation their participants displayed. What the alienated had in common in both societies—as this novel suggests—was a combination of privileged background, a sense of political and economic security and of entitlement (compatible with all sorts of neurotic needs and symptoms), and a profound belief that the prevailing social-political institutions and arrangements were self-evidently and utterly rotten and worthless. This complex of attitudes helps to explain, why, for example, most of the privileged youngsters in the book consider shoplifting both an entertaining and a lucrative hobby and a form of political protest against "the system," against capitalism. ("When he [one of the characters] arrived at the LSE [part of the University of London] he was delighted that to steal clothes, books, anything one fancied, as a means of undermining the capitalist system was taken for granted. To actually pay for something, well, how politically naive can one get?")

Lessing does not have a clear answer as to the root of this malaise, of "this rage . . . too deep in some part of the collective unconscious to reason with."

The closest she comes to pointing to a source is the British version of the generational conflict and incomplete or malfunctioning families. There are numerous glimpses of parental self-centeredness and irresponsibility, often associated with the period's grand notions of self-realization. Such parental neglect helps to explain the mentality and rootlessness of this small sample of the English "youth culture."

It is not hard to understand how children who grow up without a father or with two indifferent, uninvolved parents become susceptible to a deep sense of grievance, which may or may not take a political form, depending on the prevailing social conditions. The sons of Johnny and Frances are obvious examples, although, given their grotesquely irresponsible and largely absent father, they become scornful of his politics. Arguably, they belong to the offspring of "a generation of Believers, now discredited, [who] had given birth to children who disowned their parents' beliefs, but admired their dedication. . . . What faith! What passion! What idealism!" Here again is a close parallel with the so-called red diaper babies in this country, who became prominent 1960s radicals and subsequently politically correct academics, some of them writing reverent studies of the American communist movement without fully identifying with its failed policies.

A virtually separate part of the novel takes place in an African country named Zimlia, which closely resembles present-day Zimbabwe and is seen through the eyes of one of the novel's characters, a young, idealistic doctor who takes a job there to help the poor. Her experiences of the pervasive corruption, brutality, and economic stagnation—rarely encountered in Western works of fiction (or nonfiction) about Africa—is further illustration of the colossal and disheartening gap separating theory from practice, good intentions from good results, and of a spectacular failure of decolonialization. The new, indigenous elites are greedy, cynical, and ruthless, and no more concerned with the welfare of the masses than their predecessors were. Another sweet dream shattered.

The greatest strength of this novel is its compelling focus on the timeless tension between idealistic social-political aspiration and the dark sides of human nature. Fallible and flawed human beings, torn between conflicting values and desires, are bound to fail to create a social order in which there is no chasm between the personal and the political, good intentions and good results. As Lessing shows, "the sweetest dream" of such harmony and fulfillment will likely continue to haunt and elude us.

Chapter Thirty

Haven in Cuba

William Lee Brent was a Black Panther activist in the San Francisco Bay area in the 1960s with a substantial criminal record and many years spent in jail before joining the Panthers. A *New York Times* reporter wrote "By his own admission Mr. Brent squandered the first half of his life on petty crime, which rewarded him with nothing more than an intimate knowledge of the American prison system and a bitterness that corroded his soul" (Larry Rohter: "25 Years an Exile: An Old Black Panther Sums Up," *New York Times*, April 9, 1996). In 1969 following his arrest in a shootout with the police (which left two policemen seriously injured) while out on bail, he came to the conclusion that escaping to Cuba was the best available option and could only be accomplished by hijacking a plane. He succeeded and has lived in Cuba ever since, remaining a fugitive from American justice. He said of the hijacking: "I was at war . . . with an enemy which was the United States Government and the skyjacking was a continuation of that struggle" (Rohter, "25 Years Exile").

On his arrival in Cuba, he was treated with considerable suspicion and kept in jail for almost two years. He contrasted American jails favorably with their Cuban counterparts. Following his release he was given the privileges foreigners of similar political disposition enjoyed: free housing, full board, medical care and a small stipend. After a stint of sugarcane cutting and a laboring job in a factory he rather disliked, he succeeded in gaining admission to the University of Havana where he studied Spanish and other subjects in the humanities for four years; he graduated in 1981 with a B.A. in Hispanic languages. Earlier he met and moved in with (and later married) an American woman, a long-time supporter of Castro's Cuba and various radical-left causes in the United States; she worked for the Cuban government helping to promote tourism.

After graduation Brent was given a job teaching English in school and after 1986 he found employment at Radio Havana as announcer and disk jockey. In the late 1980s or early 1990s (not quite clear from his memoirs when) he left his job at the radio in part to avoid "stressful situations" which led to high blood pressure as did his daily consumption of "more than a quart of rum," as revealed in his memoirs (*Long Time Gone* [New York, 1996], 270, 268). He was also unhappy with the new policy of getting paid in pesos instead of dollars although he still enjoyed a good living standard as a privileged "foreign technician" as he was classified. After his retirement, given his modest pension (he did not work for the twenty-five years required for retirement with full benefits), he started to do freelance translations and give private English lessons and wrote his memoirs for an American publisher.

The memoirs make clear that Brent was well aware of and dismayed by the many flaws of Cuban socialism but given his situation, was resigned to them. There were the widespread scarcities and rationing: "Cuban pesos were plentiful because everyone worked and there was nothing to buy. This led to black marketing" (*Long Time Gone*, 204). Later on he had access to the special shops serving the "foreign technicians" and the Cuban political elite. He recalled the working conditions in the soap factory where he used to work as poor and unsafe. Moreover, "everyone worked overtime but was paid only eight hours. . . . The union never disagreed with the labor conditions set forth by the state and union members never disagreed with their leadership" (*Long Time Gone*, 207, 210–11). He learned that "once you got involved in a permanent work situation here . . . it took an act of Congress to get you out of it. You couldn't quit jobs on your own. Everything had to be approved, and if the authorities said no, you couldn't do a damned thing about it. There was no input from the bottom. . . . Everything came from the top down. The government told you what to do and you did or else" (209). The Committee for the Defense of the Revolution included "overzealous busybodies who thought their revolutionary duty was to inform on everyone they knew or came in contact with" (215). Even the foreigners who came to Cuba for political reasons were under "incredibly bureaucratic control" (228). When Brezhnev visited Cuba they all were rounded up and detained for the duration of his visit although assured that this was no reflection on their political reliability. He felt "hurt and disillusioned" (237–38). There was "complete dependence on the Soviet Union" for economic development (233). While teaching in school, he found out that students had to be retained and promoted regardless of their performance; he was rebuked for grading too hard (245). He was not happy with the compulsory farm work for both students and teachers and he "resented the fact that it was mandatory for teachers as well" (246).

On an assignment as a reporter for Radio Havana Cuba he was sent to a model prison where he "neither saw nor heard anything that made me think that these prisoners would be any better off when they were released than they had been when they came here" (263). His own years in prison led him to believe that prisons "are terrible places no matter where they are. They are vivid proof that a society cannot live up to the hopes and dreams of its people. . . . My program on RHC about the prison, however, did not reflect my true feelings because I knew my bosses would have me rewrite any negative references and they would put me on their unreliable list. I reported only the positive aspects . . ." (265). Even the vaunted health care left something to be desired: "to get a bed in a hospital, except in a life-threatening situation, you have to have a letter from your work center or the organization sponsoring you" (268).

After 1989 "profound economic and social changes were about to take place that would . . . shake our political convictions to their foundations . . . after three decades of promises that everything was going to be all right, the economy was falling apart . . ." (271, 273).

Even before the economic crisis his adaptation to life in Cuba was not altogether smooth or complete. As he explained to Huey Newton, his old boss and comrade-in-arms, with whom he had a reunion in Cuba: "I respect the Cubans . . . and I'm grateful they decided to give me asylum. The system is different, but I'm learning to concentrate on all the good things . . ." (233).

The memoir ends on a somewhat conflicted note inspired by the aftermath of the collapse of the Soviet Bloc and the ensuing economic hardships resulting from the end of the massive subsidies it used to provide. On the one hand, Brent admits:

> I felt confused and frustrated. I had believed in the revolution and considered myself part of it. The system was working fairly well when I first arrived: the basic necessities were provided. Now there didn't seem to be any guarantees at all. My faith was badly shaken. My friends felt the same way. Many of them—black and white—were turning to the ancient African religion Santeria. . . . In my need for something to help me come to grips with the new reality of my surroundings, restore my declining political convictions. . . . I began to acquaint myself with Santeria. (274)

On the other hand, he writes (on the next page), "In spite of the great disappointment at the course the Cuban revolution had taken over the many years I have lived on the island, I have not lost my resolve or my dedication to the struggle of my people and the cause of justice and equality for all.... My position is the same today as it was from the moment I joined the Black Panther Party..." (275).

In the following he writes about his continued loyalty to "the cause of black liberation" and the circumstances which led him "to challenge the system" (in the United States) rather than about his commitment to building of socialism in Cuba: "my methods were uneducated, lacking in social and political knowledge and based on intuitive resentment of unjust and abusive authority.... Through the 'clutch of circumstance' I found myself in Cuba. I have been away from my people for a quarter century. Much has changed. The flight I commandeered all those years ago is still not over" (275–76). On this ambiguous note does the book end.

Following the publication of the book, he told the *New York Times* correspondent that "his own faith that socialism is the best path for humanity remains unshaken.... So is his conviction that he must never abandon the struggle against 'the system.' I have been on a flight from depression, oppression, racism, injustice, inhumanity, cruelty. That flight is not over" (*New York Times*). These are the same sentiments expressed at the end of his book. They reflect a generalized left-liberal idealism not peculiar either to the Black Panthers or the Cuban Revolution. These sentiments have been carefully preserved and are the apparent cornerstones of his sense of identity constructed over the years.

An understanding of his political attitudes requires a consideration of practical alternatives. Brent could not return to the United States without facing criminal prosecution and even if he cut a deal he would have had to confront a new set of difficulties readjusting to American life and making a living at an advanced age. We don't know what his wife, apparently a more deeply committed and ideological leftist, would have thought of such a move; it is unlikely that she would have favored it.

Moreover, as reported in 1996 his life in Cuba was quite agreeable: "Mr. Brent now lives with his wife, a fellow American radical, who first visited Cuba in the 1960s, in a comfortable apartment with a view of the Almendares river and a tree-studded park." He has a pair of longhaired dachshunds, his wife "had become interested in the movement to establish pure dog breeds in Cuba ... [and] joined the dachshund club in Havana..." (265), a large collection of jazz and blues records, and a computer he uses to keep in touch with American political developments. A poster prominently displayed in his apartment calls "for the freedom of Mumia Abu-Jamal," convicted of killing a policeman in 1981.

Brent was neither uncritical of the Black Panthers (especially since they expelled him after the shootout) nor of conditions in Cuba but despite numerous disillusioning experiences he persevered in his beliefs, that is to say, "his own faith that socialism is the best path for humanity is unshaken," he said. So is his conviction that he must never abandon his struggle against 'the system' he still believes forced him here, even if it means that he never sets foot in the United States again" (*New York Times*). He has obviously mellowed and may be musing deep in his heart about an American road to socialism and social justice that would be less arduous than the Cuban.

Chapter Thirty-one

Demystifying Marxism

Leszek Kolakowski is one of the great thinkers of our time, author of numerous books on philosophy and religion, recipient of many honors and awards. He left his native Poland in 1968, after being dismissed from his teaching position at Warsaw University and expelled from the communist party for his unorthodox views. He went on to a distinguished academic career in the West—teaching at McGill University in Montreal, the University of California, Berkeley, and Yale—more recently dividing his time between All Souls College, Oxford, and the University of Chicago.

The publication of the new, one-volume edition of his monumental study, *Main Currents of Marxism* (W. W. Norton, 1,283 pages), is a welcome occasion for some reflections on his achievement, as well as the part played by Marxism in twentieth-century intellectual history. Not only is *Main Currents* the definitive history of Marxism, it is its definitive critique and demystification. This huge study examines every aspect of this revolutionary political philosophy: its origins, interpreters, the schools of Marxism in both the nineteenth and twentieth centuries and the disputes among them. Mr. Kolakowski conceived of the study as "an attempt to analyze the strange fate of an idea which began in Promethean humanism and culminated in the monstrous tyranny of Stalin."

It is impossible to summarize a huge work such as *Main Currents* in a brief review but some of its major propositions can be noted. The most important and instructive is that Marxism is essentially a secular religion, a product of utopian impulses influenced by nineteenth-century romantic longings and faith in the limitless perfectibility of human nature and social institutions. Living in communist Poland doubtless helped Mr. Kolakowski to recognize the unwelcome results of the attempted realization of these theories. He wrote, "The influence achieved, far from being the result or proof of its scientific character, is almost entirely due to its prophetic, fantastic and irrational elements. Marxism is a doctrine of blind confidence that a paradise of universal satisfaction is awaiting us . . . it is a certainty not based on any empirical premises . . . but simply on the psychological need for certainty. . . . Marxism performs the function of a religion and its efficacy is of a religious character."

At the present time, few political systems continue to claim that they are faithfully applying Marxist theory to their political and economic practice or are even inspired by its ideas. The exceptions are North Korea and Cuba. (China and Vietnam pay some lip service to the Marxist heritage while rapidly privatizing their economies.) In Western capitalist countries Marxism survives as an academic pursuit of intellectuals estranged from their societies. The moralistic rejection of capitalism remains the major strength and appeal of Marxism and is revitalized by the hostility to globalization.

Main Currents was written between 1968 and 1976, well before the collapse of Soviet communism, a political system that legitimated itself by Marxism and claimed to be splendidly guided by it. Mr. Kolakowski had experienced in Poland how little help Marxism offered in the creation of a more humane, rational, and just society, let alone a freer one.

Western Marxists vehemently argue that the disaster of Soviet communism has no relevance whatsoever to the great truths and insights Marx and his followers dispensed. They dispute just what kind of a contribution Marxist ideas made to the socialist states that arose and expired in Eastern Europe—what was the true relationship between theory and practice? They argue that the Eastern European communist states collapsed because of the discrepancy between Marxist theory and Soviet practice. In reality, these states failed—among other things—because they did rely on Marxist ideas in the building of a new social system.

It is possible to resolve the dispute about the effect or influence of Marxism on the policies and institutions of the various "actually existing" communist states by separating policies and the practices that diverged from the theory from those that were congruent with it. The most glaring discrepancy between theory and practice (or the theory and the anticipated results of its implementation) emerged in the economy: The nationalization of the means of production created neither a more productive nor a more efficient or humane society. As Mr. Kolakowski wrote, "Marx seems to have imagined that once capitalists were done away with, the whole world would become a kind of Athenian agora: one had only to forbid private ownership of machines or land and, as if by magic, human beings would cease to be selfish and their interests would coincide in perfect harmony."

It did not happen; instead these systems developed chronic shortages, a diminished work ethic, and a deeply alienated work force. The one-party dictatorship provided fewer avenues for political participation than the parliamentary system in pluralistic societies. The rise of supremely powerful dictators surrounded by compulsory cults flew in the face of the Marxist belief in the unimportance of the individual in the historical process. The proletariat did not become the ruling class, and the workers were not persuaded that they were the masters of their own fate or owners of means of production. Neither religion nor crime had withered away, notwithstanding the Marxist belief that the first was an opiate of the masses (produced by the hopelessness of life in a capitalist class society) and the second a direct response to the poverty, exploitation, and inequality such societies perpetuated.

Nonetheless there was no divergence between theory and practice as far as abolishing the private ownership of the means of production was concerned. It was embraced and zealously implemented in all communist states from Albania to Vietnam—despite the obvious economic price it exacted—especially in agriculture and the production of consumer goods. These may have been unintended consequences, but they originated in Marxist beliefs and presuppositions.

There was further congruence between theory and practice as regards the doctrine of class struggle. It was also embraced in all communist systems and provided historical and theoretical legitimacy for great surges of political violence and coercion. It directly led to punishing people not for what they did but for what they were—their opinions and beliefs inferred from their affiliations or social origins.

The belief in the omnipresence and inexorability of class struggle desensitized its practitioners to the results of their policies; it also succeeded in persuading them (with the help of Marx's fantasies about the ultimate withering away of the state) that the generous use of repression would pave the way toward a social system where none would be needed. Theory also became realized in the attempted coercive elimination of religious beliefs and practices—a policy adopted thanks to Marx's great contempt for organized religion.

Insofar as there was a discrepancy between theory and practice, it did not mean that no effort was made to implement Marxist ideas, but that the attempted implementation failed to yield the anticipated results; there was a yawning gulf between the promises, ideals, and expectations the theory fostered and the results of their attempted realization—but not between the theory and the policies and institutions which were devised to implement them.

Mr. Kolakowski rightly emphasized that "no political or religious movement is a perfect expression of that movement's 'essence' as laid down in its sacred writings; on the other hand these writings are not merely passive but exercise an influence of their own on the course of the movement." He has given us great help to understand what it was in these ideas that lent itself to misuse or distortion, to the institutionalization of a politicized ruthlessness dedicated to receding ends.

It is safe to say that Leszek Kolakowski's work will remain important and appreciated as long as ideas and their unanticipated consequences have an impact on history and human behavior.

Chapter Thirty-two

Public Intellectuals and the God That Failed

The collapse of communist states in Eastern Europe in 1989 and of the Soviet Union itself in 1991 was widely assumed to mark the end of the historical career of communist systems and movements; it was also expected to discredit durably the ideas that animated them. The remaining incarnations of "scientific socialism"—notably the grotesque North Korean dictatorship and the bankrupt patrimony of Fidel Castro—were hardly inspiring models of a "socialism with a human face."

The fall of communist states has been followed by a growing amnesia about the human toll exacted by their attempts to implement socialist ideals in the not-so-distant past, and coupled with a revival of anti-capitalist sentiments generated by the problematic results of globalization. No similar attempts were made at earlier times to downplay or reinterpret nonjudgmentally other major historical atrocities, including, in more recent times, the mass murders carried out by Nazi Germany. Academics did not parse the populist elements of Nazism in order to separate them from the genocidal practices in the way ideologues cull communism's egalitarian message from its gruesome applications.

In present-day Russia an abiding veneration of that great guardian of order and stability, Stalin, is coupled with ambivalence about the Soviet past and a yearning for the security and superpower status it provided. Maoist guerillas have become powerful in Nepal in recent years and remain entrenched in parts of India. Market economies failed to solve all social and economic problems in the countries where they were introduced; as a result, democratically elected leftist governments came into power in Venezuela and Bolivia, likely to be followed, according to some experts, by others of their kind in the region.

In the West no such trends can be discerned at the present time, but the rejection of capitalism and bourgeois cultural values remains entrenched among many intellectuals and in academic subcultures. Although specific communist states, extinct or surviving, are no longer widely admired by Western intellectuals, their anti-capitalist and egalitarian rhetoric remains attractive and many on the left steadfastly deny that Marxism was implicated in the moral and political-economic failures of the now defunct communist states. As Kenneth Minogue observed in 1990: "When regimes collapse . . . the principles and ideals which animated them can be glimpsed creeping stealthily away from the rubble, unscathed. Communism 'never failed'—its exponents can be heard muttering—it was 'never tried.'" This is especially the case when, as Enrique Krauze wrote in the *New Republic* a decade later, "celebrity utopians need a new address for their fantasies" and no such address is available because no political systems or movements exist upon which wishful fantasies can be readily projected. What remains are the good intentions and hopes that have proved impossible to realize. This is why Cornel West could maintain that "Marxist thought becomes even more relevant after the collapse of Communism in the Soviet Union and Eastern Europe than it was before." A flickering loyalty to the ideals that promised to transcend sordid socio-political inequities persists, as the hard-core loyalists refuse to accept that the human condition cannot be radically altered and improved, and that the failed attempts to do so required huge amounts of coercion and violence—as the history of communist states has shown. Leszek Kolakowski's observation made in 1978 (in his history of Marxism) about the influence of Marxism remains largely valid: "Almost all the prophecies of Marx . . . have already proved false, but this does not disturb the spiritual certainty of the faithful . . . for it is a certainty not based on . . . 'historical laws,' but simply on the psychological need for certainty. In this sense Marxism performs the function of religion. . . ."

THE OLD GUARD

Present-day radical leftists, anarchists, and supporters of the (leftover) counterculture continue to draw inspiration from old-guard leftist thinkers (some dead and others of an advanced age) disposed to minimize, deny, or explain away a political system that resulted in the deaths of tens of millions. Long before the fall of the Soviet Union, Western Marxists were compelled to find ways to protect their beliefs from the assault of the realities of existing communist states. The late historian and activist E. P. Thompson was one of them. He was deeply attached to communist ideals, despite disillusioning events (such as Khrushchev's revelations in 1956 and Soviet repression in Eastern

Europe in the same year). In a hundred-page "letter" to Kolakowski, Thompson proclaimed that Marxism was not discredited by the depredations of Stalinism or flaws of existing socialist states; he held up the "utopian potentials" of Marxism. He argued that "our solidarity was given not to communist states in their existence but in their potential—not for what they were but for what . . . they might become. . . ." He rebuked Kolakowski for linking "actually existing" Soviet-style systems with Marxism. Fifty years, he said, was "too short a time in which to judge a new social system." Thompson comes across as the prototypical true believer who regarded capitalism as the unchanging source of all evil and Marxism its diametrical opposite: the singular source of all that is good and honorable, to be venerated regardless of its failed applications.

Gus Hall, the general secretary of the U.S. Communist Party for several decades and a member since 1927, exemplifies unwavering commitment to the Soviet Union and a disciplined capacity to overlook its considerable blemishes. Following the fall of the Soviet communism he served all his life, he told reporters, "The world should see what North Korea has done . . . it's a miracle. If you want to take a nice vacation, take it in North Korea." He was not joking. His unwavering loyalty was rewarded by a $40 million subsidy between 1971 and 1990, provided by the Soviet authorities.

Herbert Aptheker, the Marxist historian, author of many books on black history and member of the U.S. Communist Party between 1939 and 1991, was of a similar generation. Although he broke with the party late in life, he remained a true believer in Marxism and the ineradicable evils of capitalism and American society. He believed, for instance, that higher education in the United States was "class- and race-based" and tightly controlled by the ruling classes. He succeeded in averting a major reassessment of his convictions because he managed to dissociate his pro-Soviet, communist beliefs from his lifelong struggle against racial discrimination that, he felt, legitimated all political stands he took.

Among the living, Eric Hobsbawm continues to offer another, better known example of the loyalties here discussed. Arguably, his fame and reputation rest, in part, on personifying resistance to disillusionment in the face of the vast accumulation of historical evidence calling into question old leftist articles of faith. He has shown how one may admit the deep flaws of all communist regimes that ever existed yet continue to regard the ideals inspiring and admirable. As of 1994 he still averred that even if he had known in 1934 that "millions of people were dying in the Soviet experiment," he would not have renounced it because "the chance of a new world being born on great suffering would still have been worth backing." He wrote in his autobiography, "I belonged to the generation tied by an almost umbilical cord to hope of the world revolution and its original hope, the October Revolution. . . ." He saw himself as fighter for a better world trying to make sure that mankind "will not live without the ideals of freedom and justice."

The bedrock convictions of Noam Chomsky rest on different foundations: an exceptionally fierce hatred of the United States, rather than durable admiration of an alternative political system. Although not a professed Marxist, he detects economic interests at the root of American depravities and attributes exceptional ruthlessness and cunning to American elites and policymakers. He seems incapable of contemplating any moral outrage without comparing it to some allegedly greater, far more repellent atrocity committed by the United States. He would equate 9/11 with the American bombing of the pharmaceutical factory in Sudan. He has been tirelessly disseminating his major message that no moral outrage could surpass those habitually committed by the United States (and its quasi-Nazi puppet, Israel). His attraction to communist systems has been episodic and based mainly on sympathy for the enemies of his archenemy. He repeatedly questioned the magnitude of Pol Pot's massacres in Cambodia and scorned the testimony of refugees both in an article published in 1977 in the *Nation* and a 1978 book. Chomsky also downplayed Eastern Europe's communist repression and said, "in comparison to conditions imposed by U.S. tyranny and violence, East Europe under Russian rule was practically a paradise." He considered Sandinista Nicaragua an inspiration for the downtrodden all over Latin America and even for the poor in the United States. Chomsky's quasi-celebrity status helps to explain the persistence of his political beliefs, reinforced by the favorable response of audiences who take pleasure in the combination of moral certitude and fulminations.

THE YOUNGER GENERATION

Nine years after the Soviet empire imploded, radical leftists and anarchists alike were thrilled by the publication of *Empire* (2001), written by Antonio Negri and Michael Hardt. The jargon-ridden volume was not merely an example of resistance to disillusionment, it was a major effort to revitalize radical leftist values and beliefs. As Alan Wolfe put it, "*Empire* is best understood as an attempt, using Marxist jargon, to bring back to life . . . anarchism and particularly the more destructive forms of anarchism. . . ." The major theme animating the book is the impassioned reaffirmation and romanticization of political violence, sanctified by the evil it was designed to combat. Negri and his supporters (and predecessors in the 1960s) argued that given the "essential" or "inherent" violence of capitalism, violent actions against it were morally unproblematic. Negri, a leader of the Red Brigades—which in the 1970s committed numerous high-profile terrorist acts in Italy—was charged with armed insurrection and given a prison sentence (which only required him to spend nights in jail). In the 1970s he provided a remarkable example of false consciousness, imagining himself as a member of the Italian proletariat: "I live the life of the sniper, the deviant, and the worker who doesn't show up at his job. Every time I put on my ski mask, I feel the warmth of the proletarian worker community around me. . . . Every action of destruction and sabotage seems to me a manifestation of class solidarity. Nor does the eventual risk bother me: rather it fills me with feverish excitement as one waiting for his lover. Nor does the pain of my adversary affect me. . . ."

His status as a convicted felon doubtless added to the attractions of the book, seen as he has was by his admirers as a fearless man of ideas as well as action. Rather than ignored as an expression of discredited revolutionary fantasies, *Empire* has "come as close to becoming an international best seller as a university press book . . . is likely to get," Alexander Stille noted in the *New York Review of Books*.

The shallow and muddled utopianism probably added to the appeals of the book as it promised "a revolution no power will control—because bio-power and communism, cooperation and revolution remain together, in love, simplicity and also innocence. This is the irrepressible lightness and joy of being communist."

Among other self-proclaimed former revolutionaries Bill Ayers is noteworthy. His memoir, *Fugitive Days* (2003), is a comprehensive record of the radical beliefs of his generation of activists. But he differed from many former radicals who, with the passage of time, retreated from their most virulent youthful commitments and convictions. Ayers recalled the bombing of the Pentagon with undisguised nostalgia: "Everything was absolutely ideal on the day I bombed the Pentagon; the sky was blue. The birds were singing. And the bastards were finally going to get what was coming to them." Che Guevara was among his role models, who "spoke to us every morning from a huge poster above our bed." He was among the privileged youths coming of age in the 1960s who found middle-class life unbearably stultifying and inauthentic: "I think back to my childhood, to the houses in trim rows and the identical lawns and the neat fences. . . . Where we lived . . . the grass was always green, the moms were always smiling. . . . Our kitchen was sparkling. . . ." To overcome such suburban, middle-class inauthenticity, he declared that "the personal is political, and we meant that . . . everything was part of a grand experiment in liberation. . . . I felt suddenly transported . . . swept along by the dream of peace and the captivating idea of social change. . . ." The disappointments of private and family life converged with the discovery of social-political injustices such as racism and the Vietnam War; these injustices vindicated the smoldering alienation from the suburban, upper-middle-class life that preceded the war and the discovery of racial inequalities.

Following his emergence from the underground, Ayers became a tenured professor of education at the University of Illinois at Chicago. While his current way of life is not compatible with setting off bombs or hurling rocks at policemen or shop windows, his old beliefs and commitments remain cherished and the enduring basis of his moral identity. The persistence of these commitments is underscored by his expressions of admiration for Jamil al-Amin (Rap Brown), Kathy Boudin, David Gilbert, Mumia Abu-Jamal, Anthony Ortiz, and Leonard Peltier—most of them convicted murderers.

While the "Old Guard" sought historical justification for the sufferings imposed by communist systems and movements, the young radicals were enamored and energized by heartfelt, authentic political violence in the service of lofty ends.

THE ISLAMIC FACTOR

It is among the peculiarities of the present-day cultural-political climate in the United States and other Western countries that old-style leftist sympathies for various communist states and movements have to varying degrees been transferred to the radical Islamist movements and adversaries of the United States. This development has been paradoxical, since the progressive, secular beliefs of both the old and new Left are not easy to reconcile with Islamic fundamentalism and the religious fanaticism of Islamic radicals. Nonetheless, the Arab-Islamic adversaries of the United States have become new objects of sympathy and solidarity for some figures on the left, and enlisted among the many "victims" of American policies vindicating their hostility to the United States. Lynne Stewart, a radical lawyer best known as the unsuccessful defender of Sheik Omar Abdel Rahman, the spiritual leader of the global jihad (sentenced to life in prison in 1996), exemplifies this position. Like the late William Kunstler, she became "a movement lawyer" who "didn't just defend the legal rights of her clients; she also advocated their politics," as George Packer noted in the *New York Times Magazine*. She became Rahman's lawyer at the urging of Ramsey Clark, who also deserves our attention on similar grounds. Subsequently, Stewart was indicted and sentenced to prison for helping Rahman communicate from prison with his followers. In Stewart's eyes, Packer wrote, Rahman was "a fighter for national liberation on behalf of people oppressed by dictatorship and American imperialism. She came to admire him personally too. . . ." As other radicals, she was irresistibly attracted to the enemy of her enemies. She was propelled, she said, by her true goal to always be "on the right side of history." That entailed an abiding hostility toward capitalism, which she described as "a consummate evil that unleashes its dogs of war on the helpless; an enemy motivated by insatiable greed. . . ." She also said, "I don't have any problem with Mao or Stalin or the Vietnamese leaders or certainly Fidel locking up people they see as dangerous." Her radical sympathies and support for convicted terrorists, domestic and foreign, did not make her an outcast in the legal or academic world.

Ramsey Clark, the U.S. attorney general under Lyndon Johnson, has in common with Lynne Stewart an avid interest in defending the adversaries of the United States, domestic and foreign, but the evolution of his political attitudes is more complex. After his career as attorney general, he joined William Kunstler to represent two of the so-called Attica Brothers, accused of killing a guard during the prison uprising. He provided legal assistance to Radovan Karadzic, the Bosnian Serb general indicted for war crimes, and gave legal advice to Slobodan Milosevic. Clark also joined the legal team defending Saddam Hussein, of whom he made warm remarks while he was still in power: "I've met with him four times, probably averaged two to three hours at a time. . . . [H]e is reserved, quiet, thoughtful, dignified, you might say, in the old-fashioned sense," as he was quoted in the *New York Observer*. In a *Face the Nation* interview, Clark refused to describe Saddam as an evil force. "I don't judge people as good or evil," he said. He showed no such reticence in his judgments of American policies and politicians.

It is not self-evident why Clark became an embittered critic of the United States. During the Vietnam era he prosecuted prominent war protesters such as Dr. Spock, William Sloane Coffin, and Muhammad Ali, and he might have come to regret this, given his emerging political convictions. Also significant, soon after becoming attorney general, he dropped the case against Judith Coplon, who was charged with passing secrets to a Soviet lover. It was none other than Clark's father who brought the case against Coplon when he was attorney general. Approaching eighty, it is safe to predict that Ramsey Clark will persevere in his beliefs.

WHY THESE BELIEFS ENDURED

Several conditions may be identified that contribute to the preservation of the deeply held political beliefs and ideals here discussed. Most important is that it is always easier to retain familiar, internalized beliefs, held over long periods of time, than to discard them. The more time is invested in a political cause or movement, the more difficult it becomes to abandon it. Many of the well-known representatives of these enduring beliefs are of advanced age or are deceased. What they have in common are core convictions about the corruptions and injustices that, in their view, define American society. Hatred of the enemy—the United States—prompts solidarity with the enemies of that enemy, who could be communist dictators, third-world autocrats, Islamic fanatics, or domestic terrorists.

The other major factor in the durability of these beliefs is their centrality to the sense of identity of the individuals concerned. When political beliefs and actions satisfy important emotional needs and bolster a favorable self-conception, they are likely to endure. Resisting political disillusionment was important to Western intellectuals whose sense of identity rested in large measure on their self-conception as fighters for social justice and righteous critics of the corruptions of their society. Favorable disposition toward communist systems and movements often complemented this role. While the latter has greatly diminished, the aversion toward their society did not. This aversion seemed more profoundly determining their attitudes than the alternatives embraced.

Political beliefs are also more likely to endure when they are shared with a group or subculture, and when abandoning the shared beliefs would result in the loss of important human bonds, social connections, and friendships.

Of further importance, Western intellectuals who resisted reappraisals of their leftist ideological convictions were spared the personal experience of living in communist societies. For those in the West, the unappealing attributes of communist systems—even when acknowledged—remained abstractions that could not compete with the more intimate knowledge and personal experience of the flaws of their own society. Nor was the limited awareness of the defects of communist systems sufficient to undermine high expectations nurtured by leftist ideals and ideologies.

The single most important factor that enables the individual to retain radical leftist (or other radical) beliefs is the capacity to dissociate ends from means, theory from practice, ideals from realities. Such a capacity rests on what Arthur Koestler called "the doctrine of unshaken foundations"—the overwhelming, superior moral importance attributed to the ends, which allow the individual to overlook, or altogether dismiss, the human costs of their pursuit.

V
IN CONCLUSION

Chapter Thirty-three

From a "Builder of Socialism" to "Free-Floating Intellectual": My Politically Incorrect Career in Sociology[1]

FROM BUDAPEST TO THE LONDON SCHOOL OF ECONOMICS

It is always interesting to ponder one's choice of a particular occupation or profession, assuming that it was a matter of choice. Choosing an occupation is approximately as important as choosing one's spouse, possibly more so since—at the present time at any rate—people are more likely to stay with their profession than spouse. There are several pathways to occupational choice. It may be, or used to be, a matter of following in the footsteps of parents, or, it may be inspired by the desire to do something different, interesting, exciting, or creative—that is, to find fulfillment in the occupation chosen. Another determinant may be an appetite for wealth and power or high status, recognition or fame compatible with the desire for money, and a luxurious way of life. American society, more than most, encourages such high aspirations. The desire to do good and help others is another motive for choosing a profession; it too can be combined with interest in making a good living and high status, as in the case of physicians and lawyers. One may also drift into an occupation, seizing particular opportunities, perhaps the fate of most people. The higher the skills or qualifications an occupation or profession requires, the less likely that entering it will be a matter of such drift.

There seem to be two major motives for people who become sociologists in the United States. The first is to do good, to change society or particular institutions by grasping how society and its institutions work and by discovering the roots of social problems, inequality, conflict, and human misery; it is hoped that new information and proper methodology would lead to the application of sociological insights to better lives. Any such application of the findings of sociology (and the other social sciences) rests on a conception of good society, of what constitutes social justice and human fulfillment, even of legitimate human needs. Secondly, there is the pursuit of knowledge for its own sake, the desire to become a scientist of society, to master and accumulate knowledge of human interactions, social institutions, change, and conflict but not necessarily in order to improve the world. Astronomists do not dream of altering the universe, and social scientists need not believe that their work will find application.

My own case does not quite fit these motivational patterns. The choice of sociology as a field of study and profession was certainly not the culmination of carefully nurtured aspirations, of the desire to be of some service to humanity; I aspired neither to become a virtuous critic of social injustice nor a hard-nosed scientist discovering the social facts and the imperatives of social life. But, there was a modest, lurking hope that in choosing sociology, I could eventually shed some light on some puzzling and discouraging aspects of social existence, including the painful and depriving conditions one faces in life. I was especially interested in better understanding social and political conflicts such as I experienced firsthand in my native country, Hungary, during World War II and afterwards when the country was occupied and forcibly transformed by the Soviet Union. There were finally the experiences of the crushed Revolution of 1956.

When at the ripe age of twenty-four in January 1957 I was enrolled as a first-year undergraduate at the London School of Economics (part of the University of London), I had just learned about the existence of the sociology I proposed to study. My interests in high school (gymnasium) and afterwards while in Hungary were literary. Had I been admitted to a university in Hungary and had I been free to make a choice, I would have chosen English literature, perhaps English and Russian or English and Hungarian. Upon arrival in England it seemed presumptuous and a misplaced aspiration for a Hungarian with a limited (though rapidly growing) knowledge of the English language to specialize in English literature in England. I was also interested in history, psychology, political science, and anthropology—though the latter three barely existed as academic disciplines in communist Hungary. Sociology was also unknown; although in its stead we had something called "tarsadalomtudomany" that translates as the science of society, an apparent incarnation of sociology. In reality this "science of society" was Marxism-Leninism applied to the prevailing political purposes and policies of the party-state in Hungary.

I learned of the academic existence of sociology shortly after my arrival in London in December 1956 on a visit to the London School of Economics. An English student took me there and showed the catalogue that described the programs of study, that listed specific courses, and even the readings assigned to them. I was in the privileged position to shop around, as it were, for a suitable course of study. The arrangements were flexible and generous; all of us, three hundred Hungarian student refugees flown to the U.K. from Austria in a special little airlift, were given ample choice, assistance to learn the language, and comprehensive financial support by a consortium of British universities and special funds.

The degree program in sociology entailed courses in sociological theory, social philosophy, ethics, social psychology, criminology, sociology of religion, economics, English social history, and others, all of which looked interesting in their own right though it was not clear what they all added up to. Studying sociology at LSE also allowed me to stay in London, which was an important consideration. Having grown up in a city (Budapest), but forcibly removed from it at age eighteen and compelled to spend close to five years in rural areas (more of this later), big city life had a great attraction. I had no desire to go to an English provincial university, not even to Oxford or Cambridge.

This somewhat haphazard involvement with the discipline helps to explain why being a sociologist has never been an important, defining part of my intellectual, professional, or personal identity. I believe that I could just as well have chosen political science, social psychology, cultural anthropology, social or intellectual history. In any of these fields in all probability I would have gravitated to the same professional interests that came to preoccupy me as a sociologist, addressing them presumably with different concepts and terminology.

SOCIOLOGY AND "FREE-FLOATING" INTELLECTUALS

If sociologists are considered intellectuals, and emerge from the requisite social context Karl Mannheim had specified as the breeding ground of intellectuals, I was an appropriate candidate for the sociological calling. I was "detached" all right, and quite "free-floating," having left my native country and been removed from family, friends, and a familiar subculture, without clear-cut membership in a social class, lacking organizational ties, sustaining religious beliefs, and financial security.

Similar connections between exile and the calling of the intellectual were proposed by Edward Said: "What we have here . . . is exile as metaphor, to use Said's phrase: exile as the typical condition of the modern intellectual—indeed as the only condition that should command respect. This is not an original thesis. Said's hero . . . Theodore Adorno, who was for a time a real exile, claimed that a sense of alienation, of not feeling at home even in your own home, was the only correct attitude for an intellectual to adopt. Adorno was in this respect heir to a German romantic tradition."[2]

I do not have much sympathy with the Said-Adorno position sketched above since I associate it (as did Ian Buruma, whose article I quoted from) with a certain amount of posturing. Many, if not most, of the self-consciously and boastfully "alienated" intellectuals who cherish the idea of being in exile of some kind (as Said did) are in fact all too well integrated into their social setting, showered with social and academic honors, command impressive incomes, and enjoy total job security (tenure), political and expressive freedom, and access to every conceivable media of communication. These pleasant conditions are difficult to reconcile with the original idea of "alienation" that conveys not merely a state of mind and a social-critical disposition but certain tangible deprivations associated with particular social conditions. Said and those of his disposition seem to suggest that their alienation entails something original and heroic, including willful risk-taking and victimhood. But the social criticism Said and others of similar mindset articulate does not entail any risk, it is in fact highly rewarded and respected within the intellectual-academic subcultures in which they live—and well tolerated by society at large. Moreover, the type of social criticism here referred to (I called it elsewhere "adversarial") has become highly standardized and unoriginal, a form of conventional wisdom among academic intellectuals and those left-of-center outside academia. I do not count myself among *these* alienated intellectuals (whatever the nature and degree of my "detachment" from American society).

In my case the "free-floating" condition preceded, to some degree, my departure from Hungary. It is hard to think of any collectivity to which I belonged in Hungary that contributed to a strong sense of identity. I came from a largely assimilated Jewish family; my parents were neither practicing Jews nor involved in Jewish community life. The same was true of my maternal grandfather who lived with us, though not my grandmother who, while alive, made the family observe the major Jewish holidays. Being Jewish for me meant mainly well-preserved memories of life-threatening persecution (in 1944) and a vague pride in belonging to a group that had an above average interest in learning and produced many individuals of considerable intellectual, scientific, and artistic distinction. I have somewhat similar positive feelings about my Hungarian roots when I contemplate the accomplishments of Hungarians, in and outside Hungary.

While growing up (during the postwar years), my family was steadily losing social status and financial security due to political circumstances. After finishing what was an elite high school (gymnasium) in Budapest in 1951, my parents, grandfather, and I were exiled (deported, really) to a village in Eastern Hungary. This was followed by two years of military service, much of it in the so-called construction battalions (epitozaszloalj) set up for those defined as politically unreliable by the authorities. After exile and military service I worked (as an unskilled laborer) in construction in Budapest since such an occupation entitled one to live in the city (as a former exile I needed a special permit to live there). Most of my classmates and friends managed to attend university and I felt singularly marginal and unfortunate being deprived of the same opportunity. (I had good grades and was initially admitted, but the exile made it impossible to attend.) Between 1948 and 1956 I ceaselessly fantasized about getting out of Hungary but it was not possible, either legally or illegally.

HISTORICAL EVENTS AND SOCIOLOGICAL INTERESTS

Three major political-historical events and experiences influenced my sociological interests by their impact on my life. They were the Jewish persecution in 1944, the period of communist repression between 1948 and 1956, and the Hungarian Revolution (and its defeat) in 1956. Each impressed on me the endemic nature of conflict, and the part played by lethal violence in human affairs. The latter ceased to be an abstraction when at age twelve (during the siege of Budapest) I saw corpses lying on the streets and later (after the war) when I paused on my way to school to stare at bodies exhumed from a mass grave in a park where they were buried temporarily during the siege. There were more corpses to be seen during the Revolution in 1956 when I spent most of my time as a participant observer of sorts on the streets of Budapest.

These experiences are likely to have implanted seeds of skepticism about theoretical schemes in sociology which emphasized consensus and normative integration and the rational settlement of disputes central to "conflict resolution." Not that I did not regard such possibilities praiseworthy, but they seemed historically and geographically limited to a handful of (Western) societies that managed miraculously to institutionalize the rule of law, political pluralism, and respect for the individual.

The defeat of the Hungarian Revolution was another all too obvious lesson that "might is right," that brute force can settle conflict with durable results and ideas can be silenced by naked power. To be sure, seen from the vantage point of the last decade of the twentieth century, the crushing of the revolution did not bring lasting benefits for the oppressor. Gradually the forces pressing for greater political choice and freedom and a realignment with

Western values had reasserted themselves in Hungary and elsewhere in Eastern Europe. At last, in 1989 the communist system in Hungary dissolved as it did in the Soviet Union in 1991—both developments totally unanticipated on my part and most experts on such matters. The collapse and its aftermath further contributed to my skeptical view of American sociology as this momentous historical development failed to inspire any serious analysis, discussion, or stocktaking in the sociological profession that had a long record of massive indifference toward communist systems.

I should also note here that surviving Nazism did not implant any "survivor guilt" many survivors of the Holocaust are said to suffer of. To the contrary I felt lucky and privileged; the survival and the subsequent escape from Hungary became a source of optimism, and imparted the feeling that I was in control of my life, or at any rate that I am capable of "bouncing back" after hardships.

My family and I survived the Jewish persecution because we acquired documents stating that we were gentiles and Transylvanian refugees, and these papers passed the muster of the Hungarian Nazi storm troopers looking for Jews in hiding. Getting out of Hungary and escaping communism (in November 1956) was another matter. By then I was an adult and made an entirely conscious decision to try to get out, willing to face the risk of getting caught, and if so, imprisoned. I remain convinced that it was the best decision I ever made. The following helps to understand why.

DOWN AND OUT IN HUNGARY

The five years (from June 1951 to November 1956) between finishing the gymnasium and escaping from Hungary are especially helpful explaining the interests that permeated my academic work and found expression in my publications. At the time I felt that these were totally lost, wasted years, when nothing useful was accomplished, a period of considerable physical discomfort (especially while in the army), intellectual derailment, and overall stagnation.

The exile was an old Russian-Soviet form of punishment imported to Hungary from the Soviet Union. It entailed enforced idleness combined with occasional bouts of heavy manual labor, crowded and primitive housing conditions, loss of social status and property, political stigmatization, and literal uprootedness. The exiles (or deportees), having been removed from Budapest, were left to fend for themselves in the villages but were not prevented from getting help from relatives. We were allowed to vegetate more or less undisturbed by the authorities, our movements restricted to a six-kilometer (four-mile) radius from the center of the village. There were occasional visits from the police to make sure that nobody made an unauthorized trip (given the system of personal identity documents, or internal passports, that listed residence and required registration with and permission from the police when one wanted to move, there was little practical possibility or incentive to try to escape.)

There were major sociological lessons or insights implicit in the experience of the exile and in that of the Jewish persecution. One was that human beings regardless of their individual qualities and behavior can be assigned to broad racial, ethnic, class, or political categories and treated accordingly. In effect, the authorities, both Nazi and Communist, practiced a form of applied sociology, using sociological criteria to predict individual behavior from the attributes assigned to the group the individual belonged to, or was assigned to. As the Nazis saw it, Jews were by genealogical or racial definition evil, and the good of society (and mankind) required their elimination. As to being classified as politically unreliable (or a "class enemy") by the communist regime on account of the former socioeconomic status of my maternal grandfather—in this regard the causation was more indirect. It involved the notion that class and class-consciousness is transmitted through more than one generation: if my grandfather was a capitalist with all the socially determined harmful attitudes, the latter were bound to be transmitted to his offspring, including grandson.

The deportations were an attempt to weed out groups of people seen as supportive or potentially supportive of the precommunist social-political order and hostile toward the new one; the deportations were officially justified as part of the class struggle. They also helped to alleviate the chronic housing shortage in the capital, Budapest.

The second learning experience of growing up under the communist system was that people can live for long periods of time under a political system they abhor but are capable of wearing the mask of conformity without showing signs of their dissatisfaction or hostility.

The very nature of the communist system and its massive, ongoing campaigns of propaganda and the attendant institutionalization of a gap between theory and practice (or between the official promises and reality) also made a lasting impression. It may be conjectured that the latter stimulated my subsequent interest in and awareness of the many discrepancies between appearance and reality perpetuated by both political propaganda and commercial advertising. More generally, I have retained a morbid fascination with the various institutional, cultural, as well as personal attempts at misrepresenting reality, and such interests found expression in my work.

The military service too might have contributed to my sociological interests, by illustrating the nature of hierarchies, power and powerlessness, bureaucracy at its worst, and the ability of the individual to adapt to adversity. It was an experience of deprivation, regimentation, powerlessness, and involuntary obedience to authority. Life in the army (both in the labor battalion and later in the infantry) revolved around a profusion of mindless regulations, crude as well as subtle inequalities and status distinctions, and the use of naked power. It is likely that these experiences sensitized me to the pervasive abuse of power, political inequalities and the ease with which people can be intimidated; they also contributed to my professional interest in the concept and manifestations of totalitarianism.

The Hungarian armed forces in the early 1950s combined the military traditions derived from the Austro-Hungarian Monarchy (and its Prussian aspects) and Soviet-style punitive authoritarianism with its commitment to the minute regulation of the conscripts' lives. Our hair was completely removed at the moment of induction and we remained totally shorn for an entire year. (Having a shaved head or crewcut was far from fashionable in Hungary at the time and was associated either with service in the army or incarceration.) No leaves were given during the first six months and even afterwards it was a rare privilege. The food was far worse than what inmates of maximum-security prisons or the homeless get in this country. In the labor battalion the work was quite hard and there was a great deal of harassment by the NCOs and the political commissar.[3] Our bed covers and the "mattress" (a coarse sack stuffed with straw) were almost daily thrown off by NCOs for not approximating the shape of a matchbox or brick, the official ideal. People would get up an hour before the wake-up call to have enough time to smooth and sharpen the edges and attain the ideal symmetry demanded. There were also alarms or inspections (of specks of dust under the bed, for example) in the middle of the night and nocturnal drills.

Such and other hardships were barely cushioned by group solidarity since we were intimidated and atomized. This was accomplished in part by penalizing the unit as a whole for the alleged misbehavior of an individual member (accused, for example, of not pulling his weight at work) and by encouraging his fellows to beat him up—which occasionally happened at night at the urging of the commissar.

Both the exile and military service provided opportunity to encounter a much wider range of people (i.e., peasants and other manual laborers) than would otherwise have been the case. These circumstances and encounters stimulated questions about the nature of the social and political world, the relationship between individual and society, and the part played by personal choice (or free will) versus social and political forces in one's life.

The same questions had been raised far more starkly in 1944 when my family and I stood a very good chance of being killed, and at age twelve I was well aware of the possibility and discussed it with my father who, in response to my inquiries, assured me that being shot is not painful. I never ceased to reflect on the fact that a person, because of his or her membership in (or arbitrary assignment to) an ethnic, racial, social, or religious group could be subjected to life-threatening measures, and these measures could be implemented on a large scale. Nonetheless, the experiences of Nazism and the Jewish persecution found no discernible expression in my work as a sociologist, for reasons discussed below.

POLITICAL PREOCCUPATIONS IN MY WORK

Rather than reflecting the truly traumatic experiences noted earlier, much of my work focused on Soviet totalitarianism, communism, and the attraction the latter held for Western intellectuals. This is all the more counterintuitive since the communist regime was not life-threatening—I did, however, live under it far longer. But the major explanation of these contrasting preoccupation lies elsewhere.

Already at an early age (in my teens), it seemed to me that the issue of Nazism had been settled historically and morally. No sane, decent, respectable, or moderately intelligent person would defend Nazism or try to minimize its misdeeds. After leaving Hungary and becoming an academic I noted that nobody studying or writing about any aspect of Nazism was cautioned about the danger of making value judgments (unlike those writing about communist systems or movements); refugees from Nazi Germany and former inmates of Nazi concentration camps were not considered unreliable witnesses (unlike those from communist states).[4] The condemnation of Nazism seemed, and still seems, virtually universal and unconditional (young neo-Nazis and crackpot Holocaust revisionists notwithstanding). "Nazi" became a synonym of evil, and the Holocaust its unique expression. Not only was Nazism disavowed, its evil was well documented; information of every kind—visual, statistical, documentary, eyewitness—was widely available. It did not take great intellectual discernment or moral courage in the Western world to condemn Nazism. Not only was Nazism discredited, largely due to the Holocaust, it had also been conclusively defeated on the battlefields and destroyed as a political system. This made it possible to investigate and document its misdeeds, whereas the survival of communist systems until the early 1990s contributed to their legitimacy and made it impossible to document *their* misdeeds.

In contrast to the moral assessments and condemnation of Nazism, the debate over the nature of communist systems and their supporting ideologies has persisted even after the collapse of Soviet communism. At the time of this writing many Western intellectuals and academics still have some good things to say or think about certain communist regimes (though rarely about the former Soviet Union). Castro's Cuba (an especially hellish place for critical intellectuals) retains a measure of sentimental support, and if its defects are reluctantly acknowledged, they are usually blamed on the United States. Marxism is still dominant in many departments of humanities and social sciences on American (and Western European) campuses and its relevance to the character and defects of communist systems (existing or defunct) is vigorously denied by those on the left.

For such reasons, through much of my professional career I was motivated by an impulse to enlighten my academic colleagues, and the educated public in this country about "actually existing" socialist systems, and disabuse them of illusions and the error of perceiving them as morally equivalent or superior to Western democracies. I also argued repeatedly that there was a connection between "theory and practice," that Marxism bears *some* responsibility for the form these systems took, and that it had inspired their political elites up to a point.[5]

It is indeed the case, as my late friend Stanley Milgram pointed out, that I was intellectually "energized" by what seemed to me the obtuseness, ignorance, self-deception, and wishful-thinking I encountered among many Western intellectuals and their audiences. Had there been more widespread rejection of contemporary Marxist-Leninist regimes, movements, and ideologies I would have been less likely to write about them, especially if there had also been the kind of moral consensus about them similar to that regarding Nazi Germany, apartheid-era South Africa, or various right-wing dictatorships around the world.

To this day these issues remain unsettled, morally as well as intellectually. Large numbers of Western people of good-will and idealism remain seriously uninformed about the character of communist systems (surviving or extinct) and the relationship between the ideologically inspired, if perverted, idealism that guided their rulers in undertaking the political transformations that created so much political violence and mendaciousness.

All the events, experiences, and attitudes discussed earlier also made me more aware of the significant role irrationality and aggression play in social and political affairs and human behavior.

ON BEING A "ROOTLESS COSMOPOLITAN"

The connections between being an intellectual (and the professional activities associated with it) and one's sense of identity bear further discussion. It is indisputable that uprootedness, marginality, or the outsider status were the background to (if not the direct inspiration of) my becoming a sociologist.

A specific example of the connections between life and work was a study of the process of adjustment of Hungarian students to life in Britain I undertook while still an undergraduate at LSE, which eventually became my master's thesis at the University of Illinois, Urbana, in 1960. It was obviously inspired by personal interest and made possible by the University of London underwriting the modest expenses. This was one of the very few quantitative studies I ever undertook since it was based on mail questionnaires and tabulated with the help of an early version of the computer. I only recall one finding (which certainly applied to my own case), that the best adjusted among the students were those who had good language skills and suffered some kind of political deprivation in Hungary.

The term "rootless cosmopolitan" was coined by Andrei Zhdanov, the high-ranking Soviet party functionary in charge of matters ideological and cultural in the late 1940s. It was introduced in the course of a campaign to harass and repress artists, writers, and assorted intellectuals who were, supposedly tainted by Western ideas and cultural influences, hence were "rootless cosmopolitans." The other unexpressed meaning of the term was simply "Jewish." Most of those repressed during that period were Jews and calling Jews "rootless cosmopolitans" had some historical plausibility since they were often forced to escape from one country to another. Over the years I sometimes applied the term humorously to myself. I was largely rootless, Jewish, and "cosmopolitan" in the sense of being possessed of a European cultural orientation. That is to say, I am unashamedly "Eurocentric" without being closely identified with any particular country and its culture or traditions. The rootlessness here conveyed did not prove to be particularly burdensome or problematic.

My sense of being an outsider (whether in Britain or the United States) did not prevent me from feeling sympathetic toward the social-political system in which I was able to build a new life. Freedom, or the free world, for me was not a concept placed in ironic quotation marks.[6] I could tell the difference between the presence or absence of political freedom and found ideas such as Marcuse's "repressive tolerance" irritating and unconvincing.

These political sympathies notwithstanding, I have remained largely an outsider, close to what Mannheim meant by free-floating. But, contrary to Mannheim, these circumstances did not endow me with great powers of "synthesizing" or a greater objectivity. But there were other intellectual benefits derived from growing up (and having spent my youth) in one country, my college years in another, and the rest in a third. These circumstances made me, I believe, a somewhat better observer of the social settings I lived in; I took fewer things for granted than the natives and was inclined to compare and reflect on the ways of life, institutions, attitudes, and beliefs found in different societies.

This outsider status and state of mind is perhaps best illustrated by noting that to this day, after having spent most of my adult life in the United States, I cannot say without hesitation and qualifications that I am "American." My Hungarian accent, if nothing else, reminds me that I am not. Not even an American wife and daughter born here can complete the acculturation process, although they help. I have close American friends but perhaps the closest are those who share my background, Hungarians of my generation who left in 1956, some of whom I have known since my teens or childhood, and some other foreigners who settled here.

It does not follow, however, that I have a strong sense of being Hungarian. Having spent the first twenty-four years of my life in Hungary has not been an indestructible foundation of such an identity given the difficulties I had in Hungary. At the same time, I still speak Hungarian fluently and without an accent and feel a certain pride that I can pass as a native when in Hungary. But I do not write and think in Hungarian. When I visit Hungary, which I do every year since the early 1980s, I do not feel that it is the place where I "belong."[7] On my only visit to Israel in 1968 I felt the same or an even greater distance; there was no surge of a sense of solidarity with my fellow Jews; moreover, I could not speak the language and neither the landscape nor the climate was congenial.

On my visits to Hungary as I interact with the natives I do not feel that we share important, binding ties given my long absence from Hungary, but I can still effortlessly communicate with them. I am in a country that is at once familiar and strange. I like Hungarian food, the music of Bartok and Kodaly, and the many great works of Hungarian literature untranslated and unknown outside Hungary.

When all is said and done, I feel on these visits as a well-meaning and well-regarded outsider; I do not have a love-hate relationship with Hungary and Hungarians. People I come in contact with are friendly and polite, my relatives affectionate. My parents died a long time ago; what remains is a half-sister, her son (my nephew), close cousins and a few old friends, and some newer ones as well. I never fantasized about moving back, not even after the fall of communism, although my retirement income (adequate here) would make me outright affluent there.

Being an outsider in this country is a different matter, and compatible with feeling comfortable and at home; Americans are tolerant of accents, strange food preferences, and of a certain amount of foreignness. In the academic setting such foreignness may even confer a slight advantage (less than a darker skin color). I often speculated that my freely expressed political incorrectness over the years was perhaps overlooked or excused to some degree by my colleagues as the eccentricity of a foreigner.

Apart from the accent, my outsider status is further testified to by my sketchy knowledge of American history and ignorance of popular culture. I do not know the names of famous athletes and the idols of mass entertainment; I have never been to a football, basketball, or baseball game. By contrast, my knowledge of American geography greatly exceeds that of most natives. I have been to most states, most national parks, driven across the country four times, and have a good knowledge of where major cities and geographical features are to be found. My knowledge of New England is even more impressive as I have been exploring it ever since I moved here in 1963. As to the narrower geographic confines of Western Massachusetts where I have lived since 1968, my knowledge is even more extensive and the source of some pride. I have explored most dirt roads, mountain trails, lakes, ponds, and waterways of this area by car, kayak, on foot and cross-country skis, respectively. As a matter of fact, the strongest ties that bind me to this country are geographic: cherished landscapes and the outdoors. No amount of sentimental recollection of Hungarian lands can compete with my attachment to the mountains, lakes, and seacoasts of New England.

SCHOOLS, TEACHERS, ROLE MODELS

Discussion of my intellectual development and aspirations prompts some reference to my high school, the gymnasium I attended in Budapest. By the standards of most American high schools it was a demanding and elitist institution, which (when I began) students entered at age ten and attended for eight years. At the end of the eighth year we took a much-feared comprehensive written and oral examination over several days that covered several years' work. The curriculum had virtually no electives; requirements included eight years of Latin, several years of Russian (as well some other foreign language before that was abolished), several years of mathematics, algebra, geometry, physics, biology, chemistry, zoology/botany, mostly Hungarian literature, art history, physical education, and choir. Homework was plentiful; we were given number grades. Most graduates of the school went on to university. While not everybody in my class was bookish, there were enough of us who were and who took pride in reading books well beyond what was required in school. My interests and those of my friends were literary-humanistic-philosophical but also political. In those days Hungarian schools were segregated by sex and this probably contributed to a certain intellectual male bonding and seriousness that otherwise might not have been present. We missed the company of girls badly but their absence probably made us still more bookish. My friends and I had no interest whatsoever in sports and especially team sports. While our school did have its "jocks," they had no monopoly on status and popularity, unlike in most American schools.

While the gymnasium exerted lasting influence by creating or stimulating a broad predisposition to and respect for some type of intellectual activity, the type of training I had in sociology also made a difference. It seems that having attended first a British university and later Princeton helped to make me more of a humanistic-qualitative sociologist than might otherwise have been the case, although training in sociology at LSE had a substantial positivist-empiricist component and members of the faculty were far from dismissive of quantitative methods. I think that British sociology at the time differed from American by being less polarized along the extremes of "grand theorizing" on the one hand and the pursuit of methodological refinements on the other, both famously scorned by C. Wright Mills.

From the earliest days of my sociological career I was attracted to what struck me as significant questions of social-political existence—never mind the methodological apparatus available for investigating them. I also realized over time that such an approach can degenerate into mere speculation, polemics, or journalism. At the same time, "grand theorizing" left me cold because of its abstract nature and lack of connection with concrete, substantive historical matters and situations

The teaching of sociology at LSE at the undergraduate level was more like teaching it in this country at the graduate level. Several courses were taught in the seminar format, others as medium-size lectures. There were also tutorials, better known as venerable fixtures at Oxford and Cambridge. In each year I had a different tutor (Norman Birnbaum in my first, Hilda Himmelweit, the social psychologist, in the second, and Thomas Bottomore in the third). These were indeed informal occasions; the paper and discussion topics were largely inspired by the tutor.

Most amazing from the American perspective, there were no grades, no grade-point averages, and no exams until the finals, which was the culmination of the three-year program. We did write papers for the seminars as well as for our tutor. I do not recall if those were actually graded or not but there were always written and verbal comments. The final exams were graded (or given points), which determined the type of degree received: First Class, Upper Second, Lower Second, Third, and Pass. (I got a lower second. This mediocre performance may be assessed against the fact that I did the three-year course in two-and-a-half and began with a limited knowledge of the English language.)

Also of some interest (and illustrative of the differences between British and American academic procedures at the time) is that my admission to LSE was exceedingly informal, based on a single interview with the economist Joan Robinson. I did not (and could not) even produce proof of having completed high school and with what results. I believe that my relative fluency in English at the time carried much weight.

Princeton at the time I attended graduate school (1960–1963) had an unusually permissive sociology department as far as requirements were concerned. There were no course requirements, neither regarding their number nor the kind to be taken, although it was strongly recommended we take some. I took two each semester during my two years in residence, some in political science. But we had a language requirement, reading knowledge of two languages. There was also a methods requirement but it was mercifully waived on account of my having taken such a course at LSE. The faculty members were accessible, perhaps in part because the number of graduate students in residence was small (about a dozen). My teachers at Princeton included Morroe Berger, Allen Kassof, Marion Levy, Charles Page, Mel Tumin, and Harry Eckstein in political science. I disappointed Levy on the occasion when he asked me, would I, if I had a choice, be a great scientist or creative artist/writer? I chose the latter. His seminars on theory were notable for his encouragement of comparative papers allowing us to range over the globe and almost any topic. (I recall comparing political institutions in Yemen and East Germany on one occasion, and in Tasmania and the Dominican Republic on another.)

At a time when the concept of role model enjoys great popularity, I ought to say something about particular individuals outside academia as well, whose work and ideas I admired and who significantly influenced my thinking. I knew *some* of them personally, others only through their writings. Chronologically speaking, my intellectual awakening (and exposure to the ideas of the people discussed below) began upon my arrival in England, when I became a student and gained unobstructed access to anything I wished to read. While in England, the discovery of Arthur Koestler, George Orwell, and Raymond Aron were the most memorable. I was drawn, among other things, to their thoughtful anticommunism and their understanding of what was distinctively wrong with these systems, and I resonated to their analysis of the perverted idealism these systems embodied. I was also impressed by the lives and adventures of Koestler and Orwell. In subsequent years I regularly used their writings in my teaching political sociology, sociology of literature, and the sociology of ideas and intellectuals.

Another English author that made a great impression was Isaiah Berlin, the social philosopher. Besides his style and erudition his major appeal lay in making a strong case for the importance of ideas in human affairs and in his anti-utopian and antideterministic message. He made me more fully aware of a key aspect of the human condition: that we all are prey to conflicting goals and desires that cannot be reconciled with one another.

Among my teachers, beginning with the London School of Economics, I benefited most from the lectures of and contact with T. B. Bottomore, Hilda Himmelweit, and Ernest Gellner; at the University of Illinois I had memorable graduate seminars with Joseph Gusfield (political sociology) and Bennett Berger (sociology of knowledge). At Princeton it was Harry Eckstein in political science whose course impressed me most. Alex Inkeles at Harvard was a senior colleague (not teacher) and exemplar in his disciplined pursuit of learning about important matters, such as the nature of Soviet society and global modernization. He embodied confidence in reason and systematic, hard intellectual work. I had similar admiration for the work of my late friend Stanley Milgram, one of two people with whom I ever co-authored an article. I also met and admired the work of Barrington Moore without sharing his contempt for American society, tempered later by his recognition that there were others quite a bit worse. George Kennan, whose books I repeatedly reviewed, was another figure I admired from a distance while also critical of his succumbing to notions of moral equivalence (between the United States and the Soviet Union) and of his romantic antimodernism (although I shared some of it). Sidney Hook (whom I knew) impressed me more by his personality than his philosophical writings; I admired his polemical vigor and willingness to take a public stand critical of communist systems and ideologies at a time when such a position was judged to be in poor taste and was virtually proscribed among most academic intellectuals.

Outside academia Saul Bellow (whom I visited occasionally in Vermont and Brookline, Massachusetts) was a major influence and inspiration and my favorite contemporary writer. His writings helped to understand American culture and society, including the counterculture of the 1960s; two of his novels (*Herzog* and *Mr. Sammler's Planet*) I regularly used in my sociology of literature course and three of my books begin with quotes from his writings.

MY CAREER AS A SOCIOLOGIST

My teaching experience began as a teaching assistant at the University of Illinois in Champaign-Urbana, Illinois, where I led discussion groups and graded exams in a large introductory course. The quality of students was a bit of a culture shock compared with those at LSE. I was inspired to give them a test of my own invention, which consisted of a list of the names of (what I considered) well-known artists, writers, scientists, statesmen, plus some capital cities around the world and asked them to identify them in a few words (or in case of the cities note their location). The results were comic and dismaying (I remember Bertrand Russell identified as a basketball player). At Princeton I was a TA in the social problems course known at the time as "nuts and sluts" taught by Edward Tiryakian. In the summer of 1961 I had a summer school job at Queens College, New York, teaching "crime and deviance."

My first full-time job (at Harvard) materialized while working on my dissertation at Princeton. The Department of Social Relations wanted somebody who could teach a course on Soviet society, such as Inkeles used to teach but no longer did. The other courses I taught at Harvard were the sociology of literature and crime and deviance. I was hired as a nontenured assistant professor and research fellow at the Russian Research Center.

Not surprisingly, my research and writing interests found expression in my teaching. Beginning at Harvard in 1963 I regularly taught a course on Soviet society until the end of the Soviet Union. I also taught a course at UMass entitled "Social Problems Under Socialism," which examined these problems in the Soviet, East European, Chinese, and Cuban settings. It might very well have been the only such course offered in the whole country. "Political Sociology" was another of my regular course offerings with emphasis on totalitarianism (Nazi, Soviet, and Chinese), political propaganda, the "cult of personality," political violence, and other unpleasant topics. My fourth regularly taught course was "sociology of literature and mass culture." It consisted, for the most part, of analyzing novels ranging from well-known classics such as *Robinson Crusoe, Madame Bovary,* and *Oblomov* and works of contemporary American authors like Saul Bellow and Norman Mailer to far more obscure but important authors students were unlikely to encounter in any other course. The books were treated as sources of information about matters social and historical. The "mass culture" part had a similar focus: how it reflects, intentionally and unintentionally, social realities. This was purely a teaching interest; I published nothing related to literary topics except an article (very early in my career) derived from my doctoral dissertation that was entitled "The New Man and His Enemies: A Study in the Stalinist Conceptions of Good and Evil Personified," which was based on socialist-realist novels.

At Harvard there was a congenial group of junior, nontenured faculty I was friendly with. It included Tiryakian (whose teaching assistant I used to be at Princeton), Charles Tilly, Murray Melbin, Gerald Platt, and Stanley Milgram, who became a close, lifelong friend until his untimely death in 1983. Platt has also remained a close friend and colleague having joined the Department at UMass, Amherst, two years after I left Harvard. I also met at Harvard David

Riesman, George Homans, and Talcott Parsons. Communicating face-to-face with Parsons was no less difficult than reading his books. Homans and Riesmans were another matter. I corresponded with Riesman for decades and occasionally visited him in Cambridge and later at his retirement home in Winchester.

In those days Pitirim Sorokin was still alive (in retirement) and lived in Belmont when I met him at a dinner party. He shared with me his conviction that Parsons was responsible for his being ousted as chairman of the department at Harvard and compared Parsons's alleged machinations to those of Stalin who packed the Central Committee (of the Soviet Communist Party) with his people to accomplish his designs.

I also met many people at the Russian Research Center where the lunchroom was the center for socializing that also took place during the morning coffee hour, presided over, usually, by Adam Ulam. Mrs. Helen Parsons (Talcott's wife) was the de facto head of the Russian Research Center, attending to all administrative matters; her title, if I remember correctly, was administrative secretary. When the rooms were repainted she asked what color scheme I preferred; I was deeply impressed that even a lowly nontenured assistant professor's taste was taken into consideration.

In the Center I also met Barrington Moore and had occasional conversations with him (maybe two or three times a year, which was above average as far as most of his colleagues were concerned and was considered an accomplishment given his legendary reclusiveness). I also met another young Hungarian of the 1956 generation, Peter Kenez, a graduate student in history who became a professor at Santa Cruz and has remained a very close friend.

Another Harvard experience is worth recalling. In 1963–1964 there was a visiting Soviet scholar (Yuri Asaev) in the Social Relations department. I knew him slightly through Jerry Platt, who knew him better as both worked with Parsons. At one point Asaev decided that he did not wish to return to the Soviet Union. The resulting emotional turmoil and pressures brought on him by the Soviet authorities led to two suicide attempts. In the first instance he jumped out of the window of Platt's apartment whom he was visiting, and, amazingly, injured and dazed, climbed back on a fire escape (I was present since Jerry called me for help and advice). He spent many weeks or months in the Harvard infirmary recovering. Later he tried to throw himself on the subway tracks under Harvard Square. Finally he was sent back to the Soviet Union by the State Department and those at Harvard who felt that his defection would undermine the cultural exchange programs. It was an unseemly affair, as I saw it; American authorities caved in to intense Soviet pressure (that included visits by other Soviet exchange students to his hospital room, anguished phone calls from his wife, and calls from the embassy).

At Harvard my teaching was largely limited to undergraduates, though at one point I was in charge of an interdisciplinary seminar for graduate students which featured invited speakers (one of whom was Barrington Moore).

If one may believe the *Crimson Confidential Guide* to undergraduate courses, my teaching efforts were not altogether fruitless. The following was written regarding my course on Soviet Society:

> SocRel 105 is packed with information about Soviet society and doesn't require command of the field's jargon. . . . Lecturer Paul Hollander might best be characterized as a "sleeper." His manner is quiet and his delivery at first seems soporific. His impeccable organization, however, was greatly appreciated last year, and after a few lectures the quiet charm of this one-time Hungarian refugee in his green plush sweatshirt and steel rimmed spectacles was most engaging. However, don't plan on Hollander to rouse you for the day.

Student evaluations at UMass were less favorable. There were complaints that the classes were dull, the readings too long and demanding, and the grading strict. There remained, over the years a striking and persistent contrast between students who found my courses interesting and well organized, and the exams fair, and many who thought otherwise.

Throughout my career as a sociologist, I had misgivings about both major currents informing the field: (1) the scientific, quantitative, "hardnosed" data gathering one, and (2) the idealistic, "do-gooding" orientation and its endless optimism about the perfectibility of social institutions and human beings. I had more sympathy toward the latter since at least it tended to be preoccupied with what I regarded as more important questions rather than methodological refinements. (My ineptness regarding statistics and quantitative methods also influenced these preferences.) As political correctness became pervasive in sociology and much of academic life beginning in the late 1960s and early 1970s, I became more sympathetic to the "number crunchers" who did not pursue ideological agendas.

The limitations of my professional identity as a sociologist had implications for my attitude to teaching. I never felt that the teaching of sociology or any of its subfields imparted blinding insights or that sociologists were in a position to communicate great truth to their captive audiences—shortcomings not limited to sociology. My greater interest in research and writing presumably had something to do with a lesser interest in teaching. Finally there was the matter of personality. I am not a big talker; I do not relish holding forth on social occasions, I do not enjoy performing to an audience, which is an important ingredient of being a good teacher; I told few jokes in my classes and when I did, they were rarely understood; being popular among large numbers of people has not been a high priority. In our times, when students expect to be entertained, I fell short. None of this means that I disliked teaching but only that I found it far less engrossing and stimulating than writing. The quality of the students also had something to do with these attitudes; there were rarely more than five to six students in my "advanced undergraduate" classes (of thirty to forty juniors and seniors) who were responsive, articulate, and interested in the subjects discussed in class. It was difficult to have any dialogue despite my routine entreaties to the students to ask questions, express opinions, and contribute to class discussion.

My contact with graduate students throughout my teaching career was quite limited. I regularly offered a seminar on "the sociology of knowledge and intellectuals" but often there were no takers and those who took it often came from other departments. The number of students I was advising about their dissertation was even smaller. The explanation is no mystery. The graduate students fell into two broad groups: there were the quantitatively oriented ones, and, in increasing numbers, those interested in feminism, gender studies, minorities, postmodernism, and Marxism—topics I had no interest in and could not contribute to. Presumably my politically incorrect reputation did not help either to attract students who had these interests and the political attitudes that went with them.

Following the 1960s my identification with and attachment to the discipline was further weakened as American sociology became increasingly dominated by left-of-center beliefs and agendas. During the 1970s I let my membership in ASA lapse and stopped attending (with rare exceptions) the annual meetings dominated by various leftist caucuses and topics and routinely passing political resolutions I objected to.

Although, as described earlier, I drifted into sociology in a casual and unpremeditated way, my commitment to certain values provided motivation for sociological work. My writings express beliefs I never tried to hide but I also believed that one can aspire to and approximate a degree of impartiality and that there is a social reality independent of our perceptions and preferences. Unlike so many of my fellow sociologists concerned with and determined to uncover the injustices and defects of American society, I was more interested in exploring and exposing the injustices and deformities of other political systems, notably those of Soviet-communist inspiration or design. Such an orientation followed not only from my background but also from my Western experiences. I could understand why so many Western intellectuals, including social scientists, disturbed by the inequities of their own societies paid little attention to what struck me as greater moral outrages around the world but the discrepancy still bothered me. So did the fact that they took for granted and had little appreciation of the intellectual and political freedoms they enjoyed and the political institutions and practices that sustained them.

Having come from a part of the world where repression and intolerance were endemic and where the standards of living were low, I failed to appreciate concerns with repressive tolerance and the evils of consumerism. At the same time, I am an ardent environmentalist and have a strong aversion to SUVs and the attitudes I associate with their popularity[8]—suggesting that I am not indifferent to the excesses of consumption. Nor have I remained uncritical of many other aspects of American society and culture—an attitude most recently expressed in changing the subtitle of my book *Anti-Americanism* from "critiques at home and abroad" to "irrational and rational." Doubtless, many critiques of American culture and society are *not* irrational, as is discussed at some length in the second edition of that book.

CONCLUSION

I do not regret having become a sociologist because it has allowed me to write a few books and express ideas on some subjects of importance, modest as their impact might have been. I also found academic life generally congenial especially given the abundance of free time that goes with it.

Although, as these reflections show, my background and early experiences exerted a great deal of influence on my subsequent life and work, I was never drawn to a rigorous social, or social-psychological determinism. I believe, and prefer to believe, that ideas matter as much as the standard sociological variables in shaping social and personal life and their influence often cannot be derived from these variables and from the "interests" they allegedly reflect. To be sure, ideas have social, cultural, historical, or situational sources, they do not descend from heaven. As a sociologist of knowledge, I would be the last to dispute this. Nonetheless both the origins of and affinity to ideas are much harder to pin down than, say, the relationship between delinquency and the broken family.

I always preferred and sought to link (in the spirit of Isaiah Berlin) sociopolitical events and processes to "the wishes and purposes of identifiable individuals" rather than to the impersonal forces of history, economic interest, or the grip of short-lived situations in which individuals find themselves—not that I would dismiss the importance of the latter. My predilection for emphasizing the importance of ideas doubtless has something to do with the alternative: if ideas matter little, then what matters or ought to matter? As soon as we abandon the notion of ideas being important influences over our lives, we are led to some far more deterministic scheme: the physical or material environment, the mode of production, some sort of group interest, our genes, or some combination of heredity and environment.

Taking ideas seriously and including them among the major influences on our life does not mean that we can endlessly and limitlessly reinvent ourselves or the societies we live in but it does provide a more open-ended perspective on human life and destiny.

NOTES

1. I have indulged in autobiographical writing on three previous occasions. The first was an "Epilogue" in the volume *The Survival of the Adversary Culture* (New Brunswick, N.J.: Transaction, 1988). The second occasion came when the editor of *Modern Age* asked me to contribute to a series of articles in which authors traced the major intellectual influences over their life and work ("Models and Mentors," *Modern Age*, Summer 1995). The third item focused entirely on matters political and was entitled "Growing Up in Communist Hungary" in *Red Star, Blue Star*, ed. Andrew Handler and Susan V. Meschel (New York: Columbia University Press, 1997).

2. Ian Buruma, "The Romance of Exile, *New Republic*, February 12, 2001, 33.

3. He was an officer in charge of political-ideological matters, in practice of everything. Even the building battalions designed for the socially-politically corrupt were given low-level ideological indoctrination in the form of political seminars. The commissar, barely literate, often asked me to summarize (and type out) the main points of the political pamphlets he was to use for enlightening us.

4. For example, in the early 1970s Noam Chomsky warned against believing the horror stories of Cambodian refugees who fled the massacres of the Pol Pot regime. In 1996 Nicholas Kristof, correspondent of the *New York Times* wondered if North Korean refugees' accounts of concentration camps were to be believed.

5. The connections between Marxist theory and communist repression were brilliantly summed up by Andrzej Walicky: "The habit of conceiving human liberation as a long, cruel historical process in which entire generations and classes have to be ruthlessly sacrificed for the sake of the unfettered development of human beings in the future is perhaps one of the most characteristic, although sometimes conveniently forgotten, features of Marx's thought . . . possessors of the only correct knowledge of the meaning and laws of history have a right, even a duty, to ignore the opinions of the ignorant majority; if they are in power, they have the right, the duty, to *realize* historical necessity, even against all, with the help of police, bayonets and tanks." (*Marxism and the Leap to the Kingdom of Freedom: The Rise and Fall of Communist Utopia* [Stanford University Press, 1995], 16, 205–61).

6. It may be argued that considering myself free is also a form of "false consciousness" induced by my Western social status and material comforts far superior to those in communist Hungary. If so, my "existence" determined my "consciousness" as the Marxist formulation would have it. While there is an element of truth in this, it should be pointed out that I became a critic of the communist system in Hungary well before I had any personal difficulties on account of my grandfather. I actually was an activist

in the communist youth movement and withdrew from it on my own accord well before my family or I suffered any economic setback or political discrimination.

7. See "Hungarian Paradoxes" in Paul Hollander, *Decline and Discontent: Communism and the West Today* (New Brunswick, N.J.: Transaction, 1992). For an earlier (1979) travel report, see "Public and Private in Hungary" in *The Many Faces of Socialism* (New Brunswick: Transaction, 1983).

8. I speculated about the social-cultural sources of the popularity of SUVs in American society in the introduction to *Discontents: Postmodern and Postcommunist*, 2002.

Index

Abu Ghraib, 49
Aczel, Tamas, 178
Adorno, Theodore, 260
adversary culture, 16, 22, 48, 50, 87, 201, 203–15, 227
advertising, 15–16, 22, 61, 63, 71, 75, 88, 102–17, 118, 125, 174, 192, 263
affirmative action, 82–83
Afghanistan, 39, 46, 53, 77, 206, 208–9, 213, 222, 228
Ahmad, Eqbal, 212
Albania, 150, 156, 244
Aldridge, John, 92
Ali, Ayaan Hirsi, 185–86
Ali, Tariq, 21
alienation, 15, 33, 40, 48, 69, 94, 140, 186–87, 205, 210, 213, 231–35, 244, 251, 260
Al Qaeda, 52
American Friends Service Committee, 39, 208
Americanization, 45, 47
Andropov, Yuri, 145
anti-Americanism, 1–30, 33–35, 36–40, 41–48, 49–55, 68, 173, 186, 217–18, 228, 277; domestic anti-Americanism, 44, 46, 48, 218
anticapitalism, 20, 42, 45, 204
anticommunism, 51, 223, 271

anti-Semitism, 6, 12, 34, 41–42, 129, 134–38, 144, 146, 148, 223
Applebaum, Anne, 14, 18
Aptheker, Herbert, 248
The Aquariums of Pyongyang, 164, 168
Arendt, Hannah, 225–26
Aron, Raymond, 175, 271
Asaev, Yuri, 274
Ashcroft, John, 17, 51
Atala and Renee, 94, 96
authenticity, 7, 15, 19, 72, 74, 76, 82, 95, 108, 112–16, 142, 189, 196, 199, 205, 207, 213, 221, 226–27, 231, 251
authoritarianism, 10, 264
Ayers, Bill, 16, 212, 250, 251

Baader-Meinhof Gang, 37, 228
Baker, Nicholson, 14
Balzac, Honore de, 94, 97
Barnett, Richard, 50
Baudrillard, Jean, 14, 44
Belafonte, Harry, 212
Bellow, Saul, 234, 272–73
Berger, Bennett, 272
Berger, Morroe, 98, 271
Berkeley (University of California), 52, 207, 213, 242
Berlin, Isaiah, 271, 277
Berman, Paul, 67, 206

Berrigan brothers, 20, 66, 212; Berrigan, Frida 20; Berrigan, Philip 20
bin Laden, Osama, 4, 10, 17, 52, 65, 207
Birnbaum, Norman, 270
Black Liberation Army, 37
Black Panther Party, 237, 240
blacks, 19, 34, 36, 49–50, 69, 77, 81–84, 89, 139, 169, 204, 239–40, 248
Bloom, Harold, 88, 90–92
Boorstin, Daniel, 47, 60, 63
Borenstein, Audrey, 91, 98
Bottomore, Thomas B., 270, 272
Boudin, Kathy, 251
Bradhser, Keith, 72
Brawley, Tawana, 81–84
Brent, William Lee, 237–41
Brezhnev, Leonid, 238
Britain, 3, 8, 14, 39, 74, 104, 147, 172, 194, 196, 198, 233–36, 259, 267, 270–71
Brodsky, Joseph, 145
Brooks, David, 3
Budapest, 36, 172, 257, 259, 261–63, 269
Burdick, Eugene, 126
Buruma, Ian, 185–87, 260
Bush, George H. W., 203
Bush, George W., 20, 22, 47, 51; Bush administration, 20, 209
Byron, George Gordon, 190

Calvino, Italo, 93
Cambodia, 51, 168, 218, 249
capitalism, 6–8, 12, 20, 22, 38, 42, 44–46, 50–51, 89, 153, 172, 174, 178, 180, 204, 217, 223, 230, 234–35, 243–44, 247, 248, 250, 252, 263
Carter, Jimmy, 118, 164
Cass, Leon R., 25
Castro, Fidel, 21, 67, 159, 204, 234, 246; Castro's Cuba, 67, 204, 237, 266

celebrity, 2, 13–16, 59–69, 72, 81, 209, 247, 249; cult, 13, 63; worship, 16, 61–64
censorship, 53, 93, 96
Central Committee (of the Soviet Communist Party), 141, 147–48, 274
CEO, 2, 22, 66, 124
Chandler, David, 51
Chateaubriand, Francois-Rene, 94, 96, 190, 192
Chavez, Hugo, 20–21
Chernyaev, Anatoly, 143
Chiapas (Mexico), 204, 213
China, 6, 78, 150–52, 159, 164–66, 188, 204, 218, 221, 243, 273
Chol-hwan, Kang, 164, 168
Chomsky, Noam, 9–11, 44, 50, 67–68, 168, 206, 208, 212, 216–24, 249
CIA, 50
Citizens Exchange Corps (CEC), 123–37
Clark, Ramsey, 52, 212, 251, 252
class enemy, 155, 263
classics, 89–93, 273
"classism," 81
class struggle, 155–56, 172, 244, 263
Cockburn, Alexander, 209
Coffin, William Sloane, 212, 252
Cohen, Eric, 24
Cohn, Werner, 217, 223
Colburn, Forrest, 150, 161
Cold War, 9, 17, 41, 50, 52, 123, 125–26, 204, 212, 217, 230
collectivization (of agriculture), 154, 168, 174, 222
Combs, Sean, 59. *See also* Puff Daddy
Committee for the Defense of the Revolution (Cuban), 238
communism, 3, 9, 46, 51, 142–44, 151, 156, 166, 173, 178, 184, 204, 208, 223, 243, 47–48, 250, 262, 266, 268; *Communist Manifesto*, 46; man, 182; movement, 231, 236; party, 130, 151, 154, 234, 242, 248, 274; regime, 164, 167, 171, 174,

179, 221, 248, 263, 265–66; society, 24, 173; states, 4, 7, 37, 41, 74, 86–87, 142, 150–61, 167, 176–77, 181, 228, 243–48, 251, 265; system, 1, 46, 74, 86, 92, 141, 142, 143, 150–52, 158–61, 168, 173, 174, 183, 223, 230, 244, 246, 249, 251, 253, 262–63, 265–66, 272; totalitarianism, 3, 55
computer dating, 102, 106
Cong (Vietnamese Political Police), 151
conspicuous compassion, 83
convergence, 16, 45, 51, 67, 84, 132, 175, 206, 212, 251
counterculture, 102–17, 212, 247, 272
Csurka, Istvan, 38
Cuba, 7, 21, 67, 89, 152, 159, 204, 218, 230, 237–41, 243 266, 273
cult of personality, 164, 168, 273
cultural diversity, 86, 189, 232, 235
Cultural Revolution, 6
Cumings, Bruce, 49–50, 165, 167–69
Czechoslovakia, 150, 174, 181

Daniel, Robert V., 145
dating services, 102–3
Davis, Angela, 212
Debray, Regis, 231
decadence, 8–9
deconstructionism, 12, 14, 88–90, 204
Defoe, Daniel, 96
Dellinger, David, 212
determinism, 53, 207, 277; social determinism, 53, 98
Diamond, Stanley, 83
Dickens, Charles, 94
disillusionment, disillusioning 142, 146, 178, 238, 241, 248–49, 253
dissidents, 152, 206
Djilas, Milovan, 142
Doctorow, E. L., 17, 212
Doctrine of Unshaken Foundations, 179, 253
Dorfman, Ariel, 17

Dostoevsky, Fyodor, 92, 156–57
Dow, Mark, 49–50
Dowd, Maureen, 203
Dreiser, Theodore, 95
Duke University, 81–84, 263

Eagelton, Terry, 88
Eastern Europe, 10, 39, 151, 174–75, 180, 182, 209, 222, 243, 246–49, 273, 262
East Germany, 150, 174, 179, 271
Eckstein, Harry, 271–72
egalitarianism, 15, 18, 54, 61, 75, 180, 246, 247; rhetoric, 180, 247
Ehrenreich, Barbara, 204, 212
Eichman, Adolf, 225
Eliot, George, 90
elitism, 6, 12–13, 54, 61–63, 67–68, 79, 89, 91, 103, 105, 132–34, 142, 146, 156, 158–61, 166, 178, 180, 211, 216, 236, 238, 249, 261, 266, 269; anti-elitism, 13, 15, 63; ruling elites, 89, 142, 159, 161, 180
Ellis, John, 89
Empire, 211–12, 249–50
Engels, Frederick, 130, 147, 152
Enlightenment, 42, 45, 186, 190, 235
entertainment, 12–17, 21–22, 42, 47, 59–61, 63, 65–66, 75–76, 100, 103, 109, 113, 119, 269; orientation, 12–13, 17, 47, 66, 113
Eorsi, Istvan, 179
equality, 18, 22, 54, 80, 155, 176, 213, 240,
escapism, escapist, 119, 94
Ethiopia, 150, 153, 159
ethnocentrism, ethnocentric, 79, 187
Eurocentric, 11, 92, 267

Fahrenheit 9/11, 65–68
Falk, Richard, 206, 212
false consciousness, 2, 64, 68, 250
fanaticism, 1, 4, 35, 86, 185–86, 232, 251
Fanon, Franz, 231

fascism, 10, 11, 17, 92, 138, 148, 206, 210, 223, 226, 235
Faurisson, Robert, 218, 223
feminism, 18, 33, 53, 78–79, 90, 110–11, 115, 204–5, 209, 211, 233, 276; radical feminists, 53, 204, 233
Fish, Stanley, 12, 212
Flaubert, Gustave, 94–97, 99, 190
Foley, Barbara, 210
Foner, Eric, 34, 208
Forbes, Malcolm, 51
Freud, Sigmund, 94, 123
Frey, James, 13–14
Fuentes, Carlos, 51, 91, 231
fundamentalism, 3, 11, 53, 55, 68, 251
Fussell, Paul, 190–91
future orientation, 157

Gallaudet University, 19
Galloway, George, 14
Gellner, Ernest, 272
genocide, 38, 40, 52, 54, 127, 156, 208, 222, 226, 246
Gere, Richard, 39, 208
Gestapo, 51, 226
Gimes, Miklos, 179
glasnost, 143, 180
globalization, 12, 35, 38, 52, 189, 205, 223, 229, 243, 246; antiglobalization, 35, 204, 213, 243
Goethe, Johann Wolfgang, 94, 96, 190
Gonzales, Elian, 67
Goodheart, Eugene, 99
Gorbachev, Mikhail, 141, 143, 156, 180
Gordimer, Nadine, 21
Gornick, Vivian, 39, 208
great books, 88, 100
Greece, 189–99
Green Guide, 194. *See also* Michelin Guide
Green Party, 207
Grenada, 218
Grossman, Vasily, 176
Guantanamo, 49

Guevara, Che, 7, 65, 235, 250
Gulag, 36–37, 49, 54, 164–69, 188, 235
Gusfield, Joseph, 272

Halfin, Igal, 150–51
Hall, Gus, 248
Hamas, 3, 34
Hampshire College, 208–9
Hardt, Michael, 212, 249
Harvard University, 11, 18, 21, 33, 172; *Educational Review*, 222, 272–75
hatred, 1–9, 34–38, 44, 66–69, 88, 160, 184–85, 204, 204–7, 218, 220, 225–27, 249, 253
Havel, Vaclav, 222
Haverford College, 210
Hayden, Tom, 212
Hegedus, Andras, 179
Heine, Heinrich, 190
Heller, Agnes, 178–79
Hendel, Samuel, 127
Hertzberg, Hendrik, 205
Hilton, Paris, 63
Himmelweit, Hilda, 270, 272
Hitchens, Christopher, 17, 206
Hitler, Adolf, 10, 14, 51
Hobsbawm, Eric, 11, 248
Ho Chi Minh, 159
Holocaust, 6, 14, 35, 40, 69, 91–92, 126, 208, 216–18, 223, 225, 262, 265; Holocaust deniers, 216–18, 223; Holocaust revisionist, 223, 265
Homans, George, 274
Hook, Sidney, 272
Hungarian Revolution of 1956, 138, 170–73, 261
Hungary, 36–38, 91, 109, 138, 159, 170–82, 198, 258–69, 274–75
Hussein, Saddam, 20–21, 52, 68, 73, 76, 252

identity, 4, 12, 19, 20, 33, 54, 66, 78, 83–84, 89, 92, 94, 97, 107, 187, 191,

205–6, 211–12, 218, 227, 240, 251, 253, 259, 260, 263, 266–68, 275
identity politics, 12, 19, 78
inauthenticity, 45, 204, 212, 227, 250
individualism, 2, 12, 15, 45, 61, 112, 160, 190–91, 230; radical individualism, 2, 12
inequality, 18, 22, 44, 52, 54, 82, 95, 98, 153, 175–76, 206–7, 244, 251, 258, 264
Inkeles, Alex, 272–73
Inquisition, 155, 181
intellectuals/intelligentsia 5, 7, 10–15, 21, 38–39, 41–44, 53–55, 83, 105, 143, 145, 160, 167, 169, 186, 190, 198, 203, 211, 219, 222, 225, 229–33, 242–43, 246–53, 259–60, 265–67, 271–72, 276; academic, 11, 39, 53, 83, 105, 167, 169, 211, 229, 260, 272; public, 14–15, 218, 246–53; Western, 7, 11, 21, 143, 167, 230–31, 247, 253, 265–66, 276
Internet, 102, 106
Iraq, 20–21, 46, 52, 65, 68, 73–76, 187, 229
Iron Curtain, 39, 171, 174, 209
Ishiguro, Kazuo, 95
Islam, 4, 6, 9, 19, 21, 35, 37, 43–44, 46, 52–53, 55, 68, 79–80, 85–87, 184–88, 206–7, 225–29, 232, 251, 253; Islamic fanaticism, 1, 4, 44, 87, 253; Islamic radicals, 184, 251
Israel, 3, 6, 11–12, 20, 35, 37–38, 44, 52, 78, 157, 204, 212, 216–24, 227–31, 249, 268; anti-Israeli, 6, 11–12, 44, 204, 228

Jackson, George, 50,
Jacoby, Russell, 205, 211
Jameson, Frederick, 207, 212
Jews, 6, 11, 35, 44, 77–78, 89, 91–92, 108, 116, 129, 145, 156, 178, 217–18, 229–30, 260–68
Johnson, Chalmers, 52

Kadar, Janos, 159
Kakutani, Michiko, 14
Kassof, Allen, 128, 271
Kelly, Michael, 205
Kenez, Peter, 274
Kennan, George, 8–9, 52, 272
Kernan, Alvin, 88
KGB, 37, 50, 130, 151, 155, 174
Khrushchev, Nikita, 50, 138, 140, 143, 146, 147, 180, 248
Kim Il Sung, 7, 21, 159, 165
Kim Jong Il, 168
Kirkpatrick, Jeane, 50
Klare, Michael, 208
Koestler, Arthur, 179, 253, 271
Kolakowski, Leszek, 242–45, 247–48
Koran, 19, 85–86, 188
Kozol, Jonathan, 212
Kramer, Hilton, 160
Krauze, Enrique, 247
Kunstler, William, 212, 251–52
Kushner, Tony, 17

Laguna Woods (California), 23
Lapham, Lewis, 10, 11, 51
Laqueur, Thomas, 52, 207
Lauren, Ralph, 61
Leisure World (California), 23–24
Leites, Nathan, 157–58
Lenin, Vladimir, 51, 130, 144, 147–48, 152–54, 157
Leninism, 142, 151, 156, 158, 178, 181, 258, 266
Leonhard, Wolfgang, 179
Lessing, Doris 233–36
Levine, Robert, 216–17, 220
Levy, Marion, Jr., 271
Leys, Simon, 151
Lifton, Robert Jay, 52
Litvan, Gyorgy, 177, 181
Llosa, Mario Vargas, 90–91
London School of Economics (LSE), 172, 235, 257–59, 270–72
Lon Nol, 51

"lookism," 110
Lukacs, George, 178

Maceda, Jim, 73
MacFarquhar, Larissa, 117, 220
Madame Bovary, 96, 235, 273
Magic Mountain, 94
Mailer, Norman, 15, 53, 207, 212, 231, 273
Mandel, Michael, 39, 208
Mann, Thomas, 94
Mannheim, Karl, 259, 267
Mao Zedong, 159, 204, 221, 252; Mao's China, 165, 218
Maoism, 188, 204, 213, 246
Marcuse, Herbert, 10, 267
Margalit, Avishai, 185
Markovits, Andre, 11
Marx, Karl, 24, 37, 86, 108, 130, 147, 156, 188, 228, 243, 247
Marxism, 4, 27, 42, 45, 86–87, 97, 141–43, 181, 187–88, 204, 228, 242–45, 246–53, 258, 266, 276
Marxism-Leninism, 151, 156, 158, 266
mass culture, 1, 42, 45, 47, 52, 66, 90, 112, 119, 273
mass media, 13, 15, 37, 54, 60, 63, 93, 96, 168, 176, 217, 218, 227
mass murder, 35–37, 39, 43–44, 158, 225–28, 246
mass society, 225
matchmaking, 102–3
McCarthyism, 54
Mead, Russell, 39, 209
Melbin, Murray, 273
mendacious, 142, 164, 167, 171, 177, 266
Mendelsohn, Daniel, 14
Mengistu, Haile Mariam, 159
Meray, Tibor, 178
Merkin, Daphne, 24
Michelin Guide, 193. *See also* Green Guide
Middle East Studies Association, 210
Milgram, Stanley, 225, 266, 272–73

Mills, C. Wright, 231, 270
Milosevic, Slobodan, 204, 252
Minogue, Kenneth, 247
mirror image, 50
Mishra, Pankaj, 4
modernity and modernization, 2, 4, 7, 16–17, 20, 23–25, 35, 37, 43–47, 63, 77, 78, 80, 94, 97, 102–3, 108, 112, 117, 119, 133, 153, 160, 188–92, 197–99, 206, 213, 225–26, 259, 272
Modern Language Association, 17
Molotov, Vyacheslav, 145
Moore, Barrington, Jr., 272, 274–75
Moore, Michael, 65–70, 220
moral equivalence, 10, 39, 41, 49–55, 126, 169, 208–9, 222–23, 230, 266, 272
Morales, Evo, 7
moral indignation, 7–8, 34, 54, 66, 95, 142, 175, 207, 220, 229
Morgan, Robin 33
Mother Jones, 67
multiculturalism, 11–12, 18–19, 42, 53–54, 78, 80, 87, 92, 204
Muslim, 3, 4, 5, 9, 43, 79–80, 185–86, 188

Nader, Ralph, 67, 209, 212
The Nation, 104, 209, 218, 249
national character, 42, 196
National Review, 104
Navasky, Victor, 212
Nazi Germany, 10, 41, 51, 53, 223, 226, 246, 265–66
Nazism, 3, 14, 51, 147, 155–56, 158, 173, 184, 187, 220, 223, 225–26, 228, 246, 249, 262–63, 265–66, 273
NBC, 13, 73
Negri, Antonio, 212, 249–50
new socialist man, 176
Newton, Huey, 239
New York Review of Books, 103, 250
Nicaragua, 67, 150, 204, 208–9, 218, 249
Niebuhr, Richard, 53

noble savage, 192, 230
nomenklatura, 143, 146, 179
North Korea, 7, 21, 49, 145, 159, 164–66, 167–69, 243, 246, 248; North Korean Gulag, 164–66, 167–69
North Vietnam, 20, 221, 231
nuclear war, 50, 123–26

obedience to authority, 36, 225, 264
Oblomov, 273
Ochab, Edward, 157
October Revolution, 153, 249. *See also* Russian Revolution
old age, 25, 75, 79, 117, 119, 120
Orwell, George, 211, 271

Packer, George, 33, 205, 251
Page, Charles, 271
Palestine, 6, 7, 35, 37–38, 44, 157, 187, 208, 210, 227, 229–32
Parenti, Michael, 212
Parsons, Helen, 274
Parsons, Talcott, 274
party functionary (communist), 171, 267
Pasternak, Boris Leonidovich, 145
perestroika, 141, 143–44
Peretz, Martin, 229
personals, 102–17
Pinter, Harold, 9–11, 21
Pipes, Richard, 54
Platt, Gerald, 273–74
Poland, 174, 242–43, 157, 178
Politburo (of Soviet Communist Party), 141
political conflict, 1, 6, 153–54, 226–27, 258
political correctness, 16, 18, 51, 53, 78–80, 85, 87, 89–90, 92, 104, 110–11, 187, 236, 275
political crimes, 36, 151–52, 159
political culture, 3, 5, 15, 37, 154, 160, 225–28
political disillusionment, 146, 253
political elite, 146, 156, 178, 238, 266

political jokes, 178
political pilgrims, 21, 230
Political Pilgrims (Hollander), 74, 125
political police, 151–52, 174
political violence, 37, 42, 79, 87, 150–63, 188, 225–28, 229–32, 244, 249, 251, 266, 273
Pollitt, Katha, 33, 209
Pol Pot, 51, 168, 218, 222, 249
popular culture, 6, 14, 16, 54, 61, 88, 92, 269
positive hero, 176
Postal, Paul, 216–17, 220
postcommunist, 12, 41, 46, 136, 143–44
postmodernism, 5, 12, 14, 42, 89, 204, 211, 276
propaganda, 6, 10, 21, 46, 50, 67, 73–74, 89, 137, 141, 148, 156, 167, 171, 174, 176–78, 180–82, 263, 273
publicity, 15–16, 61, 63, 81
Puff Daddy, 59–61. *See also* Combs, Sean
purge trials, 35, 37, 54, 154, 171

racial profiling, 79
racism, 34, 41–42, 69, 79, 81–83, 89, 168, 187, 204, 240, 251
radical left, 9, 104, 227, 230, 237, 247, 249, 253
radicals, 6, 184, 226, 236, 250–52
Rahman, Omar Abdel, 251
Rakosi, Mathias, 159
Rapoport, Anatol, 126
Reagan, Ronald, 47, 51, 67
Red Brigades, 37, 228, 250
Red Diaper Babies, 236
Riesman, David, 274
relativism, 13–15, 18–19, 61, 204; aesthetic, 60, 61, 63; cultural, 20, 35, 60, 92, 185; intellectual, 61; moral, 5, 8, 12, 53, 60–63; selective, 12
relativist, 18, 185
The Remains of the Day, 95
repressive tolerance, 10, 267, 277
reverse discrimination, 83

revolutionary violence, 213
Richmond, Yale, 128
Rigoulot, Pierre, 164, 168
Rilke, Rainer Maria, 45
Robinson, Joan, 271
Robinson Crusoe, 95–96, 273
role models, 16, 92, 250, 269, 271
Rolland, Romain, 145
romanticism, 23, 45, 47, 94, 96, 102–3, 109, 112, 116, 147, 189, 190, 192, 196–97, 243, 249, 260, 272
root causes, 4, 34, 39, 44, 52, 87, 153, 206–8, 227, 228, 230, 232
rootless cosmopolitan, 173, 266–69
Rosenberg, Ethel, 17, 235
Rosenberg, Julius, 17, 235
Roszak, Theodore, 212
Rushdie, Salman, 53
Russell, Bertrand, 273
Russia, 9–10, 46, 52, 77–78, 91, 123–40, 141–49, 156, 158, 165, 181, 208, 222, 246, 249, 258, 262, 269, 273–74
Russian Research Center (Harvard University), 273–74
Russian Revolution, 181, 208. *See also* Russian Revolution
Rwanda, 6, 157

Said, Edward, 17, 40, 208, 212, 259–60
Sandinista Nicaragua, 67, 150, 204, 218, 249
Sandinistas, 67, 150, 204, 218, 249
Sartre, Jean-Paul, 231
Savio, Mario, 213
scapegoats, 35, 38, 160; scapegoating impulse, 5–6, 9, 34, 43, 224, 227
Schucking, Levin, 97
secularization, 4, 7, 9, 24, 25, 43, 66, 80, 91, 117, 159, 176, 180, 184–85, 193, 224, 242, 251
secular religion, 242, 184
selective perception, 168, 220

self-esteem, 83, 198, 211
self-realization, 23, 112, 234, 236
September 11, 2001, 33–35, 36–40, 44, 203–15, 227
sexism, 34, 41–42, 79, 81, 89
Shakespeare, William, 88–92, 155
Shapiro, Raymond, 104
Sharia (Laws), 86
Sharpton, Al, 83
Sheehan, Cindy, 20–21
Sheehy, Gail, 24
Shelley, Percy Bysshe, 190
Shining Path, 213
show trials, 36, 151, 155, 179
Sinyavsky, Andrei, 145
social criticism, 10, 12, 15, 18, 48, 65–66, 68, 83, 99, 132, 205, 212, 216, 218, 226, 260
socialism, 4, 21, 46, 50–51, 92–93, 145, 147, 150–63, 165, 170–73, 176, 178, 182, 204, 218, 220, 222, 234, 238, 240–41, 243, 246, 248, 257, 266, 273; state, 46, 51, 204; system, 153, 204, 222, 266
social isolation, 45, 64, 103, 112, 117
socialist realism, 92–93, 176, 273
Solzhenitsyn, Aleksandr Isaevich, 140, 145, 155
Sontag, Susan, 15, 52, 69, 206–7, 212, 231
Sorokin, Pitirim, 274
Soros, George, 51
The Sorrows of Young Werther, 96, 190
Soviet: bloc, 239; communism, 9, 46, 143, 154, 166, 173, 204, 243, 248, 266, 274, 276; Communist Party, 154, 274; dissidents, 140; experiment, 142, 234, 248; purges, 54; regime, 142; society, 24, 173; system, 1, 46, 74, 86, 92, 141–43, 150–52, 158–61, 168, 173–82, 223, 230, 244, 246, 249, 251, 253, 262–66, 272, 278; totalitarianism, 265; Union, 4, 8–10, 17, 39, 41–42,

46, 50–51, 53, 69, 92–93, 123–40, 141–49, 150–63, 175, 180, 204, 222, 230, 238, 246–48, 258, 262, 266, 272–74. *See also* USSR
Spivak, Gayatri, 231
Spock, Benjamin, 252
spontaneity, 46, 74, 90, 103, 108–9, 112, 116, 127, 138
Srebrenica, 6
Stalin, Joseph, 35, 37, 51, 96, 130, 138, 144–45, 147–48, 154–59, 165, 173–74, 242, 246, 252, 274
Stalinism, 3, 142, 177, 188, 248, 273
Stasi, 151
state security, 130, 151, 155
status seeking, 2, 13, 33
status symbol, 72
Steele, Shelby, 84
Stendhal (Henri-Marie Beyle), 94, 97
stereotyping, 8, 42, 47, 77–80, 117, 131, 187
Stewart, Lynne, 251–52
Stewart, Martha, 61
Stille, Alexander, 250
Stone, I. F., 212
Stone, Oliver, 208
Stotsky, Sandra, 51
superpower, 4, 8–9, 46, 51–52, 143, 207, 246
SUVs, 22, 71–72, 277
Sweezy, Paul, 212

Taliban, 23, 53, 204, 208–9, 222
Terkel, Studs, 16
terrorism, 2–4, 6, 10, 17, 19, 21, 33–35, 36–40, 44–45, 51–52, 68, 78–80, 85–87, 145, 150–62, 174, 187, 203, 205–15, 217–18, 221–22, 228–30, 250–53
Thackeray, William Makepeace, 94
theocracy, 80
third world,12, 41, 46, 52, 118, 151, 169, 218, 221–22, 230, 232, 234, 253,

Thompson, E. P., 247–48
Tilly, Charles, 273
Tiryakian, Edward, 273
Tolstoy, Leo, 94
totalitarianism, 3, 7, 44, 53, 55, 67, 133, 139, 152, 155, 159, 166–69, 177, 181, 209, 264, 265, 273; mentality, 181; regimes, 155; systems, 44
tradition, 4, 11, 13, 21, 23–24, 35, 41–45, 52, 83, 89, 92, 112, 119, 144, 150–51, 159–60, 167, 169, 175, 180, 187, 189–92, 197, 198, 204–5, 230, 260, 264, 267
traditional societies, 23–24, 35, 43–44, 52, 119, 169, 175, 190–92, 198
Trilling, Lionel, 203
Trotsky, Leon, 142, 148, 158
Trotskyites, 145, 204
Trout, Paul, 11
true believer, 220, 235, 248
Trump, Donald, 16
Tumin, Mel, 271
Twentieth Party Congress (Soviet Communist), 143, 146–47, 180

Ulam, Adam, 274
University of Massachusetts, Amherst, 33, 172, 209–10, 273, 275,
University of North Carolina, 3, 19, 85–87, 210
Updike, John, 92
USSR, 52, 128, 130, 132, 137, 148, 154, 223. *See also* Soviet Union
utopianism, 51, 157, 160–61, 180, 186, 233, 243, 247–48, 250, 272

Van Gogh, Theo, 185–87
Venezuela, 20–21, 246
victimization, 82, 144; victim culture, 17; victimhood, 18–19, 82, 260
Vietcong, 20, 221, 227, 231
Vietnam, 20–21, 38–39, 127, 159, 205–6, 218, 221, 226, 235, 243–44, 251–52

Vietnam War, 20, 39, 206, 218, 226, 235, 251
Vidal, Gore, 10, 15, 45, 52, 206–7, 209

Walker, Alice, 208
Walzer, Michael, 206
Wat, Alexander, 178
Watt, Ian, 95
Weathermen, 16, 37, 212, 228
West, Cornel, 14, 16, 247
Western Europe, 4, 9, 22, 46, 189, 195–96, 266
Wharton, Edith, 95
white guilt, 82–84
Wieseltier, Leon, 15
Willis, Ellen, 206

Windschuttle, Keith, 221
withering away of the state, 153, 244
Wolf, Naomi, 17–18
Wolfe, Alan, 249
Wolin, Richard, 12
Wordsworth, William, 190
World Trade Center (WTC), 34, 37, 207, 209
World War II (WWII), 14, 51, 116, 145–46, 151, 179, 220, 233, 258

Yakovlev, Alexander, 141–49, 156

Zhdanov, Andrei, 173, 267
Zimbabwe, 236
Zinn, Howard, 212–13
Zola, Emile, 95

About the Author

Paul Hollander is professor emeritus of sociology at the University of Massachusetts at Amherst and a center associate of the Davis Center for Russian and Eurasian Studies at Harvard University. He lives in Northampton, Massachusetts. Hollander attended high school in Budapest, college in London (London School of Economics), and graduate school in the United States (Princeton University). His books include *Soviet and American Society: A Comparison*, *Political Pilgrims*, *Anti-Americanism*, *Political Will and Personal Belief: The Decline and Fall of Soviet Communism*, and *The End of Commitment: Intellectuals, Revolutionaries, and Political Morality*.